THE GENERATION OF SYNTACTIC STRUCTURES
FROM A SEMANTIC BASE

NORTH-HOLLAND
LINGUISTIC SERIES 2
Edited by S. C. DIK and J. G. KOOIJ

THE GENERATION OF SYNTACTIC STRUCTURES FROM A SEMANTIC BASE

W. J. HUTCHINS

*Postgraduate School of Librarianship
and Information Science,
University of Sheffield*

1971

NORTH-HOLLAND PUBLISHING COMPANY
AMSTERDAM · LONDON

Library of Congress Catalog Card Number 78-146187

ISBN 0 7204 6182 0

Publishers:
NORTH-HOLLAND PUBLISHING COMPANY – AMSTERDAM
NORTH-HOLLAND PUBLISHING COMPANY, LTD. – LONDON

PRINTED IN THE NETHERLANDS

CONTENTS

I. INTRODUCTION

The initial stimulus for the work described in this monograph was a concern with the linguistic problems in mechanised information retrieval systems. The rapid and continuing exponential increase in all kinds of publications makes it imperative that the processes of abstracting, indexing, classifying and searching for documents are automated to a considerable degree. Whereas human indexers and abstractors are able to interpret and analyse the content of documents without needing to know the workings of language, the mechanisation of any of these processes demands detailed knowledge of language structure. Linguists have contributed much to knowledge about syntactic structures, in particular the transformational-generative grammarians, but for the purposes of informational retrieval the more urgent need is for insight into semantic structures. No really effective information retrieval system is possible if only syntax is taken account of: 'content' can be represented only in semantic terms. Thus, we find in many experimental systems the use of semantic graphs to represent document content, e.g. Syntol (Cros et al., 1964), the sophisticated SMART system (Salton, 1968) and the inference and question-answering systems of Quillian (1966), Simmons (1965) and others (Minsky, 1968).

The attempt by some transformational-generative grammarians to attach semantic information onto syntactic structures (Katz and Postal, 1964) is not satisfactory, from the point of view of information retrieval at least, since while it is sufficient enough for the explanation of anomaly, tautology, etc. and for the resolution of homonymy it does not adequately account for the many utterances which are not anomalous or tautological and in which homonyms cannot be explicated solely by recourse to syntactic relationships. The present work has a different approach. It describes a language model in which semantic graphs are the base for the generation of the syntactic structures of sentences.

The model adopted is 'stratificational' in that it hypothesises between a linguistic utterance (spoken or written) and its extra-linguistic reference a series of strata: sememic, lexemic, morphemic, etc. However, it differs in many ways from the stratificational model of Lamb (1966) and Gleason (1964), particularly in that the structure of an 'expression' on any stratum is directly determined by its structure on higher strata and not by 'tactics' applicable to elements on that stratum only. The model is also 'generative' in that syntactic structures are derived (generated) from semantic graphs and strings of graphemes (sentences) are derived from syntactic structures. It is not 'transformational' since there are no rules for the conversion of one syntactic structure into another: as we shall see, 'synonymous' syntactic structures are generated from the same underlying semantic network or graph.

A general outline of the model is followed by an introduction to the kind of rules required for the derivation of syntactic structures from 'sememic formulae'. The subsequent chapters illustrate a variety of syntactic and semantic features working from relatively simple structures to more complex ones. On the whole, those aspects which cause most difficulty in information retrieval systems have been treated in greater detail than those of less concern. The concluding chapter touches upon some deeper issues raised during the exposition including certain parallels with the formulations of logicians.

Throughout, my debt to the work of linguists from many different 'schools' will be very evident both in the theoretical aspects of the model and in the particular analyses of English I have adopted. The list of references is merely an indication of the main sources for my approach to syntax and semantics.

II. THE MODEL AND THE SEMOLEXEMIC RULES

Before outlining the language model which underlies the work presented in this monograph some preliminary remarks must be made about structural semantics in general.

A. Semantic structure

1. A number of philosophers and linguists who have investigated the place of meaning in language structure, e.g. Antal (1963), Baldinger (1966), Hjelmslev (1961), Katz and Fodor (1963), Leech (1969), Lyons (1963, 1968), Morris (1938) and Quine (1960), have demonstrated conclusively that any semantic theory must keep distinct the notions of 'sense' and 'reference'. The former embraces the complex semantic interrelationship of lexemes (items of vocabulary) and the latter the relationships between lexemes and the objects, concepts, events, etc. to which they may refer. Furthermore, the primacy of 'sense' over 'reference' must be recognised. For the correct application and understanding of a given lexeme it is not necessary to know all its actual or potential referents. Indeed, many lexemes have no referents — whether real, imaginary or conceptual — and yet they do and must have 'sense': "while every sign [= lexeme] has a designatum not every sign has a denotatum [= referent] " (Morris, 1938).

2. For the 'sense' of a particular lexeme (Morris' 'designatum') we adopt the term 'sememe' used by Baldinger (1966) and Lamb (1964) among others. Since the sememe of a lexeme is a linguistic unit and the referents of a lexeme are extralinguistic, we cannot define the sememe in terms of the common

characteristics (attributes or properties) of its set of referents, i.e. the 'sememe' is not the same as the philosopher's 'intension'. Instead, it can be defined only relative to other sememes. [1]

3.   The paradigmatic relationships between sememes, e.g. those of synonymy, antonymy, hyponomy, can be accounted for if we hypothesise 'atomic' semantic components, called here 'semons'. Sememes with a large number of semons in common will be more closely related (be more alike in meaning) than sememes with few semons in common. (Lexemes which are synonymous will have the same set of semons, i.e. the same sememe.) By procedures such as componential analysis (e.g. Leech, 1969; Lyons, 1968: 470 ff.) it should be possible to isolate a group of semons sufficient for the definition of all sememes. Hypothetically, the group should be relatively small in number, because every semon must occur in a number of different sememes (in order that paradigms of 'similar' sememes can be drawn up) and because one sememe is sufficiently distinguished from another if it has just *one* semon lacking in the other. As Lyons (1968: 476) points out, such definitions of sememes would enable us to achieve more precise formulations of concepts such as synonymy, hyponomy, analyticity, syntheticity, tautology and 'semantic distance' (e.g. why *car* can be said to be closer in meaning to *bus* than to *train*), which are at present to a greater or lesser extent intuitive.

4.   Although semons are not the same 'entities' as the characteristics of referents there must be clearly a considerable parallelism between them. For example, from a componential analysis of the sememes for *boy*, *girl*, *man*, *woman*, *bull*, *cow*, *calf*, *sheep*, *lamb* we may obtain the semons '⟨male⟩', '⟨female⟩', '⟨young⟩', etc. The counterparts of these semons are the conceptual characteristics 'maleness', 'femaleness', 'youth', etc. The parallelism between semons and referential characteristics enables us to account for the 'act of referring'. A lexeme is used to refer to an object, event, etc. (e.g. BOY) if its sememe contains semons ('⟨male⟩', '⟨young⟩', etc.) which are counterparts of some of the characteristics ('maleness', 'youth', etc.) which have been discerned, by the language user, in that object (BOY). Not all the characteristics discerned in an object need to have semon counterparts in the sememe of an appropriate

---

[1] In fact, any intensional definition must resort to some notion of 'sense' because it can be formulated only with knowledge of the referential extension of the lexeme and this implies that at some earlier stage a partitioning of some universe (of percepts or concepts) has taken place which took account of the conventional 'senses' of a group of lexemes.

lexeme. Whereas the number of semons is only that sufficient and necessary for the distinction of the sememe from other sememes, the number of characteristics common to a set of objects can be very large. [2] Which characteristics have in fact semon counterparts in the sememe for a particular lexeme is an 'arbitrary' decision on the part of a language community. The referents of a lexeme do not necessarily constitute a 'natural' class since the community may choose to group together objects which according to some 'scientific' criterion should be distinguished, e.g. it may consider that the class of referents denoted by *fish* includes all the referents of *whales*. The confusion resulting from the natural, almost subconscious, tendency to define lexemes according to 'real' characteristics common to its referents rather than through some kind of componential analysis bedevils the whole field of semantics.

5. The characteristics which are present in a lexeme's referents but which have no semon counterparts may be called the lexeme's 'connotations'. Not all connotations need to be accepted by the whole community since they are not essential to the use or understanding of the lexeme. On the whole, connotations tend to be personal or shared only by a small group of the community. [3] However, some are more widespread. For example, it is unlikely that the sememe for *pig* contains the semon(s) '⟨dirty⟩'. However, for many members of the community one characteristic of all its referents is 'dirty', i.e. *pig* evokes the immediate connotation of dirtiness. Connotations, then, are semantic features added to the core 'cognitive meaning' of a lexeme (its sememe) for the expression of contempt, affection, reprobation and other 'emotive meanings' (Lyons, 1968: 448 ff.).

The presence of connotations for nearly all items in the vocabulary is naturally a considerable hindrance in componential analysis. This is particularly so in the case of 'abstract' terms such as *democracy, freedom, virtue*, etc. Standing alone these lexemes are undoubtedly vague, but it is always possible to specify them exactly by adding descriptive phrases, e.g. *democracy as practised in Athens in the age of Pericles* or *democracy as understood by Lenin.*

---

[2] Hence, while the possible classifications of extralinguistic entities are almost infinite, the classifications of sememes are limited by the relatively small number of semons. This suggests that any information retrieval system would be improved if it adopted a classification based on a componential analysis of vocabulary instead of the present classifications based on (largely intuitive) conceptual analyses of referents – analyses which in the nature of things change at every advance of scientific knowledge.

[3] Truly personal connotations, i.e. those held by one particular individual, are recognised by psychologists and literary critics to be valuable indicators of an individual's 'attitude to society', 'philosophy of life', etc.

These phrases may be said to make explicit the connotations intended by a speaker (in his subsequent use of *democracy*) and thus may be said to narrow down the potential referents to one specific referent. In componential analysis, the sememes (the core 'cognitive meanings') of *democracy*, *freedom*, etc. must be extracted somehow from their plethora of widely-diverging connotations: obviously a very difficult task, but not theoretically an impossible one.

As we have mentioned, many connotations are shared by members forming a subgroup of the language community. Where such subgroups represent distinct social communities with common interests — professional, intellectual, recreational, etc. — these connotations may become semantic components essential for communication in the group, i.e. the connotations become semons. Thus, we find the creation of specialist vocabularies (e.g. legal jargon, slang, medical terminology, etc.) and we must accept that certain lexemes may have one sememe for the community as a whole and another found only in a subgroup of the community.

6.   Since a lexeme can express any one of a number of referents it is usually necessary for a speaker to specify exactly the one intended. This can be done either (i) by deixis, e.g. adding to *book* (which may refer to any one of millions of possible referents) a deictic article *this* or *that* to form a phrase *this book* or *that book*, (ii) by a descriptive phrase, e.g. *a red book on the top shelf of John's bookcase* (in the same way that *democracy* was specified), or (iii) by anaphoric reference to an earlier description (see chapter VI). In every case the speaker links together a number of lexemes to form phrases. A speaker will also link lexemes together when he wants to express relationships between referents — the expression of a 'cognitive experience' or an 'event' frequently takes the form of a sentence. We called the 'sense' of a single lexeme its sememe; for the 'sense' of a sentence, a syntagmatic structure of linked sememes, we coin the term 'sememic formula' (often abbreviated as SF).

7.   A number of lexemes have only one referent, e.g. proper names. While these lexemes must have sememes it would seem that only a restricted number of their semons are identifiable. For example, *John* may have the semon '⟨male⟩' and *Washington* the semon '⟨city⟩' but other semons are more doubtful. We cannot add, for example, the semon '⟨capital⟩' to the sememe for *Washington* because we are not justified in assuming the synonymy of *Washington* and *capital of the United States*. The two expressions are 'referentially' synonymous but not synonymous in 'sense' — at some future date the capital may be another city.

8. This monograph considers only the synchronic aspects of semantic structure, in the belief that diachronic semantics can proceed only from a secure
synchronic base. As far as the semon constitution of the language is concerned, however, we may hypothesize that it changes relatively slowly. New
lexemes (i.e. neologisms) can usually be paraphrased in terms of old lexemes:
the method usually found in dictionaries. We may presume that their sememes
consist essentially of new groupings of 'old' semons. Although we must suppose that new semons are required from time to time it may well be that this
is not frequent. Certainly not as frequent as the apparently rapid change in
vocabulary might suggest. Whether semons are as stable as phonemic and syntactic structure is, of course, very much an open question to which there can
be no answer at present.

B. The language model

1. In fig. 1 a schematic presentation of the language model is given which
shows how a speaker (or writer) passes through a number of strata from the
awareness of a 'cognitive experience' to its expression in speech (or writing).
By the very use of 'cognitive' we already indicate that no discussion will be
found here of the communication of 'emotive' states.
1.1. To express an extralinguistic 'cognitive experience' a speaker or writer
considers, firstly, which characteristics he wishes to communicate. The semon
counterparts of these characteristics (or rather of those characteristics which
have available semons) are then organised in some, as yet undefinable, way as
a network of semons indicating the interrelationships between the semons.
1.2. From a semon network he constructs a pattern of sememes by selecting
those sememes which can contain the semons in the network while retaining
the relationships specified. A pattern of sememes may constitute one or more
sememic formulae (SFs) according to the complexity of the semon network
and the available sememes and sememic structures. The sememic formulae
derived from one semon network will usually (but not necessarily) be inter-
related in some way, e.g. anaphorically (see chapter VI).
1.3. Each sememic formula is converted into a linear string of lexemes containing information on syntactic structure. Some sememes in SFs are realised
as lexemes and others as syntactic functions or grammatical categories. (In
the graph representation of SFs employed in this monograph the latter are
generally links and the former are generally nodes.) This, the semolexemic
transformation, is the topic of the present work.

Fig. 1

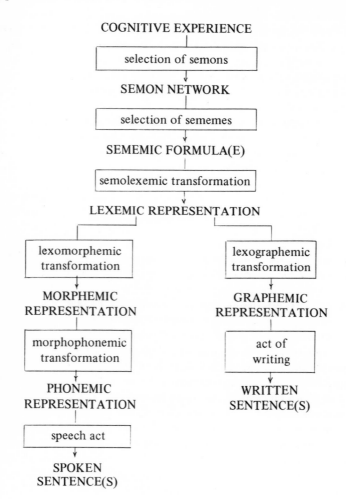

1.4. From the lexemic representation a speaker derives a string of morphemes and from these a string of phonemes which he can transform into a spoken utterance. From the same lexemic representation a writer derives a string of graphemes which he transforms into a written sentence.

2. At every stage in the process a speaker or writer is faced with a number of selectional restrictions but, at the same time, he has available to him a large number of options.

2.1. In selecting semons he is restricted by the range of semons recognised by the community and these may not be adequate for the expression of the characteristics of his 'cognitive experience'. In the selection of sememes and in constructing sememic formulae he is similarly restricted by the sememes available, i.e. he cannot choose a group of semons at random and expect to find a sememe to contain them. At the same time, however, for a given semon network there may be many different ways of grouping into sememes. His choice will depend on many factors. Chief of these are his knowledge of the vocabulary, since in selecting sememes he is essentially selecting lexemes. Other factors are his emotional state at the time and his stylistic inclinations. Some features of style are often common to large subgroups of the community, even to whole generations, i.e. there is fashion in language use and some fashionable practices may impose severe restrictions on choice of sememes.

In other linguistic contexts the restrictions placed upon any speaker by the availability of semons and sememes have been described as the factors which reveal the influence of language upon thought and culture (the Sapir-Whorf hypothesis). This view presupposes that semons are not universal to all languages. This is not the place to discuss the universality of semons. Indeed, until we know far more about semantic structure such a discussion would be premature.

2.2. In semolexemic transformation the speaker or writer is restricted by the syntactic structures available for the expression of a semantic relationship represented in a SF. On the other hand, he is often faced with a wide choice. Almost any part or node of a SF can be emphasised and for each variant there is a syntactic structure available. As in sememe selection the choice of one structure rather than another may be made for 'emotive' or stylistic reasons.

2.3. The restrictions further down in the process are well known and need not be elaborated. Some are intra-lingual, e.g. the absence of a phonemic or graphemic form for a lexeme in a given grammatical function; others are extra-lingual, e.g. the inability for whatever reason of a particular speaker to pronounce certain sounds.

2.4. In so far as the model attempts to account for all the choices open to a speaker or writer and all the restrictions 'imposed' upon him by the language itself it is a model of "competence" (in Chomsky's terms) or of "langue" (in de Saussure's terms). A description of the choices made by a particular speaker on a particular occasion and an explanation of why certain options were not pursued would be dealing with "performance" or "parole". The model underlying this study follows the current practice in linguistics in being a model of "competence".

2.5. All the choices made by a speaker after his initial selection of semons have no effect on the 'cognitive' sense of what he wishes to express. Some choices, perhaps most, do however introduce matters of style and overtones of 'emotive' meaning. Since these are aspects of "performance" we ignore them here and treat all utterances derived from a common semon network as synonymous.

3. Understanding a sentence can be considered as the inverse of the process of expression. Starting, for example, from a written sentence the reader forms a graphemic representation. This is converted by 'grapholexemic transformation' into a lexemic representation, which in turn is changed by 'lexosememic transformation' into a sememic formula. From the SF a semon network is constructed which enables him to discover the characteristics by which he can identify the 'cognitive experience' intended by the writer. Naturally, there are as many restrictions and choices in this process as there are in expression and it should not be surprising that a reader often makes choices leading to an interpretation which the writer did not intend.

4. Only one part of this model is investigated in detail, the transformation of sememic formulae into lexemic strings. The main emphasis is on the realisation of syntactic structures from representations of semantic relationships in SFs. From time to time brief allusions are made to semon networks, but there is no attempt to deal with problems of sememe formation since this would require a systematic componential analysis of vocabulary. Statements in the text about the semon constitution of sememes are based largely on the semantic analysis of syntactic structures. However, as I show in chapter XV, some information about the nature of semon networks and about certain semantic relationships such as anomaly, tautology, etc. can be gleaned from the structures and interrelationships of sememic formulae.

C. Semolexemic transformations

Semolexemic transformation is a two-stage process. The first stage forms a linearisation of the sememic formula and the second converts the linearised SF by semolexemic rules into a lexemic realisation containing all the necessary syntactic information for transformations into lower strata.

1. As already described, a sememic formula is an organisation of sememes in the form of a graph. Both the nodes and the links of the graph are sememes: the former usually being realised as lexemes, the latter usually as grammatical categories attached to lexemes. An example of a SF is given in fig. 2. It is one we shall have occasion to use frequently in following sections.

Fig. 2

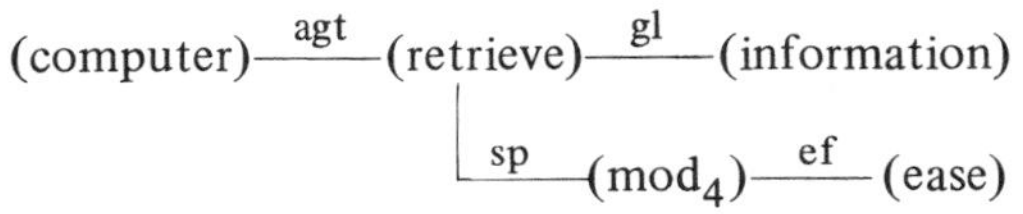

$$(\text{computer}) \xrightarrow{\text{agt}} (\text{retrieve}) \xrightarrow{\text{gl}} (\text{information})$$
$$\big|_{\text{sp}} (\text{mod}_4) \xrightarrow{\text{ef}} (\text{ease})$$

1.1. The similarities and differences between my sememic formulae and the graphs of Lamb (1964) will be obvious from fig. 3 which represents part of the SF in fig. 2. In Lamb's graph the nodes only are sememes and the links are directed:

Fig. 3

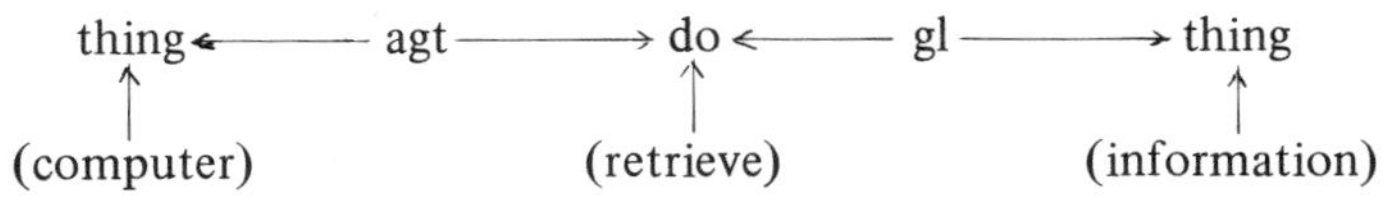

$$\text{thing} \longleftarrow \text{agt} \longrightarrow \text{do} \longleftarrow \text{gl} \longrightarrow \text{thing}$$
$$\uparrow \qquad\qquad\qquad \uparrow \qquad\qquad\qquad \uparrow$$
$$(\text{computer}) \qquad (\text{retrieve}) \qquad (\text{information})$$

1.2. The sememic links found in SFs are of the following kinds:
  (i) 'agt': indicating the relationship between the agent of a process and the process itself.
  (ii) 'gl': the relationship between a process and the patient of a process.
  (iii) 'sp' and 'ef': these links always occur together. They indicate that the sememe linked by 'sp' is modified in some way by the sememe attached to 'ef' — the kind of modification being specified by the sememe between the two links.
  (iv) 'co' and 'oc': also only occurring together. They indicate co-ordination, the nature of the co-ordination being specified by the sememe between 'co' and 'oc'.

 (v) 'ana': the anaphoric relationship.
 (vi) 'dat': the relationship between a process and the beneficiary of the
      process.
  All of these links may be traced in the reverse direction thus forming a
further set of sememic links:
(vii) 'tga': the relationship between a process and the agent of a process.
(viii) 'lg': the relationship between the patient of a process and the process
      itself.
 (ix) 'fe' and 'ps': the inverse of the 'sp–ef' modification link.
  (x) 'tad': the relationship between the beneficiary of a process and the
      process itself.
  These must be seen as only preliminary definitions of the meaning of these
links — their full significance can be appreciated only after the realisation of
SFs including them.
  A few other links which have not been mentioned here will be explained
when they arise.
1.3. In the course of the description I will often speak of "the sememe at the
end of the 'tga' link". In the case of the SF in fig. 2 the sememe intended
would be '(computer)'. Similarly, "the sememe at the end of the 'agt' link"
would be '(retrieve)'; "the sememe at the end of the 'ps' link" would also be
'(retrieve)'; "the sememe at the end of 'ef' " would be '(ease)'. As a variant for
sememe when talking about SFs I also use "node". Thus, "the node at the
end of the 'gl' link in fig. 2" is '(information)'.

2. The linearisation of a SF involves the choice of a point of entry in the
graph and of the path which is to be traced through it. Choices made during
linearisation do not affect 'cognitive' meaning but, as I have already mentioned, they do result in different emphases and stylistic variants in realisations.
2.1. Firstly, nodes in the SF are selected which are to be the 'theme' node
and the 'pivot' node. I follow Halliday (1967: 212) in using theme for "what
is being talked about, the point of departure for the clause as a message". It is
the sememe which a speaker or writer considers the most effective connector
with what has gone previously and its lexeme often becomes the 'grammatical
subject' of the sentence.
2.2. The 'pivot' node must be one either appearing at the end of a 'agt' or
'lg' link or appearing between a 'sp' and a 'ef' link. In fig. 2 the pivot can be
either '(retrieve)' or '(mod$_4$)'.
2.3. The theme node must be a node at the other end of a link from the
pivot node. It can be no other node in the SF. If '(retrieve)' is chosen as pivot,

the theme can be either '(computer)' at the end of 'tga', or '(information)' at
the end of 'gl', or '(mod$_4$)' at the end of 'sp'. If '(mod$_4$)' is the pivot, then
the theme can be either '(retrieve)' at the end of 'ps' or '(ease)' at the end of
'ef'.

2.4. Next, the theme node and all nodes leading from it except the pivot
node are placed in one all-embracing bracket. Thus, if '(mod$_4$)' is chosen as
pivot and '(retrieve)' as theme we obtain the following:

Fig. 4 (i)

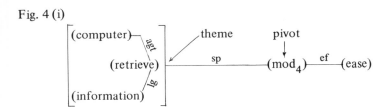

The nodes '(computer)' and '(information)' are included in the bracket
because they both lead from '(retrieve)' but neither of them is the pivot
node.

If the theme node has no nodes leading from it, then it alone is bracketed:

Fig. 4 (ii)

theme   pivot
↓   ↓
[(computer)]——agt——(retrieve)——gl——(information)
|__sp__(mod$_4$)——ef——(ease)

Fig. 4 (iii)

pivot   theme
↓   ↓
(computer)——agt——(retrieve)——gl——[(information)]
|__sp__(mod$_4$)——ef——(ease)

Fig. 4 (iv)

(computer)——agt——(retrieve)——gl——(information)
|__sp__(mod$_4$)——ef——[(ease)]
↑   ↑
pivot   theme

On a number of occasions I shall refer to the 'tail' node in a SF of a linearisation. It may be defined as the sememe linked to the pivot by 'gl' or 'tga' when the theme is the node at the end of 'tga' or 'gl' respectively. For example in fig. 4 (ii) the 'tail' node would be '(information)' and in fig. 4 (iii) it would be '(computer)'.

2.5. After these preliminaries the SF can be linearised. In the course of linearisation further bracketing takes place:

(i) when a node at the end of a 'tga', 'gl' or 'dat' link is encountered it is bracketed together with any other nodes leading from it. If a single node has already been bracketed because it is the theme node it is not further bracketed.

(ii) when a node at the end of an 'ef', 'ps' or 'oc' link is encountered it is bracketed with the other nodes leading from it. But if the node stands alone it is not bracketed.

To the theme node and bracket is attached a 'decl' link (indicating that the sentence is 'declarative' − in this monograph I do not deal with interrogatives or imperatives). From the theme node a path is traced through all the links and nodes in the theme bracket, then to the pivot node and through all the other links and nodes in the SF. If there is a choice of paths, one is selected and traced to its end node. Then the linearisation returns to the node where the paths divided, a symbol 'b' (indicating 'branch') is added followed by the name of the node and the other path is traced to its end.

2.6. To illustrate, take the bracketing of fig. 4 (i).

(a) To the theme node and bracket is attached 'decl':

$$\text{decl} \longrightarrow [(\text{retrieve})$$

(b) One path from '(retrieve)' is selected:

$$\text{decl} \longrightarrow [(\text{retrieve}) \xrightarrow{\text{tga}} [(\text{computer})]$$

Since '(computer)' is at the end of a 'tga' link it must be bracketed (rule (i) above).

(c) Returning to the node where there was a choice of paths, i.e. '(retrieve)', we add 'b' and the name of the node:

$$\text{decl} \longrightarrow [(\text{retrieve}) \xrightarrow{\text{tga}} [(\text{computer})] \, b(\text{retrieve})$$

(d) The other path is now traced:

decl $\longrightarrow$[(retrieve)$\xrightarrow{\text{tga}}$[(computer)]] b (retrieve)$\xrightarrow{\text{gl}}$[(information)]]

Standing at the end of a 'gl' link, '(information)' must be bracketed.
(e) As all the paths within the theme bracket have now been traced, the bracket is closed and the linearisation proceeds to the pivot node:

decl$\longrightarrow$[(retrieve)$\xrightarrow{\text{tga}}$[(computer)]] b (retrieve)——

——$\xrightarrow{\text{gl}}$[(information)]]]$\xrightarrow{\text{sp}}$(mod$_4$)

(f) Finally, the path to the remaining node is traced:

decl$\longrightarrow$[(retrieve)$\xrightarrow{\text{tga}}$[(computer)]] b (retrieve)——

——$\xrightarrow{\text{gl}}$[(information)]]]$\xrightarrow{\text{sp}}$(mod$_4$)$\xrightarrow{\text{ef}}$(ease)

As this node at the end of 'ef' has no other links leading from it there is no bracketing (see rule (ii)).
2.7. If at (b) above the path selected had been the 'gl' link, the following linearisation would have been obtained:

decl$\longrightarrow$[(retrieve)$\xrightarrow{\text{gl}}$[(information)]] b (retrieve)——

——$\xrightarrow{\text{tga}}$[(computer)]]]$\xrightarrow{\text{sp}}$(mod$_4$)$\xrightarrow{\text{ef}}$(ease)

The linearisation resulting from the alternative choices of theme and pivot nodes are, from fig. 4 (ii):

decl$\longrightarrow$[(computer)]$\xrightarrow{\text{agt}}$(retrieve)$\xrightarrow{\text{gl}}$[(information)]] b (retrieve)—

——$\xrightarrow{\text{sp}}$(mod$_4$)$\xrightarrow{\text{ef}}$(ease)

decl$\longrightarrow$[(computer)]$\xrightarrow{\text{agt}}$(retrieve)$\xrightarrow{\text{sp}}$(mod$_4$)$\xrightarrow{\text{ef}}$(ease)

b (retrieve)$\xrightarrow{\text{gl}}$[(information)]]

From fig. 4 (iii):

decl$\longrightarrow$[(information)]$\xrightarrow{\text{lg}}$(retrieve)$\xrightarrow{\text{tga}}$[(computer)]] b (retrieve)—

——$\xrightarrow{\text{sp}}$(mod$_4$)$\xrightarrow{\text{ef}}$(ease)

$$\text{decl} \longrightarrow [(\text{information})] \xrightarrow{\text{lg}} (\text{retrieve}) \xrightarrow{\text{sp}} (\text{mod}_4) \xrightarrow{\text{ef}} (\text{ease})$$

$$\text{b} (\text{retrieve}) \xrightarrow{\text{tga}} [(\text{computer})]$$

(Note the inverse tracing of 'agt' and 'gl' to produce 'lg' and 'tga' links.)
Finally, from fig. 4 (iv):

$$\text{decl} \longrightarrow [(\text{ease})] \xrightarrow{\text{fe}} (\text{mod}_4) \xrightarrow{\text{ps}} [(\text{retrieve}) \xrightarrow{\text{tga}} [(\text{computer})]$$

$$\text{b} (\text{retrieve}) \xrightarrow{\text{gl}} [(\text{information})]]$$

$$\text{decl} \longrightarrow [(\text{ease})] \xrightarrow{\text{fe}} (\text{mod}_4) \xrightarrow{\text{ps}} [(\text{retrieve}) \xrightarrow{\text{gl}} [(\text{information})]$$

$$\text{b} (\text{retrieve}) \xrightarrow{\text{tga}} [(\text{computer})]]$$

These last two illustrate the bracketing of a node at the end of 'ps' when
other links and nodes lead from it (see rule (ii)).

3.   A linearisation is converted into a lexemic realisation by means of semolexemic rules. A full list of all the rules employed in this publication is given
in appendix B.
3.1.   Semolexemic rules are of two basic kinds:

(i) $\alpha : X(x) \rightarrow X(x) + Y$

   $\alpha : X(x) \rightarrow Y + X(x)$

where 'α' is a sememic link in a linearisation, '$X(x)$' is a grammatical category
plus a sememe, and 'Y' is another grammatical category. Informally, the rules
may be read as "the operation of 'α' upon '$X(x)$' produces the lexemic string
'$X(x) + Y$' or the lexemic string '$Y + X(x)$' ".

(ii) $\alpha : Y \rightarrow Z$

where 'α' is a sememic link or a bracket in a linearisation, 'Y' is a grammatical
category and 'Z' is another grammatical category or group of categories.
3.2.   Sememes, i.e. nodes of a SF, may be attached only to 'lexical' grammatical categories (a list of which is given in appendix A) by rule (1), viz:

$$(x) : C \rightarrow C(x)$$

where '(x)' is any sememe occurring in a linearisation and 'C' is any 'lexical'
category produced by an earlier (usually the immediately preceding) semo-

lexemic rule. Sememes are always attached to the last (i.e. the right-most) 'lexical' category in a lexemic string which has not yet had any sememe attached to it.

3.3. Semolexemic rules are applied strictly in the order in which the sememic symbols (links or brackets) occur in the linearisation. The grammatical categories on which they operate are: in the case of sememic links, the last 'lexical' category plus sememe in the string so far produced or occasionally the last 'non-lexical' category; and, in the case of brackets, the last 'lexical' category without a sememe or the last 'non-lexical' category. The whole process of semolexemic transformation of a linearised SF is triggered off by the introduction of an initial category 'S'. Upon this category operates the first semolexemic rule, generally 'decl'.

I have not attempted a mathematical formulation of these rules since it would seem to be premature. However, in general, the kind of rules outlined are dealt with by Hockett (1967: 114 ff.).

4. Since the above description is necessarily abstract I will quickly pass on to a concrete illustration of how the rules operate. Our example shall be one of the linearisations in section 2.7 above:

$$\text{decl} \longrightarrow [(\text{computer})] \xrightarrow{\text{agt}} (\text{retrieve}) \xrightarrow{\text{gl}} [(\text{information})]$$

$$\text{b (retrieve)} \xrightarrow{\text{sp}} (\text{mod}_4) \xrightarrow{\text{ef}} (\text{ease})$$

For reference the full realisation is summarised in fig. 6; the following serves as a commentary upon the procedures.

4.1. The first sememe in the linearisation, 'decl', operates upon the initial category:

$$(7) \quad \text{decl} \ : \ S \rightarrow NPs$$

(Here and in all later examples the rule number in appendix B is given in brackets before its statement.)

4.2. The next sememic symbol is the righthand bracket '[', which operates on the 'non-lexical' category 'NPs':

$$(30) \quad [\quad : \ NPs \rightarrow NP \ (N^0$$

The rule introduces a 'lexical' category 'N' to which the following sememe in the linearisation, '(computer)', may be attached:

$$(1) \quad (\text{computer}) \ : \ N^0 \rightarrow N^0 (\text{computer})$$

4.3. The lefthand bracket ']' which follows closes the bracket opened by '[', thus:

(2)   ]   :   NP(N^0(computer) → NP(N^0(computer))

This is stated as a general rule in the appendix as

]   :   K (... → K(...)

where 'K' is any 'non-lexical' category.

4.4. The next rule is the operation of the link 'agt' upon 'NP (...)':

(50)   agt   :   NP (...) → NP (...) + V

'V' is a 'lexical' category to which the following sememe '(retrieve)' may be attached. Upon 'V (retrieve)' operates the next sememic symbol 'gl':

(199)   gl   :   V (retrieve) → V (retrieve) + NPt

4.5. The bracket '[' can be applied to 'NPt', thus:

(35)   [:   NPt → NP(N^0

The other options available will be treated later, for the present we will ignore them.

By the same process described above, the next sememe '(information)' is attached to the category 'N^0' and the brackets are closed by ']', producing:

NP(N^0 (information))

4.6. With the next symbol 'b' we can introduce the branching rules (3) and (4). These are of general application and occur frequently in the examples.

(3)   b(x)   :   C(x) → C(x)

(4)   b(x)   :   C(y) → C(y) + C$_x$(Δ)

4.6.1. Rule (3) is fairly simple. If the sememe '(x)' which follows 'b' is the same as the sememe attached to the last 'lexical' category 'C' in the lexemic string produced so far, then the branching rule makes no change. The next rule will then operate on the last category plus sememe 'C(x)'. This will happen, for example, if an earlier rule of the form 'α : X(x) → Y + X(x)' has placed the branch node '(x)' in the final position of a string. There are numerous examples of this in later sections and I need not elaborate further.

4.6.2. In this particular case, however, the sememe following 'b' is '(retrieve)' and it is not the same as the sememe attached to the last 'lexical' category in the string: '(information)'. Therefore rule (4) is applicable. This adds a dummy sememe to the string with the category which has been attached earlier to the branch node — in this case, '(retrieve)' has been assigned the category 'V', so the effect of rule (4) is to add 'V(Δ)' to the lexemic string:

b(retrieve) : N^0 (information)) → N^0 (information)) + V (Δ)

4.7. As we shall see a dummy sememe is not realised graphemically, its purpose is to permit the derivation of 'discontinuous' structures, e.g. the modification of a verb by an adverb following the 'object' of the verb, as in this example.

Next : (329)   sp   : $V(\Delta) \rightarrow V(\Delta) + Z_{034}$

The sememe '(mod_4)' may be attached to 'Z_{034}' as it has a numerical subscript matching one of those attached to the category 'Z'. This operation is expressed in the general rule:

$$(5) \quad (\text{mod}_n) : C_n \rightarrow C_n(\text{mod}_n)$$

where 'n' is any one particular numerical subscript and 'C' any 'lexical' category. In this case: $(\text{mod}_4) : Z_4 \rightarrow Z_4(\text{mod}_4)$.

Finally, rule (167) is applied — also expressed in the appendix as a general rule, viz. (167) ef : $Z_n(\text{mod}_n) \rightarrow \text{Adv}_n$. In our example, therefore:

$$\text{ef} \quad : \quad Z_4(\text{mod}_4) \rightarrow \text{Adv}_4 \ .$$

Since the last sememe '(ease)' belongs to the adjective-adverb class A_4 (see chapter IV) it can be attached to this category.

4.8. The full lexemic realisation which has been generated and which includes a 'discontinuous' adverbial modification, is thus: $NP(N^0(\text{computer})) + V(\text{retrieve}) + NP(N^0(\text{information})) + V(\Delta) + \text{Adv}_4(\text{ease})$.

4.8.1. At this stage the items in round brackets are no longer sememes but lexemes, since all the semolexemic rules have been applied. In this particular instance the lexemes happen to have the same physical form as the sememes from which they are derived, but in a number of later examples we will find lexemes with forms different from their sememic origins. (It is in fact mainly a matter of convenience to 'name' sememes by their most usual graphic realisations.)

4.8.2. As a 'bracketed labelled string' a lexemic realisation can be represented as a tree structure, e.g. fig. 5. We might say that semolexemic rules transform a sememic graph into a syntactic tree with appended lexemes.

Fig. 5

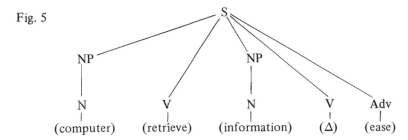

As in a Chomskyan grammar, this tree could be generated by 'rewrite rules'. However, a direct comparison with the kind of phrase-markers found in transformational-generative grammars would not be legitimate; their purposes and generative 'histories' differ too much.

4.9. To conclude this general outline of the semolexemic rules, two further points need to be made.

In certain cases the attachment of a sememe to a category, by rule (1), modifies the category itself. A common example is the attachment of a semon containing a semon '⟨v⟩' (= 'verbal') to the category 'N'. This results in the modification of 'N' to 'Nv', i.e. $N(v ...) \rightarrow Nv(...)$. Such category modification is completed always before the operation of the next semolexemic rule. Secondly, with certain categories numerical superscripts are used N^0, N^1, N^2, Nv^0, Nv^1, Nv^2, Vpp^0, Vpp^1, Vpp^2, etc. As we shall see, they have an important role in ensuring that only 'correct' syntactic structures are realised.

D. Lexographemic transformations

Although my principle aim is to describe the processes of semolexemic transformation, I cannot ignore completely the next stage, lexographemic transformation. This is because lexographemic rules must eliminate certain constructions if the vocabulary has no graphic form for a particular lexeme/category group.

1. The first stage of lexographemic transformation is the validation of the lexemic realisation. A lexemic realisation may be invalidated on two counts. Firstly if it has any lexeme (including the dummy) attached to a 'non-terminal' category. In appendix A 'lexical' categories are divided into 'terminal' and 'non-terminal' — the latter should occur only during the semolexemic transformations, thus if any remain after all rules have been applied the realisation must be invalid.

Secondly, a lexemic realisation is invalidated if it contains any 'non-lexical' category to which no valid lexemic string within round brackets is attached. Thus, a realisation containing ' ... + NP + ... ' would be invalid, but one containing ' ... + NP(Adj(x) + N(y)) + ... ' would be accepted since 'Adj(x) + N(y)' is a valid lexemic string (i.e. it has lexemes attached to 'terminal' categories).

2. The second stage converts the realisation into a form acceptable for direct

transformation into graphemes. The validated lexemic realisation is stripped (i) of all 'non-lexical' categories and brackets enclosing lexemic strings, i.e. 'NP(N^0(computer))' becomes 'N^0(computer)'; (ii) of all dummy sememes with their attached categories; and (iii) of all subscripts and superscripts, i.e. 'N^0(computer)' becomes 'N(computer)' and 'Adv_4(ease)' becomes 'Adv(ease)'.

3. The final stage is the conversion of each category-plus-lexeme group in the resulting string into a graphic form. This may be envisaged as 'lexicon look-up'.

From a lexicon containing entries such as:

V(retrieve)	= G/retrieves	N(information)	= G/information
Vpp(retrieve)	= G/retrieved	Adj(ease)	= G/easy
Nv(retrieve)	= G/retrieval	Adv(ease)	= G/easily
N(computer)	= G/computer		

We are able to transform our final lexemic realisation:

$$N(computer) + V(retrieve) + N(information) + Adv(ease)$$

into   *computer retrieves information easily*.

If the lexicon does not contain an entry for any particular lexeme-plus-category in a realisation, then the whole realisation is unproductive. For example, if 'V(computer)' or 'Adj(computer)' occur in a lexemic realisation it cannot be converted into graphic form.

4. All these stages of lexographemic transformation are given in fig. 6. But in all future examples only the final graphic form of a realisation will be given.

In addition, general semolexemic rules such as (1), (2), (3), (4) and (5) will not be stated in future realisations. Instead the processes will be abbreviated: the steps described in detail in the last few pages would be presented in the following more succinct form.

(30)	[	:	NPs $\rightarrow$ NP(N^0
(50)	agt	:	NP(...) $\rightarrow$ NP(...) + V
(199)	gl	:	V(retrieve) $\rightarrow$ V(retrieve) + NPt
(35)	[	:	NPt $\rightarrow$ NP(N^0
(329)	sp	:	$V(\Delta) \rightarrow V(\Delta) + Z_{034}$
(167)	ef	:	$Z_4(mod_4) \rightarrow Adv_4$

[*the*] *computer retrieves information easily*

Fig. 6

Semolexemic rule	No. of rule in app. B	Lexemic string generation
		S = initial category
decl	7	NPs
[	30	$NP(N^0$
(computer)	1	N^0(computer)
]	2	NP(...)
agt	50	NP(...) + V
(retrieve)	1	V(retrieve)
gl	199	V(retrieve) + NPt
[	35	$NP(N^0$
(information)	1	N^0(information)
]	2	NP(...)
b(retrieve)	4	N(information)) + $V(\Delta)$
sp	329	$V(\Delta) + Z_{034}$
(mod_4)	5	$Z_4(mod_4)$
ef	167	Adv_4
(ease)	1	Adv_4(ease)

lexemic realisation	$NP(N^0$(computer)) + V(retrieve) + $NP(N^0$(information)) + $V(\Delta) + Adv_4$(ease)

elimination of 'non-terminal' categories	N(computer) + V(retrieve) + N(information) + Adv(ease)

graphemic realisation	*computer* *retrieves* *information* *easily*

III. SENTENCES AND NOMINALISATIONS

One linearisation of the SF in fig. 2 has been realised in some detail in order to illustrate the operations of the semolexemic rules. To demonstrate their flexibility we will work through all the possible realisations of the other seven linearisations. By this means we can show how the rules derive only 'correct' sentences and no 'incorrect' ones.

A. Sentences

1. The linearisation we used in the last chapter was one from fig. 4 (ii). A second linearisation of this figure is:

$$\text{decl} \longrightarrow [(\text{computer})] \xrightarrow{\text{agt}} (\text{retrieve}) \xrightarrow{\text{sp}} (\text{mod}_4) \xrightarrow{\text{ef}} (\text{ease})$$

$$b\,(\text{retrieve}) \xrightarrow{\text{gl}} [(\text{information})]$$

It has two possible realisations:

(30)	[	:	$\text{NPs} \rightarrow \text{NP}(\text{N}^0$
(50)	agt	:	$\text{NP}(...) \rightarrow \text{NP}(...) + \text{V}$
(325)	sp	:	$\text{V}(\text{retrieve}) \rightarrow \text{V}(\text{retrieve}) + \text{Z}_{034}$
(167)	ef	:	$\text{Z}_4(\text{mod}_4) \rightarrow \text{Adv}_4$
(200)	gl	:	$\text{V}(\Delta) \rightarrow \text{V}(\Delta) + \text{NPt}$

computer retrieves easily information

and, with the application of rule (326) after (50):

(326)   sp   : $V(\text{retrieve}) \rightarrow Z_{469} + V(\text{retrieve})$

(167)   ef   : $Z_4(\text{mod}_4) \rightarrow \text{Adv}_4$

(199)   gl   : $V(\text{retrieve}) \rightarrow V(\text{retrieve}) + \text{NPt}$

computer easily retrieves information

1.1. In both realisations 'NPt' is changed into 'NP(N^0' by rule (35). On consulting appendix B the reader will note that rules (36) and (37) also apply '[' to 'NPt', producing 'NPq(Vinf^0' and 'NPr(Conj(that) + Vrel' respectively. However, the attachment of '(information)' to either category would be unproductive: in the case of 'Vinf' because there is no graphemic realisation for 'Vinf(information)' and in the case of 'Vrel' because it is a 'non-terminal' category and there are no further semolexemic rules to operate on it (see D.1 in chapter II above).

Apart from rule (30) there are other rules in which '[' operates on 'NPs'. Rule (31) produces 'NPc(Vger', rule (32) 'NPe(Vfor', rule (33) 'NPf(Vinf^1' and rule (34) 'NPr(Conj(that) + Vrel'. For similar reasons the attachment of '(computer)' to any of these categories is unproductive: there are no graphic forms for 'Vger(computer)' or 'Vinf(computer)' and 'Vfor' and 'Vrel' are non-terminal categories.

Needless to say these rules will be illustrated in other realisations where they are productive: those operating on 'NPs' later in this section, and those operating on 'NPt' in section B of this chapter.

1.2. One further point may be noted. In the first realisation we see the use of branching rule (4) to produce 'V(Δ)' on which rule (200) operates. In the second realisation branching rule (3) is found. Its application has been made possible by the preceding rule (326) which placed the branch node '(retrieve)' in the final position in the string (see C 4.6 above).

2.   In fig. 4 (iii) the sememe '(information)' was selected as theme node. From both its linearisations we can realise 'passive' sentences synonymous (cognitively) with the 'active' sentences produced from 4 (ii).

2.1. The linearisation:

$$\text{decl} \longrightarrow [(\text{information})] \xrightarrow{\text{lg}} (\text{retrieve}) \xrightarrow{\text{tga}} [(\text{computer})]$$

$$\text{b (retrieve)} \xrightarrow{\text{sp}} (\text{mod}_4) \xrightarrow{\text{ef}} (\text{ease})$$

can be realised in two different ways:

$$[\quad:\quad NPs \to NP(N^0)$$

(216) lg : $NP(...) \to NP(...) + V(be) + Vpp^0$

(380) tga : $Vpp^0(retrieve) \to Vpp^0(retrieve) + Pr(by) + NP$

(348) sp : $Vpp^0(\Delta) \to Vpp^0(\Delta) + Z_{034}$

ef : $Z_4(mod_4) \to Adv_4$

information is retrieved by computer easily

and, instead of rule (348):

(347) sp : $Vpp^0(\Delta) \to Vpp^0(\Delta) + W_{034}$

(102) ef : $W_4(mod_4) \to Pr(with) + N^0$

information is retrieved by computer with ease

As many later examples will show a prepositional phrase headed by *with* is a common alternative to the adverbial realisation.

2.2. From the second linearisation:

$$decl \longrightarrow [(information)] \xrightarrow{lg} (retrieve) \xrightarrow{sp} (mod_4) \xrightarrow{ef} (ease)$$

$$b\ (retrieve) \xrightarrow{tga} [(computer)]$$

2.2.1. We can realise:

$$[\quad:\quad NPs \to NP(N^0)$$

lg : $NP(...) \to NP(...) + V(be) + Vpp^0$

(343) sp : $Vpp^0(retrieve) \to Vpp^0(retrieve) + Z_{034}$

ef : $Z_4(mod_4) \to Adv_4$

(381) tga : $Vpp^0(\Delta) \to Vpp^0(\Delta) + Pr(by) + NP$

information is retrieved easily by computer

or, instead of (343), we may have:

(346) sp : $Vpp^0(retrieve) \to Z_{3469} + Vpp^0(retrieve)$

ef : $Z_4(mod_4) \to Adv_4$

(380) tga : $Vpp^0(retrieve) \to Vpp^0(retrieve) + Pr(by) + NP$

information is easily retrieved by computer

This example shows the facility with which semolexemic rules can be devised to permit 'discontinuous' structures — in this case the insertion of an adverb within the passive form of a verb – thus fulfilling one of Yngve's conditions for a satisfactory generative grammar (Yngve, 1960).

2.2.2. Two other realisations have interesting ramifications.

$$\text{lg} \quad : \quad NP(...) \rightarrow NP(...) + V(be) + Vpp^0$$

$$(345) \quad \text{sp} \quad : \quad Vpp^0(\text{retrieve}) \rightarrow X_{478} + Vinf^1(\text{retrieve})$$

$$(125) \quad \text{ef} \quad : \quad X_4(\text{mod}_4) \rightarrow Adj_4$$

$$(375) \quad \text{tga} \quad : \quad Vinf^1(\text{retrieve}) \rightarrow Pr(for) + NP[obl]^0 \\ + Vinf^1(\text{retrieve})$$

information is easy for [a] *computer to retrieve* [4]

or, instead of using (375):

$$(376) \quad \text{tga} \quad : \quad Vinf^1(\text{retrieve}) \rightarrow Vinf^0(\text{retrieve}) + Pr(by) + NP$$

information is easy to retrieve by computer

Here we find that the sememe '(ease)' is realised not as an adverb (*easily*) or adverbial phrase (*with ease*) but as an adjective. A frequent example in the literature is Chomsky's *John is easy to please*. The rules above show how this sentence can be derived from the SF in fig. 7 in which '(John)' is correctly identified as the patient of '(please)'.

Fig. 7

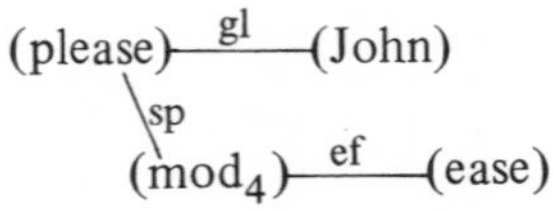

2.3. Not all adjectives, of course, can occur in such structures, just as not all adverbs can occur in all the positions which *easily* can occupy in sentences. This is indicated by the different subscripts present with W, X and Z (see next chapter).

3. In realising the linearisations of fig. 4 (i), where the theme node was '(retrieve)', we find that the other categories generated by '[' from 'NPs' are now productive.

---

[4] If the lexeme attached to 'N[obl]^0' (derived from 'NP[obl]' through '[') has a form in the 'oblique' case, e.g. the English prepositions *him*, *her*, *us* (for their derivation see chapter XIII.D), it is used. Otherwise the uninflected form is produced. Similarly with 'N[gen]' in later examples, a genitive is produced only if the lexeme has such a form. Strictly speaking rule (35) should read [: NPt → NP(N[obl]^0 since pronominal objects are always oblique.

3.1. From the linearisation

$$\text{decl} \longrightarrow [(\text{retrieve}) \xrightarrow{\text{tga}} [(\text{computer})] \text{ b (retrieve)} —$$

$$\xrightarrow{\text{gl}} [(\text{information})]\ ]\ \vdash^{\text{sp}} \rightarrow (\text{mod}_4) \xrightarrow{\text{ef}} (\text{ease})$$

(31)	[	:	$\text{NPs} \rightarrow \text{NPc(Vger}$
(368)	tga	:	$\text{Vger(retrieve)} \rightarrow \text{NPgen} + \text{Vger(retrieve)}$
(202)	gl	:	$\text{Vger(retrieve)} \rightarrow \text{Vger(retrieve)} + \text{NPt}$
(317)	sp	:	$\text{NPc(...)} \rightarrow \text{NPc(...)} + \text{Y}_{46789}$
(139)	ef	:	$\text{Y}_4(\text{mod}_4) \rightarrow \text{V(be)} + \text{Adj}_4$

[*the*] *computer's retrieving information is easy*

The choice of rule (369) instead of (368) would have been unproductive

(369)	tga	:	$\text{Vger(retrieve)} \rightarrow \text{Vger(retrieve)} + \text{Pr(by)} + \text{NP}$

because 'gl' cannot operate on $\text{Vger}(\Delta)$. Thus we do not find

* *retrieving by computer information is easy*

3.2.	(32)	[	:	$\text{NPs} \rightarrow \text{NPe(Vfor}$
	(367)	tga	:	$\text{Vfor(retrieve)} \rightarrow \text{Pr(for)} + \text{NP[obl]}$ $+ \text{Vinf}^1(\text{retrieve})$
	(204)	gl	:	$\text{Vinf}^1(\text{retrieve}) \rightarrow \text{Vinf}^0(\text{retrieve}) + \text{NPt}$
	(318)	sp	:	$\text{NPe(...)} \rightarrow \text{NPe(...)} + \text{Y}_{46789}$
		ef	:	$\text{Y}_4(\text{mod}_4) \rightarrow \text{V(be)} + \text{Adj}_4$

for [*a*] *computer to retrieve information is easy*

3.3. The use of rule

(33)	[	:	$\text{NPs} \rightarrow \text{NPf(Vinf}^1$

and rule

(375)	tga	:	$\text{Vinf}^1(\text{retrieve}) \rightarrow \text{Pr(for)} + \text{NP[obl]}$ $+ \text{Vinf}^1(\text{retrieve})$

produces the same realisation. The necessity for these rules in addition to (32) and (367) will be evident shortly.

3.4. Rule (34) generates from 'NPs' the category string 'NPr(Conj(that) + Vrel'. Although 'tga' can operate on 'Vrel(x)' and 'gl' can operate on the resultant string — later examples show how — the process is in this case un-

productive because the next sememe 'sp' cannot produce from 'NPr(...)' the
category 'Y_4' required by '(mod$_4$)'.

Therefore we do not have * *That the computer retrieves information is
easy*. With other adjectives, however, the structure is perfectly acceptable (see
next chapter).

3.5. Lastly, of course, rule (30) is operative producing 'NP(N^0' from 'NPs'.
Since '(retrieve)' contains the verbal semon '⟨v⟩' the category 'N^0' is modified
to 'Nv^0' (see chapter II.C.4.9). This introduces nominal structures, which will
be more fully illustrated in the next section.

$$[\quad : \quad NPs \rightarrow NP(N^0$$

(357)	tga	:	$Nv^0(\text{retrieve}) \rightarrow NPgen + Nv^1(\text{retrieve})$
(195)	gl	:	$Nv^1(\text{retrieve}) \rightarrow NP[gen] + Nv^2(\text{retrieve})$
(316)	sp	:	$NP(...) \rightarrow NP(...) + Y$
(138)	ef	:	$Y(\text{mod}_4) \rightarrow V(\text{be}) + Adj_4$

computer's information retrieval is easy

Here we have an example with one genitive form realised (*computer's*) and
one not realised (*information*). Instead of (195) we could have:

(194)   gl   : $Nv^1(\text{retrieve}) \rightarrow Nv^2(\text{retrieve}) + Pr(\text{of}) + NP$

giving   *computer's retrieval of information is easy*

There are two other rules in which 'tga' can be applied to 'Nv^0(x)'. Using rule

(356)   tga   : $Nv^0(\text{retrieve}) \rightarrow Nv^3(\text{retrieve}) + Pr(\text{by}) + NP$

and   (198)   gl   : $Nv^3(\Delta) \rightarrow Nv^2(\Delta) + Pr(\text{of}) + NP$

produces   *retrieval by computer of information is easy*

Secondly, there is rule (355), viz.

tga   : $Nv^0(x) \rightarrow AJ + Nv^1(x)$

In this instance its use is unproductive because there is no graphic form for
'Adj(computer)'. If, however, the node were '(machine)' we can see how the
rule permits the generation of a sentence such as

Mechanical retrieval of information is easy.

4.   The other linearisation of fig. 4 (i) is:

$$\text{decl} \longrightarrow [(\text{retrieve}) \xrightarrow{\text{gl}} [(\text{information})] \, b \, (\text{retrieve})$$

$$\xrightarrow{\text{tga}} [(\text{computer})] \,] \xrightarrow{\text{sp}} (\text{mod}_4) \xrightarrow{\text{ef}} (\text{ease})$$

4.1.   [: $NPs \rightarrow NPc(Vger$

    (202)   gl   : $Vger(retrieve) \rightarrow Vger(retrieve) + NPt$

    (370)   tga : $Vger(\Delta) \rightarrow Vger(\Delta) + Pr(by) + NP$

and then (317) and (139):

            retrieving information by computer is easy

4.2.   [: $NPs \rightarrow NPe(Vfor$

    (201)   gl   : $Vfor(retrieve) \rightarrow Pr(for) + NP[obl] + Vinf(be)$
                               $+ Vpp^0(retrieve)$

    (380)   tga : $Vpp^0(retrieve) \rightarrow Vpp^0(retrieve) + Pr(by) + NP$

and then (318) and (319):

            for information to be retrieved by computer is easy

4.3.   [: $NPs \rightarrow NPf(Vinf^1$

    (204)   gl   : $Vinf^1(retrieve) \rightarrow Vinf^0(retrieve) + NPt$

    (372)   tga : $Vinf^0(\Delta) \rightarrow Vinf^0(\Delta) \rightarrow Pr(by) + NP$

and then (319) and (139):

            to retrieve information by computer is easy

These last two examples show why we need to have both categories 'Vfor' and 'Vinf^1'.

If instead of using (372) we chose rule (374) a rather interesting construction can be illustrated.

              [: $NPs \rightarrow NPf(Vinf^1$

             gl   : $Vinf^1(retrieve) \rightarrow Vinf^0(retrieve) + NPt$

    (374)   tga : $Vinf^0(\Delta) \rightarrow Vinf^0(\Delta)) + T + PRP(Pr(for) + NP$

             ]   : $PRP(... \rightarrow PRP(...)$

    (323)   sp   : $T \rightarrow Y_{4789}$

    (139)   ef   : $Y_4(mod_4) \rightarrow V(be) + Adj_4$

        to retrieve information is easy for [a] computer

In rule (374) the bracket opened by the '[' immediately following 'decl' is closed and a new 'PRP' bracket is opened. Between the two the rule places the category 'T' allowing for the generation of *is easy* between two phrases. Basically, then, rule (374) and its companion rule (373) — productive only when a '(mod_6)' node appears in the SF (see next chapter) — are further means for generating 'discontinuous' structures.

4.4. The nominals derived from the linearisation are as follows:

information retrieval by computer is easy

(rules 193, 358, 316, 138)

retrieval of information by computer is easy

(rules 192, 361, 316, 138)

and using rules which introduce the 'T' category, viz.

$$(360) \quad tga \quad : \quad Nv^2(retrieve) \to Nv^2(retrieve)) + T \\ + PRP(Pr(for) + NP$$

$$(363) \quad tga \quad : \quad Nv^2(\Delta) \to Nv^2(\Delta)) + T + PRP(Pr(for) + NP$$

information retrieval is easy for [a] *computer*

(rules 193, 360, 323, 139)

retrieval of information is easy for [a] *computer*

(rules 192, 363, 323, 139)

5. To conclude the linearisations of fig. 2 we have those from the choice of '(mod_4)' as pivot node and '(ease)' as theme node.

5.1. One linearisation from 4 (iv) was:

$$decl \longrightarrow [(ease)] \xrightarrow{fe} (mod_4) \xrightarrow{ps} [(retrieve) \xrightarrow{tga} [(computer)]$$

$$b \,(retrieve) \xrightarrow{gl} [(information)] \,]$$

It can be realised:

$$(8) \quad decl \quad : \quad S \to Pron(it) + V(be) + AJ$$

$$(12) \quad [\quad : \quad AJ \to AJ(Adj$$

$$(180) \quad fe \quad : \quad AJ(...) \to AJ(...) + G$$

$$(261) \quad ps \quad : \quad G(mod_4) \to NPe$$

$$(23) \quad [\quad : \quad NPe \to NPe(Vfor$$

$$tga \quad : \quad Vfor(retrieve) \to Pr(for) + NP[obl] \\ + Vinf^1(retrieve)$$

$$gl \quad : \quad Vinf^1(retrieve) \to Vinf^0(retrieve) + NPt$$

it is easy for [a] *computer to retrieve information*

This realisation introduces a number of new rules. Instead of rule (7) producing 'NPs' we find rule (8) generating an 'anticipatory' *it* followed by an adjective. Its use in earlier realisations would be unproductive, firstly because neither '(computer)' nor '(information)' have adjectival forms and secondly because the following 'agt' or 'lg' cannot operate on 'AJ(...)'. On the other hand, the use of rule (7) would be unproductive here, for reasons which will be found in chapter IV.C.6 below.

There is obviously a parallelism between this realisation and that of *For a computer to retrieve information is easy*. Just as we found two methods for the derivation of this sentence from the same linearisation (3.2 and 3.3), we have an alternative for *It is easy for a computer to retrieve information*:

(262)   ps   : $G(mod_4) \rightarrow NPf$

(24)   [: $NPf \rightarrow NPf(Vinf^1$

   tga   : $Vinf^1(retrieve) \rightarrow Pr(for) + NP[obl]$
   $+ Vinf^1(retrieve)$

As before, the reason for rules (262) and (24) are apparent when we consider other realisations.

5.2. The second linearisation of fig. 4 (iv) was:

decl $\longrightarrow$ [(ease)] $\xrightarrow{fe}$ (mod$_4$) $\xrightarrow{ps}$ [(retrieve) $\xrightarrow{gl}$ [(information)]

b (retrieve) $\xrightarrow{tga}$ [(computer)]]]

(261)   ps   : $G(mod_4) \rightarrow NPe$

(23)   [: $NPe \rightarrow NPe(Vfor$

   gl   : $Vfor(retrieve) \rightarrow Pr(for) + NP[obl]$
   $+ Vinf(be) + Vpp^0(retrieve)$

   tga   : $Vpp^0(retrieve) \rightarrow Vpp^0(retrieve) + Pr(by) + NP$

it is easy for information to be retrieved by computer

(262)   ps   : $G(mod_4) \rightarrow NPf$

(24)   [: $NPf \rightarrow NPf(Vinf^1$

   gl   : $Vinf^1(retrieve) \rightarrow Vinf^0(retrieve) + NPt$

   tga   : $Vinf^0(\Delta) \rightarrow Vinf^0(\Delta) + Pr(by) + NP$

it is easy to retrieve information by computer

In the last realisation, the use of rule (374) introducing the category 'T'

would be obviously unproductive because the resultant lexemic string would
be invalidated by the presence of this unresolved 'non-lexical' category (see
chapter II.D.1).

6.   From the SF of fig. 2 we have generated 25 sentences differing from each
other not in their 'cognitive meaning' but in their emphases (deriving from
different selections of pivot and theme nodes) and in their styles (deriving
from different paths in linearisation and the choice of semolexemic rules).
The rules introduced will recur in later sections but rarely in the same combinations. They have been formulated so that easy linkages can be made with
rules for the derivation of other syntactic structures.
      I have not attempted to account for the generation of articles or different
verb forms at this stage as it would have introduced greater complexity into
the presentation. I have left these aspects for treatment in chapters VI, VIII
and IX.

B. Nominalisations

To illustrate the applications of some of the semolexemic rules rather more
fully I shall show how certain fairly complex nominalisations can be realised.

1.   If the SF in fig. 2 appeared as a subgraph in a larger SF we might find the
node '(retrieve)' attached to another node '(b)' by a 'agt' or 'gl' link. In fig.
8 (i) '(retrieve)' is the theme node of such a SF; and in fig. 8 (ii) it is the 'tail'
node (or 'object' of the 'verbal' node '(b)').

Fig. 8 (i)

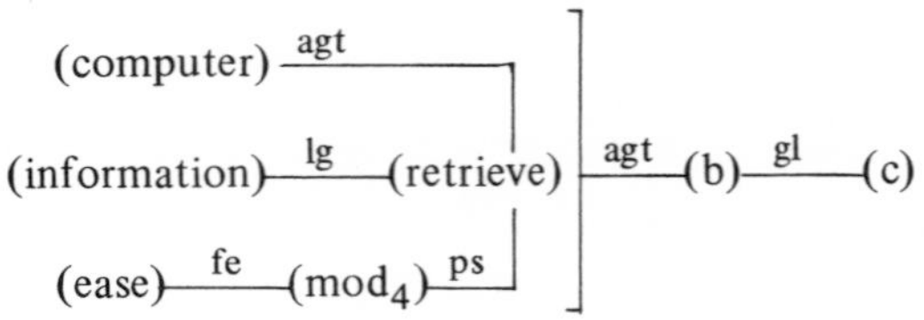

Fig. 8 (ii)

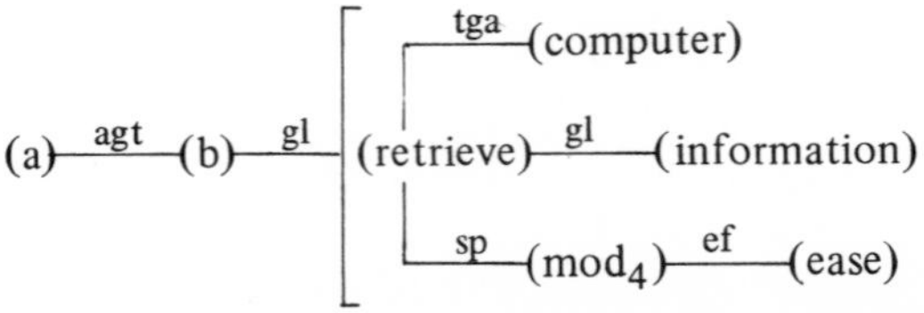

I will illustrate the realisation of nominalisations from linearisations of fig. 8 (ii). Those from fig. 8 (i) are very similar to those already illustrated in Section A and I leave them for the reader to work through.

On the whole the exposition will be brief and will not include any unproductive rule applications, the chief aim of this section being to demonstrate the use of the superscripts with 'Nv' and 'Vinf'. There are six possible linearisations of fig. 8 (ii) as there are three paths from '(retrieve)'.

2. $\quad$ (b)$\xrightarrow{\text{gl}}$[(retrieve)$\xrightarrow{\text{tga}}$[(computer)] b (retrieve)$\xrightarrow{\text{gl}}$[(information)]

$\quad$ b(retrieve)$\xrightarrow{\text{sp}}$(mod$_4$)$\xrightarrow{\text{ef}}$(ease)]

$\quad\quad\quad$ gl $\quad$: $\quad$ $V(b) \to V(b) + NPt$

$\quad\quad\quad$ [$\quad$: $\quad$ $NPt \to NP(N^0$

2.1. $\quad$ (357) $\quad$ tga $\quad$: $\quad$ $Nv^0(retrieve) \to NPgen + Nv^1(retrieve)$

$\quad\quad\quad$ (195) $\quad$ gl $\quad$: $\quad$ $Nv^1(retrieve) \to NP[gen] + Nv^2(retrieve)$

$\quad\quad\quad$ (313) $\quad$ sp $\quad$: $\quad$ $Nv^2(retrieve) \to Nv^4(retrieve) + Wh(s) + Y$

$\quad\quad\quad$ (138) $\quad$ ef $\quad$: $\quad$ $Y(mod_4) \to V(be) + Adj_4$

$\quad\quad\quad$ ... *computer's information retrieval which is easy*

2.2. $\quad$ Instead of (195) we can use (194):

$\quad\quad\quad$ tga $\quad$: $\quad$ $Nv^0(retrieve) \to NPgen + Nv^1(retrieve)$

$\quad\quad\quad$ (194) $\quad$ gl $\quad$: $\quad$ $Nv^1(retrieve) \to Nv^2(retrieve) + Pr(of) + NP$

$\quad\quad\quad$ (314) $\quad$ sp $\quad$: $\quad$ $Nv^2(\Delta) \to Nv^4(\Delta) + Wh(s) + Y$

$\quad\quad\quad$ ef $\quad$: $\quad$ $Y(mod_4) \to V(be) + Adj_4$

$\quad\quad\quad$ ... *computer's retrieval of information which is easy*

2.3. $\quad$ Or at one step further back, we could use (356) instead of (357):

$\quad\quad\quad$ (356) $\quad$ tga $\quad$: $\quad$ $Nv^0(retrieve) \to Nv^3(retrieve) + Pr(by) + NP$

$\quad\quad\quad$ (198) $\quad$ gl $\quad$: $\quad$ $Nv^3(\Delta) \to Nv^2(\Delta) + Pr(of) + NP$

$\quad\quad\quad$ sp $\quad$: $\quad$ $Nv^2(\Delta) \to Nv^4(\Delta) + Wh(s) + Y$

$\quad\quad\quad$ ... *retrieval by computer of information which is easy*

2.4. $\quad$ Besides these realisations with the 'verbal noun' *retrieval* there are also the following:

$$\text{(371)} \quad \begin{array}{ll} [& : \quad \text{NPt} \rightarrow \text{NPq}(\text{Vinf}^0 \\ \text{tga} & : \quad \text{Vinf}^0(\text{retrieve}) \rightarrow \text{NP}[\text{obl}] + \text{Vinf}^1(\text{retrieve}) \\ \text{gl} & : \quad \text{Vinf}^1(\text{retrieve}) \rightarrow \text{Vinf}^0(\text{retrieve}) + \text{NPt} \\ \text{sp} & : \quad \text{Vinf}^0(\Delta) \rightarrow \text{Vinf}^0(\Delta) + Z_{034} \\ \text{ef} & : \quad Z_4(\text{mod}_4) \rightarrow \text{Adv}_4 \end{array}$$

[scientists require a] *computer to retrieve information easily*

or, of course, with a prepositional phrase:

$$\text{sp} \quad : \quad \text{Vinf}^0(\Delta) \rightarrow \text{Vinf}^0(\Delta) + W_{034}$$

... *computer to retrieve information with ease*

2.5.
$$\text{(384)} \quad \begin{array}{ll} [& : \quad \text{NPt} \rightarrow \text{NPr}(\text{Conj}(\text{that}) + \text{Vrel}) \\ \text{tga} & : \quad \text{Vrel}(\text{retrieve}) \rightarrow \text{NP} + \text{V}(\text{retrieve}) \\ \text{gl} & : \quad \text{V}(\text{retrieve}) \rightarrow \text{V}(\text{retrieve}) + \text{NPt} \\ \text{sp} & : \quad \text{V}(\Delta) \rightarrow \text{V}(\Delta) + Z_{034} \end{array}$$

... *that [a] computer retrieves information easily*

The category 'Vrel' occurs whenever there is the necessity to ensure the realisation of a clause containing a finite verb. It is thus found with relative and subordinate clauses as well as here in *that*-clauses. Probably not all verbs which can take an infinitive construction (2.4) can also accept a *that*-clause and vice versa. I do not go into the problems of verb classification in this study, merely touching upon it briefly in chapter XIII.

3. A second linearisation of fig. 8 (ii) is:

$$\xrightarrow{\text{gl}} [(\text{retrieve}) \xrightarrow{\text{gl}} [(\text{information})] \text{ b } (\text{retrieve}) \text{\textemdash}$$

$$\xrightarrow{\text{tga}} [(\text{computer})] \text{ b } (\text{retrieve}) \xrightarrow{\text{sp}} (\text{mod}_4) \xrightarrow{\text{ef}} (\text{ease})]$$

$$\begin{array}{lll} & [& : \quad \text{NPt} \rightarrow \text{NP}(\text{N}^0 \\ \text{(193)} & \text{gl} & : \quad \text{Nv}^0(\text{retrieve}) \rightarrow \text{NP}[\text{gen}] + \text{Nv}^2(\text{retrieve}) \\ \text{(358)} & \text{tga} & : \quad \text{Nv}^2(\text{retrieve}) \rightarrow \text{Nv}^3(\text{retrieve}) + \text{Pr}(\text{by}) + \text{NP} \\ \text{(315)} & \text{sp} & : \quad \text{Nv}^3(\Delta) \rightarrow \text{Nv}^4(\Delta) + \text{Wh}(s) + Y \end{array}$$

... *information retrieval by computer which is easy*

(192)   gl   : $Nv^0(\text{retrieve}) \to Nv^2(\text{retrieve}) + Pr(\text{of}) + NP$

(361)   tga : $Nv^2(\Delta) \to Nv^3(\Delta) + Pr(\text{by}) + NP$

   ... retrieval of information by computer which is easy

   [: $NPt \to NPr(\text{Conj}(\text{that}) + Vrel$

(215)   gl   : $Vrel(\text{retrieve}) \to NP + V(\text{be}) + Vpp^0$

   tga : $Vpp^0(\text{retrieve}) \to Vpp^0(\text{retrieve}) + Pr(\text{by}) + NP$

   ... that information is retrieved by computer easily

Rule (215) is the 'passive' equivalent of rule (384) introduced in the last section.

4.   Next, the linearisation:

$$\underline{\quad}\xrightarrow{\text{gl}}[(\text{retrieve})\xrightarrow{\text{tga}}[(\text{computer})]\ b\ (\text{retrieve})\xrightarrow{\text{sp}}(\text{mod}_4)\underline{\quad}$$

$$\underline{\quad}\xrightarrow{\text{ef}}(\text{ease})\ b\ (\text{retrieve})\xrightarrow{\text{gl}}[(\text{information})]\,]$$

4.1.   [: $NPt \to NP(N^0$

(357)   tga : $Nv^0(\text{retrieve}) \to NPgen + Nv^1(\text{retrieve})$

(312)   sp   : $Nv^1(\text{retrieve}) \to X + Nv^2(\text{retrieve})$

(124)   ef   : $X(\text{mod}_4) \to Adj_4$

(196)   gl   : $Nv^2(\text{retrieve}) \to Nv^2(\text{retrieve}) + Pr(\text{of}) + NP$

   computer's easy retrieval of information

or (197)   gl   : $Nv^2(\text{retrieve}) \to NP[\text{gen}] + Nv^2(\text{retrieve})$

   ... computer's easy information retrieval

Here we encounter for the first time the category 'X' used in the formation of very many adjectival realisations, as later examples will illustrate.

4.2.   [: $NPt \to NPq(Vinf^0$

   tga : $Vinf^0(\text{retrieve}) \to NP[\text{obl}] + Vinf^1(\text{retrieve})$

(337)   sp   : $Vinf^1(\text{retrieve}) \to Vinf^2(\text{retrieve}) + Z_{034}$

(204)   gl   : $Vinf^2(\Delta) \to Vinf^0(\Delta) + NPt$

   ... computer to retrieve easily information

4.3.   [:   NPt → NPr(Conj(that) + Vrel

                      tga   :   Vrel(retrieve) → NP + V(retrieve)

and then by rules already illustrated in section A.1 to produce either ... *that*
[a] computer retrieves easily information or ... *that [a] computer easily re-*
trieves information.

5.   From the linearisation:

$$\xrightarrow{\text{gl}} [(\text{retrieve}) \xrightarrow{\text{gl}} [(\text{information})]\, b\, (\text{retrieve}) \xrightarrow{\text{sp}} (\text{mod}_4)\text{---}$$

$$\xrightarrow{\text{ef}} (\text{ease})\, b\, (\text{retrieve}) \xrightarrow{\text{tga}} [(\text{computer})]\,]$$

we can realise

                      [:   NPt → NPq(Vinf^0

                      gl   : $\text{Vinf}^0(\text{retrieve}) \rightarrow \text{Vinf}^0(\text{retrieve}) + \text{NPt}$

       (336)   sp   : $\text{Vinf}^0(\Delta) \rightarrow \text{Vinf}^0(\Delta) + Z_{034}$

       (372)   tga   : $\text{Vinf}^0(\Delta) \rightarrow \text{Vinf}^0(\Delta) + \text{Pr(by)} + \text{NP}$

                      ... *to retrieve information easily by computer*

and   [:   NPt → NPr(Conj(that) + Vrel

                      gl   : $\text{Vrel(retrieve)} \rightarrow \text{NP} + \text{V(be)} + \text{Vpp}^0(\text{retrieve})$

                      ... *that information is easily retrieved by computer*

6.   From

$$\xrightarrow{\text{gl}} [(\text{retrieve}) \xrightarrow{\text{sp}} (\text{mod}_4) \xrightarrow{\text{ef}} (\text{ease})\, b\, (\text{retrieve})\text{---}$$

$$\xrightarrow{\text{tga}} [(\text{computer})]\, b\, (\text{retrieve}) \xrightarrow{\text{gl}} [(\text{information})]\,]$$

is realised   [:   NPt → NP(N^0

       (310)   sp   : $\text{Nv}^0(\text{retrieve}) \rightarrow X + \text{Nv}^2(\text{retrieve})$

                      ef   : $X(\text{mod}_4) \rightarrow \text{Adj}_4$

       (358)   tga   : $\text{Nv}^2(\text{retrieve}) \rightarrow \text{Nv}^3(\text{retrieve}) + \text{Pr(by)} + \text{NP}$

       (198)   gl   : $\text{Nv}^3(\Delta) \rightarrow \text{Nv}^2(\Delta) + \text{Pr(of)} + \text{NP}$

                      ... *easy retrieval by computer of information*

7. Finally, from the sixth linearisation:

$$\xrightarrow{gl}[(\text{retrieve})\xrightarrow{sp}(\text{mod}_4)\xrightarrow{ef}(\text{ease}) \, b \, (\text{retrieve})\text{——}$$

$$\xrightarrow{gl}[(\text{information})] \, b \, (\text{retrieve})\xrightarrow{tga}[(\text{computer})] \,]$$

we can derive

	[	:	$NPt \rightarrow NP(N^0$
	sp	:	$Nv^0(\text{retrieve}) \rightarrow X + Nv^2(\text{retrieve})$
(197)	gl	:	$Nv^2(\text{retrieve}) \rightarrow NP[\text{gen}] + Nv^2(\text{retrieve})$
	tga	:	$Nv^2(\text{retrieve}) \rightarrow Nv^3(\text{retrieve}) + Pr(by) + NP$

          ... easy information retrieval by computer

or	(196)	gl	:	$Nv^2(\text{retrieve}) \rightarrow Nv^2(\text{retrieve}) + Pr(of) + NP$
	(361)	tga	:	$Nv^2(\Delta) \rightarrow Nv^3(\Delta) + Pr(by) + NP$

          ... easy retrieval of information by computer

C. Relative clauses and other nominalisations

The semolexemic rules for the realisation of relative clauses and related structures can also be illustrated with the aid of the SF in fig. 2. As well as '(retrieve)', other nodes in the SF may appear attached by 'lg' to a node within a larger SF.

1. In fig. 9 (i) we find '(computer)' attached by a 'lg' link to '(b)':

Fig. 9 (i)

$$(a)\xrightarrow{agt}(b)\xrightarrow{gl}(\text{computer})\xrightarrow{agt}(\text{retrieve})\xrightarrow{gl}(\text{information})$$

$$\xrightarrow{sp}(\text{mode}_4)\xrightarrow{ef}(\text{ease})$$

Since some of the realisations of this SF are rather awkward (from a stylistic point of view) the rules will be illustrated also with other SFs:

Fig. 9 (ii)

$$(a)\xrightarrow{agt}(b)\xrightarrow{gl}(\text{machine})\xrightarrow{agt}(\text{wash})\xrightarrow{gl}(\text{clothes})$$

Fig. 9 (iii)

$$\text{(a)} \xrightarrow{\text{agt}} \text{(b)} \xrightarrow{\text{gl}} \text{(boy)} \xrightarrow{\text{agt}} \text{(read)} \xrightarrow{\text{gl}} \text{(book)}$$

2. Linearisations of these SFs are:

$$\xrightarrow{\text{gl}} [\, [(\text{computer})] \xrightarrow{\text{agt}} (\text{retrieve}) \xrightarrow{\text{gl}} [(\text{information})]] \, b \, (\text{retrieve}) \text{---}$$

$$\xrightarrow{\text{sp}} (\text{mod}_4) \xrightarrow{\text{ef}} (\text{ease})]$$

$$\xrightarrow{\text{gl}} [\, [(\text{machine})] \xrightarrow{\text{agt}} (\text{wash}) \xrightarrow{\text{gl}} [(\text{clothes})] \,]$$

$$\xrightarrow{\text{gl}} [\, [(\text{boy})] \xrightarrow{\text{agt}} (\text{read}) \xrightarrow{\text{gl}} [(\text{book})] \,]$$

Firstly, there are the relative clause realisations:

$$
\begin{array}{llll}
 & \text{gl} & : & V(b) \to V(b) + \text{NPt} \\
 & [& : & \text{NPt} \to \text{NP}(N^0 \\
(14) & [& : & N^0 \to \text{NPw}(N^0 \\
(53) & \text{agt} & : & \text{NPw}(...) \to \text{NP}(...) + \text{Wh}(s) + V
\end{array}
$$

and, by (199) and (329) ... *computer which retrieves information easily,*
... *machine which washes clothes,* ... *boy who reads* [*a*] *book.* The graphic
realisation of 'Wh(s)', which we have met in earlier examples, depends on the
lexemic context in which it occurs: *who* if it refers back to an animate object,
which if it does not. (For a treatment of anaphoric reference see chapter VI.)

3. From the same linearisations we can realise the 'passive' equivalents of
these phrases:

$$
\begin{array}{llll}
 & [& : & \text{NPt} \to \text{NP}(N^0 \\
 & [& : & N^0 \to \text{NPw}(N^0 \\
(54) & \text{agt} & : & \text{NPw}(...) \to \text{NP}(...) + \text{Pr(by)} + \text{Wh}(s) + \text{Vrel} \\
(215) & \text{gl} & : & \text{Vrel}(x) \to \text{NP} + V(\text{be}) + \text{Vpp}^0(x)
\end{array}
$$

... computer by which information is easily retrieved

... machine by which clothes are washed

... boy by whom a book is read

4. As further alternatives we can generate nominalisations incorporating present participle forms:

$$[\quad : \quad NPt \rightarrow NP(N^0$$
$$[\quad : \quad N^0 \rightarrow NPw(N^0$$
$$(55) \quad agt \quad : \quad NPw(...) \rightarrow Vprp^1 + NP(...)$$

From this we can derive ... *washing machine* since the graphic form of 'Vprp(wash)' is the participle *washing*. In this derivation there is some similarity with the approach of Lees (1960) to this kind of nominalisation. Further, upon the group 'Vprp^1(x)' we can apply

$$(214) \quad gl \quad : \quad Vprp^1(x) \rightarrow NP + Vprp^1(x)$$

to produce ... *clothes washing machine*, and also ... *information retrieving computer*, ... *book reading boy* (although they are admittedly awkward in style).

5. In the rather similar constructions when the participle follows the noun, e.g. *computer retrieving information*, *machine washing clothes*, *boy reading a book*, there is an implication of 'continuous' or 'progressive' action, i.e. "machine is (in the process of) washing the clothes". The constructions cannot be considered synonymous with *machine which washes clothes*, etc. because there the notion of 'continuity' is absent. Similarly, constructions in which the participle precedes the noun do not imply a 'continuous' tense: *washing machine* is "a machine which is for washing" not "a machine in the process of washing". (For the treatment of 'continuous' verb forms see chapter IX.)

6. When the node '(information)' of the SF in fig. 2 is attached by 'lg' to a node in a larger SF we have:

Fig. 10 (i)

(a)—^{agt}—(b)—^{gl}—(information)—^{lg}—(retrieve)—^{tga}—(computer)
                                                              |
                                                     —^{sp}—(mod$_4$)—^{ef}—(ease)

And in our other examples:

Fig. 10 (ii)

(a)—^{agt}—(b)—^{gl}—(clothes)—^{lg}—(wash)—^{tga}—(machine)

Fig. 10 (iii)

$$(a) \xrightarrow{\text{agt}} (b) \xrightarrow{\text{gl}} (\text{book}) \xrightarrow{\text{lg}} (\text{read}) \xrightarrow{\text{tga}} (\text{boy})$$

7.   These are linearised:

$$\xrightarrow{\text{gl}} [[(\text{information})] \xrightarrow{\text{lg}} (\text{retrieve}) \xrightarrow{\text{tga}} [(\text{computer})] \, b \, (\text{retrieve}) -$$

$$\xrightarrow{\text{sp}} (\text{mod}_4) \xrightarrow{\text{ef}} (\text{ease})]$$

$$\xrightarrow{\text{gl}} [[(\text{clothes})] \xrightarrow{\text{lg}} (\text{wash}) \xrightarrow{\text{tga}} [(\text{machine})]\,]$$

$$\xrightarrow{\text{gl}} [[(\text{book})] \xrightarrow{\text{lg}} (\text{read}) \xrightarrow{\text{tga}} [(\text{boy})]\,]$$

Firstly, there are the relative clause realisations:

[	:	$NPt \rightarrow NP(N^0$
[	:	$N^0 \rightarrow NPw(N^0$
(218)	lg	: $NPw(...) \rightarrow NP(...) + Wh(s) + V(be) + Vpp^0$
(380)	tga	: $Vpp^0(x) \rightarrow Vpp^0(x) + Pr(by) + NP$

   ... *information which is retrieved by* [*a*] *computer easily,*

   ... *clothes which are washed by* [*a*] *machine,*

   ... *book which is read by* [*the*] *boy*

and the 'active' equivalents

(219)	lg	: $NPw(...) \rightarrow NP(...) + Wh(s) + Vrel$
(384)	tga	: $Vrel(x) \rightarrow NP + V(x)$

   ... *information which* [*a*] *computer retrieves easily,*

   ... *clothes which* [*a*] *machine washes,*

   ... *book which* [*the*] *boy reads*

In these realisations the presence of the relative pronoun is optional. As an alternative to (219) we can have:

(220)	lg	: $NPw(...) \rightarrow NP(...) + Vrel$

to produce ... *information a computer retrieves,* ... *clothes a machine washes,* ... *book the boy reads.*

8.   Just as the linearisations of fig. 9 have present participle realisations, the

linearisations of fig. 10 have past participle realisations:

$$(222) \quad \text{lg} \quad : \quad \text{NPw}(...) \to \text{Vpp}^1 + \text{NP}(...)$$

From this we can derive ... *washed clothes*, ... *retrieved information*. The only rule operating on '$\text{Vpp}^1(x)$' with 'tga' is:

$$(382) \quad \text{tga} \quad : \quad \text{Vpp}^1(x) \to \text{ADV} + \text{Vpp}^1(x)$$

by which we can produce ... *mechanically washed clothes*. There are no realisations for the other linearisations because neither 'Adv(computer)' nor 'Adv(boy)' have graphic forms.

As with the present participle constructions, there are rather similar constructions with past participles following the noun. It seems likely that *clothes washed by machine* is not synonymous with *mechanically washed clothes* since the former appears to imply a past event, i.e. "the clothes have been washed", which the latter does not imply. However, there is some doubt whether this is always the case: the phrase may be synonymous with *clothes which are washed by machine*. If the two constructions are considered synonymous then it is a simple matter to add the rule:

$$(221) \quad \text{lg} \quad : \quad \text{NPw}(...) \to \text{NP}(...) + \text{Vpp}^0$$

by which, with the application of:

$$\text{tga} \quad : \quad \text{Vpp}^0(\text{wash}) \to \text{Vpp}^0(\text{wash}) + \text{Pr(by)} + \text{NP}$$

we can derive the required *clothes washed by machine*.

9. Finally, we may find the node '(ease)' of the SF in fig. 2 attached by 'lg' to another node:

Fig. 11

$$(a) \xrightarrow{\text{agt}} (b) \xrightarrow{\text{gl}} (\text{ease}) \xrightarrow{\text{fe}} (\text{mod}_4) \xrightarrow{\text{ps}}$$

$$(\text{computer}) \xrightarrow{\text{agt}} (\text{retrieve}) \xrightarrow{\text{gl}} (\text{information})$$

From the linearisation:

$$\xrightarrow{\text{gl}} [(\text{ease}) \xrightarrow{\text{fe}} (\text{mod}_4) \xrightarrow{\text{ps}} [(\text{retrieve}) \xrightarrow{\text{tga}} [(\text{computer})]$$

$$\text{b}\,(\text{retrieve}) \xrightarrow{\text{gl}} [(\text{information})]\,]\,]$$

we can realise:

$$(182) \quad \text{fe} \quad : \quad N^0(\text{ease}) \rightarrow N^0(\text{ease}) + B$$

$$(249) \quad \text{ps} \quad : \quad B(\text{mod}_4) \rightarrow \text{Pr}(\text{with}) + \text{Wh}(s) + \text{NPp}$$

$$(29) \quad [\quad : \quad \text{NPp} \rightarrow \text{NPp}(\text{Vrel}$$

$$\text{tga} \quad : \quad \text{Vrel}(\text{retrieve}) \rightarrow \text{NP} + \text{V}(\text{retrieve})$$

$$\text{gl} \quad : \quad \text{V}(\text{retrieve}) \rightarrow \text{V}(\text{retrieve}) + \text{NPt}$$

ease with which [a] computer retrieves information

Two new rules are introduced here. We have seen the employment of 'Vrel' earlier but not its derivation through 'NPp'. This method is found in subordinate clasues and various related constructions (see chapter V.B).

Rule (182) is also new but it will not be discussed further at this point, as it will be amply illustrated in the next chapter when adjectival realisations are described.

IV. ADJECTIVES AND ADVERBS

A. General

1. A valuable classification of adjectives (and adverbs) has been made by Vendler (1968). One of his objectives was to define the order in which classes of adjectives occur as pre-modifiers of nouns. By the procedures of distributional analysis (some of the results of which have been used elsewhere in this monograph), Vendler identified nine main classes $A_1 - A_9$, one of which, A_1, is divided into the subclasses $A_a - A_m$ and A_x. It should be noted that the classes are not exclusive since some adjectives occur in more than one, e.g. *good* belongs to A_3, A_4, A_6 and A_8. Vendler established that the order of the classes when used attributively is: $A_9 A_8 A_7 \ldots A_2 A_x A_m A_1 \ldots A_b A_a N$. Whenever two adjectives in the same class modify a noun they are always co-ordinated. For example, the colour-adjectives belong to A_f so we have *black and white, red and yellow* etc. When adjectives from different classes are juxtaposed co-ordination is optional. (For co-ordination see chapter VII below.)

2. So far we have illustrated only one adjective-class, namely A_4 with the example *easy*. Other adjectives in this class are *difficult, pleasant, un-pleasant*, etc. As we have seen, *easy* was realised from a SF containing the link ' $\underline{\text{sp}}$ (mod$_4$) $\underline{\text{ef}}$ '. The subscript 4 in '(mod$_4$)' specifies that any adjective realised must belong to A_4. If the node is '(mod$_6$)' then the adjective must belong to A_6, etc. In this chapter I will illustrate these other classes: $A_2 - A_9$ are realised from '(mod$_{2-9}$)', but in the case of A_1 I have abandoned Vendler's letter subscripts — some adjectives of this class are realised from '(mod$_1$)' but others are derived from sememes such as '(poss)', '(orig)', etc.

On the whole, only differences from adjective-class A_4 are explained in any detail. The similarities are largely left for the reader to explore with the rules given in appendix B.

B. Adjective classes

1. Vendler's class A_6 includes adjectives such as *clever, stupid, reasonable, kind, nice, thoughtful, considerate*. Fig. 12 gives a SF including the sememe '(kind)':

Fig. 12

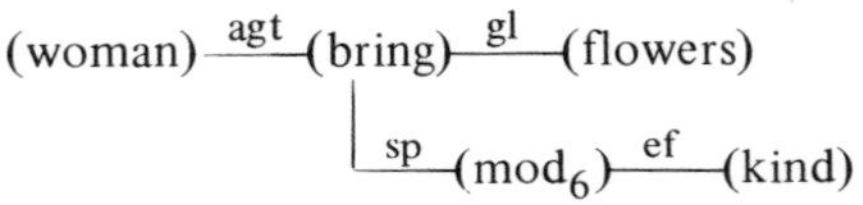

$$(\text{woman}) \xrightarrow{\text{agt}} (\text{bring}) \xrightarrow{\text{gl}} (\text{flowers})$$
$$\xrightarrow{\text{sp}} (\text{mod}_6) \xrightarrow{\text{ef}} (\text{kind})$$

1.1. With '(bring)' as theme and '(mod_6)' as pivot we can realise:

the woman's bringing of the flowers is kind

for the flowers to be brought by the woman is kind

These are generated by the same (or similar) rules to those used for *computer's retrieval of information is easy* and *for information to be retrieved by computer is easy*.

1.2. We can also realise:

to bring flowers is kind of the woman

This sentence is comparable with *to retrieve information is easy for a computer*. The same principle is involved in the generation, but instead of rule (374) introducing 'T' we have:

(373)   tga   : $\text{Vinf}^0(\Delta) \rightarrow \text{Vinf}^0(\Delta)) + R + \text{PRP}(\text{Pr}(\text{of}) + \text{NP}$

and then

(322)   sp   : $R \rightarrow Y_6$

         ef   : $Y_6(\text{mod}_6) \rightarrow V(\text{be}) + \text{Adj}_6$

1.3. Whereas with '(mod_4)' it is incorrect to have realisations such as * *that [a] computer retrieves information is easy* and * *that information is retrieved by computer is easy*, we find that sentences like these are quite acceptable with adjectives in A_6:

that the woman brings flowers is kind

that the flowers are brought by the woman is kind

Hence, the rules permit the generation of Y_6 from an operation of 'sp' on 'NPr(...)':

$$(320) \quad \text{sp} \quad : \quad \text{NPr}(...) \to \text{NPr}(...) + Y_{69}$$

1.4. From the SF of fig. 12 with the theme on '(kind)' and with '(mod_6)' as pivot, we can realise:

	fe	:	$NP(...) \to NP(...) + G$
(263)	ps	:	$G(\text{mod}_6) \to \text{NPh}$
(25)	[	:	$\text{NPh} \to \text{NPh}(\text{Vof}$
(379)	tga	:	$\text{Vof(bring)} \to \text{Pr(of)} + \text{NP[obl]} + \text{Vinf}^1(\text{bring})$
	gl	:	$\text{Vinf}^1(\text{bring}) \to \text{Vinf}^0(\text{bring}) + \text{NPt}$

it is kind of the woman to bring the flowers

This is parallel to *it is easy for the computer to retrieve information* but with an obligatory *of* instead of *for*.

1.5. When the pivot is on '(bring)' we find that the position of the adverb *kindly* relative to the verb is more restricted than in the case of adverbs in A_4. We have *the woman kindly brings the flowers* and *the flowers are kindly brought by the woman* but not * *the woman brings kindly the flowers,* * *the woman brings the flowers kindly* or * *the flowers are brought kindly by the woman*. Therefore, the rules specify that the operation of 'sp' on '$V(x)$' or '$Vpp(x)$' produces only '$Z_6 + V(x)$' and '$Z_6 + Vpp(x)$' and never '$V(x) + Z_6$', '$Vpp(x) + Z_6$', etc.

1.6. Finally there is one structure not available to SFs with '(mod_4)' when the pivot is on the 'verbal' node: '(bring)' in fig. 12

	agt	:	$NP(...) \to NP(...) + V$
(327)	sp	:	$V(\text{bring}) \to V(\text{be}) + X_{69} + \text{Vinf}^0(\text{bring})$

the woman is kind to bring the flowers

2. The adjectives in class A_9 e.g. *probable, likely, certain*, occur in all structures where A_6's are found except that we find *to retrieve information is likely for a computer*, i.e. this structure follows the pattern of the A_4's with *for* instead of the *of* found with the A_6's (section 1.2 above).

3. Vendler's class A_7 includes *possible* and *impossible* and his class A_8 includes *useful, profitable* and *necessary*. Adjectives from both classes occur in

the same structures as adjectives from class A_4. However, for neither class are there any adverbial realisations: * *computer retrieves impossibly information*, * *information is impossibly retrieved by computer*. Thus, no 'Adv' can be derived by the operation of 'ef' on Z_7 or Z_8. (As we shall see later, Z_7 and Z_8 are employed for other realisations.) The reader can confirm that the following sentences are all realisable from a SF containing '(mod_7)':

information retrieval by computer is impossible

to retrieve information by computer is impossible

it is impossible to retrieve information by computer

it is impossible for a computer to retrieve information

information is impossible to retrieve by computer

4. To illustrate Vendler's class A_3, which includes *slow, fast, good, bad, weak, careful, beatiful*, I give the SFs:

Fig. 13 (i)

$$(woman) \xrightarrow{agt} (dance) \xrightarrow{gl} (waltz)$$
$$\quad\quad\quad\quad\quad\;\; \Big|\xrightarrow{sp} (mod_3) \xrightarrow{ef} (beautiful)$$

Fig. 13 (ii)

$$(man) \xrightarrow{agt} (play) \xrightarrow{gl} (chess)$$
$$\quad\quad\quad\quad\; \Big|\xrightarrow{sp} (mod_3) \xrightarrow{ef} (care)$$

4.1. The structures accepting A_3 are all those found with A_4 with the exception of * *to dance the waltz is beautiful for the woman*, * *to play chess is careful for the man*, * *the waltz is beautiful to dance by the woman* and * *chess is careful to play by the man*. Some possible realisations of fig. 13 (i) and fig. 13 (ii) are:

the woman dances the waltz beautifully

the waltz is beautifully danced by the woman

the woman's dancing of the waltz is beautiful

the man plays chess carefully

the man's chess playing is careful

4.2. In addition, '(mod_3)' has realisations involving 'nomina agentis' and 'gerundive' forms which are not found with '(mod_4)'.

$$decl \longrightarrow [(man)] \xrightarrow{\text{agt}} (play) \xrightarrow{\text{sp}} (mod_3) \xrightarrow{\text{ef}} (careful)\, b\, (play) \relbar\joinrel\relbar$$

$$\xrightarrow{\text{gl}} [(chess)]$$

(51)	agt	:	$NP(...) \to NP(...) + V(be) + Nag$
(307)	sp	:	$Nag(play) \to X_3 + Nag(play)$
(125)	ef	:	$X_3(mod_3) \to Adj_3$
(190)	gl	:	$Nag(play) \to Nag(play) + Pr(of) + NP$

the man is a careful player of chess

or:　(191)　gl　:　$Nag(play) \to NP[gen] + Nag(play)$

the man is a careful chess player

While rule (51) can operate on any '$NP(...)$' for the generation of 'nomina agentis', e.g. from '$(man) \xrightarrow{\text{agt}} (drive)$' we have *the man is a driver*, the only adjective-class which can modify the noun is A_3. Therefore, rule (307) specifies that 'sp' operating on '$Nag(x)$' can derive only '$X_3 + Nag(x)$'. The 'gerundive' form is realised by:

(52)	agt	:	$NP(...) \to NP(...) + P + Pr(at) + Vger$
(321)	sp	:	$P \to Y_3$
	ef	:	$Y_3(mod_3) \to V(be) + Adj_3$
	gl	:	$Vger(play) \to Vger(play) + NPt$

the man is careful at playing chess

Again, while rule (52) could operate on any '$NP(...)$' the only derivative from 'P' by 'sp' is 'Y_3', thus ensuring that only adjectives of class A_3 may occur. (On the string produced by (52), 'sp' could be applied to '$Vger(x)$'. However, in that case, 'P' would remain unresolved in the lexemic realisation, which would consequently be rejected.)

5. Vendler's class A_5 is treated quite differently. As he himself says (p. 102-3) adjectives such as *ready, willing, anxious* are best considered as variants of verbal forms such as *want, wish, be ready, be eager*, etc. They can, therefore, be easily accommodated as nodes between 'agt' and 'gl' links (with some slight variation in the semolexemic rules – see also chapter XIII.A).

Vendler's classes A_i and A_j (subclasses of A_1), which he calls verb-derivatives, can be treated similarly. In fact, *washing* in *washing machine* (section III.C.4) is an example of class A_i and *washed* in *washed clothes* (section III.C.8) an example of A_j.

C. Modification of nouns

So far we have illustrated realisations of '$\xrightarrow{\text{sp}}(\text{mod}_n)\xrightarrow{\text{ef}}(x)$' structures only when they are attached to potential 'pivot' nodes, i.e. those occurring between 'agt' and 'gl' links. However, they are also found (perhaps more commonly?) attached to nodes at the end of 'tga' or 'gl'. It seems, in fact, that adjectives in Vendler's classes A_1 and A_2 are never attached to 'pivot' nodes, i.e. they have no adverbial realisations. Those members of Vendler's class A_1 which I derive via '(mod_1)' are the colour and shape adjectives. With '(mod_2)' are derived the adjectives of A_2, the 'contrastive' (or 'polar') adjectives *long–short*, *thick–thin*, *big–little*, *wide–narrow*, etc.

1. The realisations of a SF with any '(mod)' sememe attached to a non-'pivot' node follows a general pattern. Consider the SF:

$$(a)\xrightarrow{\text{sp}}(\text{mod}_n)\xrightarrow{\text{ef}}(b)$$

Firstly there are the two kinds of linearisations:

(i)   decl $\longrightarrow[(a)]\xrightarrow{\text{sp}}(\text{mod}_n)\xrightarrow{\text{ef}}[(b)]$

(ii) $\longrightarrow[(a)\xrightarrow{\text{sp}}(\text{mod}_n)\xrightarrow{\text{ef}}(b)]$

In the first the SF stands as an individual structure; in the second it is a substructure in a larger SF.

2. From the linearisation (i) we can generate:

$$(316)\quad \text{sp}\quad:\quad NP(N^0(a)) \to NP(...) + Y$$
$$\text{ef}\quad:\quad Y(\text{mod}_n) \to V(\text{be}) + Adj_n$$
$$(a)\quad \underline{NP(N^0(a)) + V(\text{be}) + Adj_n(b)}$$

From the linearisation (ii) we have two realisations:

$$(300) \quad \text{sp} \quad : \quad N^0(a) \rightarrow N^0(a) + Wh(s) + Y$$
$$\text{ef} \quad : \quad Y(mod_n) \rightarrow V(be) + Adj_n$$
$$\text{(b)} \quad \underline{N^0(a) + Wh(s) + V(be) + Adj_n(b)}$$
$$(301) \quad \text{sp} \quad : \quad N^0(a) \rightarrow X + N^0(a)$$
$$\text{ef} \quad : \quad X(mod_n) \rightarrow Adj_n$$
$$\text{(c)} \quad \underline{Adj_n(b) + N^0(a)}$$

3. For each '(mod)' class we can illustrate realisations with the structures of (a), (b) and (c):

(mod_1):   (a) *ball is red* (b) *ball which is red* (c) *red ball*

(mod_2):   (a) *elephant is small* (b) *elephant which is small* (c) *small elephant*

(mod_3):   (a) *king is weak* (b) *king who is weak* (c) *weak king*

(mod_4):   (a) *problem is easy* (b) *problem which is easy* (c) *easy problem*

(mod_6):   (a) *man is reasonable* (b) *man who is reasonable* (c) *reasonable man*

(mod_7):   (a) *problem is impossible* (b) *problem which is impossible* (c) *impossible problem*

(mod_8):   (a) *object is useful* (b) *object which is useful* (c) *useful object*

(mod_9):   (a) *event is probable* (b) *event which is probable* (c) *probable event*

These realisations are obviously the 'normal' adjectival realisations of sememes and we might well doubt the status of a lexeme classified as 'adjective' which did not appear in at least one of these environments.

4. In addition to these structures, the sememes attached to '(mod_2)' and '(mod_3)' have realisations not available to the other adjective-classes. Beside *Henry is a weak king* and *Jumbo is a small elephant* we have *Henry is weak as a king* and *Jumbo is small for an elephant* [but big for an animal]. Assuming for the present (leaving the explanation until chapter XII.A) that this use of *is* is realised from ' $\xrightarrow{\text{fe}}$(cop, mem)$\xrightarrow{\text{ps}}$ ' the linearisations underlying both forms are:

$$\text{decl} \rightarrow [(Henry)] \xrightarrow{\text{fe}} (cop, mem) \xrightarrow{\text{ps}} [(king) \xrightarrow{\text{sp}} (mod_3) \xrightarrow{\text{ef}} (weak)]$$

$$\text{decl} \longrightarrow [(\text{Jumbo})] \xrightarrow{\text{fe}} (\text{cop, mem}) \xrightarrow{\text{ps}} [(\text{elephant})\underline{\quad\quad}$$

$$\xrightarrow{\text{sp}} (\text{mod}_2) \xrightarrow{\text{ef}} (\text{small})]$$

	fe	:	$NP(...) \rightarrow NP(...) + J$
(275)	ps	:	$J(\text{cop, mem}) \rightarrow V(\text{be}) + N^0$
	[	:	$N^0 \rightarrow NPw(N^0$
	sp	:	$N^0(\text{king/elephant}) \rightarrow X + N^0(\text{king/elephant})$

Henry is a weak king,   Jumbo is a small elephant

(276)	ps	:	$J(\text{cop, mem}) \rightarrow V(\text{be}) + N^2$
(16)	[	:	$N^2 \rightarrow NPw(N^2$
(305)	sp	:	$N^2(\text{king}) \rightarrow X_3 + Pr(\text{as}) + N^0(\text{king})$

Henry is weak as a king

(304)	sp	:	$N^2(\text{elephant}) \rightarrow X_2 + Pr(\text{for}) + N^0(\text{elephant})$

Jumbo is small for an elephant

5. The other linearisations of the SF $(a) \xrightarrow{\text{sp}} (\text{mod}_n) \xrightarrow{\text{ef}} (b)$ are:

(iii) $\text{decl} \longrightarrow [(b)] \xrightarrow{\text{fe}} (\text{mod}_n) \xrightarrow{\text{ps}} [(a)]$

(iv) $\longrightarrow [(b) \xrightarrow{\text{fe}} (\text{mod}_n) \xrightarrow{\text{ps}} (a)]$

Linearisation (iv) has two possible realisations:

(182)	fe	:	$N^0(b) \rightarrow N^0(b) + B$
(247)	ps	:	$B(\text{mod}_n) \rightarrow Pr(\text{of}) + N^0$
		(d)	$\underline{N^0(b) + Pr(\text{of}) + N^0(a)}$
(181)	fe	:	$N^0(b) \rightarrow A + N^0(b)$
(239)	ps	:	$A(\text{mod}_n) \rightarrow \text{Ngen}$
		(e)	$\underline{\text{Ngen}(a) + N^0(b)}$

Illustrating for each '(mod)' class:

   (mod_1):   (d) *redness of the ball* (e) *ball's redness*

   (mod_2):   (d) *smallness of the elephant* (e) *elephant's smallness*

(mod_3):	(d) *weakness of the king* (e) *king's weakness*
(mod_4):	(d) *easiness of the problem* (e) *problem's easiness*
(mod_6):	(d) *reasonableness of the man* (e) *the man's reasonableness*
(mod_7):	(d) *impossibility of the problem* (e) *problem's impossibility*
(mod_8):	(d) *usefulness of the object* (e) *object's usefulness*
(mod_9):	(d) *probability of the event* (e) *event's probability*

6. There are no realisations of linearisation (iii) because 'ps' does not operate on '$J(mod_n)$', which would be produced from

$$fe \quad : \quad NP(...) \rightarrow NP(...) + J$$

Therefore we do not have * *redness is the ball's*, * *weakness is the king's*, * *the impossibility is the problem's*, etc. Their unacceptability may lie in the explicit indication of 'possession' by constructions of the form *N is N's* (cf. the realisation of '(poss)' below) and this notion is by no means necessarily present in '(mod)' linkages. However, even if such sentences were realisable they would have to be considered synonymous with realisations (a), *the ball is red, the king is weak, the problem is impossible*, etc., which would be obviously not acceptable. (Note that (d) and (e) are not synonymous with (b) and (c), in the same way that *computer which retrieves information* is not synonymous with *information which is retrieved by computer*.)

7. It will be noted that the lexemic realisation of '(ease)' in (d) and (e) above, i.e. *easiness*, differs from its realisation elsewhere, e.g. in *computer retrieves information with ease* and *ease with which information is retrieved by computer*. This more 'abstract' form seems to be obligatory: instead of *easiness of the problem* we cannot have *ease of the problem*. Apparently the 'N' category attached to the '(b)' sememe in all (d) and (e) realisations must be more closely specified, perhaps as 'Nab'. This would entail the replacement of rules (181) and (182) by the following:

$$(185) \quad fe \quad : \quad Nab^0(b) \rightarrow A + Nab^0(b)$$

$$(186) \quad fe \quad : \quad Nab^0(b) \rightarrow Nab^0(b) + B$$

8. It seems that rule (186) is also required in the derivation of structures analogous to *ease with which computer retrieves information* (chapter III.C.9) from SFs containing '(mod_7)', '(mod_8)' and '(mod_9)' attached to 'verbal' nodes.

$$\longrightarrow [(use) \xrightarrow{\text{fe}} (mod_8) \xrightarrow{\text{ps}} [(solve) \xrightarrow{\text{gl}} [(problem)]]]$$

$$(186) \quad \text{fe} \quad : \quad \text{Nab}^0(\text{use}) \rightarrow \text{Nab}^0(\text{use}) + \text{B}$$

$$(251) \quad \text{ps} \quad : \quad \text{B}(\text{mod}_8) \rightarrow \text{Pr}(\text{of}) + \text{NPc}$$

$$[\quad : \quad \text{NPc} \rightarrow \text{NPc}(\text{Vger}$$

$$\text{gl} \quad : \quad \text{Vger}(\text{solve}) \rightarrow \text{Vger}(\text{solve}) + \text{NPt}$$

usefulness of solving the problem

Similarly for *impossibility of solving the problem* and *probability of solving the problem.*

Clearly *use of solving the problem* is unacceptable here. The reason appears to be connected with the occurrence of 'Pr(of)'; thus 'Nab' is required here and in realisation (d), *easiness of the problem* and *usefulness of the object*, but it is not required in *ease with which* ... etc.

D. Other adjectives

1. Many of the adjectives in Vendler's A_1 have equivalent prepositional realisations in which the notion of 'possession' is definitely present. The generation of 'possessive' constructions, as well as adjectival constructions, can be illustrated by a SF containing the most general 'possessive' node '(poss)':

$$(\text{Mary}) \xrightarrow{\text{ sp }} (\text{poss}) \xrightarrow{\text{ ef }} (\text{beauty})$$

(The close connection between '(poss)' and many of the '(mod)' nodes needs more detailed examination than I can give here).

1.1. $(316) \quad \text{sp} \quad : \quad \text{NP}(...) \rightarrow \text{NP}(...) + \text{Y}$

$(300) \quad \text{sp} \quad : \quad \text{N}^0(\text{Mary}) \rightarrow \text{N}^0(\text{Mary}) + \text{Wh}(s) + \text{Y}$

$(158) \quad \text{ef} \quad : \quad \text{Y}(\text{poss}) \rightarrow \text{V}(\text{be}) + \text{Adj}$

Mary (who) is beautiful

or $(159) \quad \text{ef} \quad : \quad \text{Y}(\text{poss}) \rightarrow \text{V}(\text{have}) + \text{N}^0$

Mary (who) has beauty

1.2. $(299) \quad \text{sp} \quad : \quad \text{N}^0(\text{Mary}) \rightarrow \text{N}^0(\text{Mary}) + \text{K}$

$(96) \quad \text{ef} \quad : \quad \text{K}(\text{poss}) \rightarrow \text{Pr}(\text{with}) + \text{N}^0$

Mary with beauty

1.3.   (301)   sp   : $N^0(Mary) \to X + N^0(Mary)$

       (133)   ef   : $X(poss) \to Adj$

                     ... beautiful Mary

1.4.   (187)   fe   : $NP(...) \to NP(...) + J$

       (183)   fe   : $N^0(beauty) \to N^0(beauty) + Wh(s) + J$

       (281)   ps   : $J(poss) \to V(be) + Ngen$

                 beauty (which) is Mary's

1.5.   (182)   fe   : $N^0(beauty) \to N^0(beauty) + B$

       (259)   ps   : $B(poss) \to Pr(of) + N^0$

                    beauty of Mary

1.6.   (181)   fe   : $N^0(beauty) \to A + N^0(beauty)$

       (243)   ps   : $A(poss) \to Ngen$

                    Mary's beauty

2.   Two other 'possessive' nodes, '(posq)' and '(posh)' are more restricted in scope, but they are also more explicitly 'possessive'. Their realisations follow the general pattern of '(poss)' and can be illustrated briefly:

2.1.   (star)——^{sp}——(posq)——^{ef}——(light)

       (316) or (300) and (156)   :   *star (which) is luminous*

       (316) or (300) and (157)   :   *star (which) has much light*

       (299) and (95)   :   *star with much light*

       (301) and (132)   :   *luminous star*

The adjective *luminous* belongs to Vendler's class A_h.

       (182) and (258)   :   *light of [the] star*

       (181) and (242)   :   *star's light*

2.2.   (table)——^{sp}——(posh)——^{ef}——(rectangle)

       (316) or (300) and (154)   :   *table (which) is rectangular*

       (316) or (300) and (155)   :   *table (which) has shape of rectangle*

| (299) and (94) | : | *table with shape of rectangle* |
| (301) and (131) | : | *rectangular table* |

The adjective in this case belongs to Vendler's class A_g.

| (182) and (257) | : | *rectangle of [the] table* |
| (181) and (241) | : | *table's rectangle* |

2.3. As we shall see later, the realisations of 'locatives' are remarkably similar to those of the 'possessives', hence the presence in their sememes of "pos" (see XI.D.5).

3. One other sememe will serve to illustrate the remaining subclasses of A_1 which are not 'possessive'

$$(\text{box}) \underline{\quad \text{sp} \quad} (\text{orig}) \underline{\quad \text{ef} \quad} (\text{wood})$$

3.1. From this SF we can realise, by rules (316) or (300), and:

| (148) | ef | : | $Y(\text{orig}) \rightarrow V(\text{be}) + \text{Adj}$ |
| | | | *box (which) is wooden* |

or   (149)   ef   : $Y(\text{orig}) \rightarrow V(\text{be}) + V\text{pp}(\text{make}) + \text{Pr}(\text{of}) + N^0$

box (which) is made of wood

by rule (299) and:

| (88) | ef | : | $K(\text{orig}) \rightarrow \text{Pr}(\text{of}) + N^0$ |
| | | | *box of wood* |

or: (89)   ef   : $K(\text{orig}) \rightarrow V\text{pp}(\text{make}) + \text{Pr}(\text{of}) + N^0$

box made of wood

and, by rule (301) and:

| (128) | ef | : | $X(\text{orig}) \rightarrow \text{Adj}$ |
| | | | *wooden box* |

This adjective and others such as *iron, steel, metal*, etc. belong to Vendler's class A_a. They should be distinguished from adjectives of classes A_b and A_c derived from SFs containing '(like)' or '(like, sb)' which are illustrated in chapter XII.

3.2. From the reverse linearisation we have:

by rule (182) and:

$$(254) \quad \text{ps} \quad : \quad B(\text{orig}) \rightarrow \text{Pr}(\text{of}) + N^0$$

wood of [*the*] *box*

and by rule (181) and:

$$(204) \quad \text{ps} \quad : \quad A(\text{orig}) \rightarrow \text{Ngen}$$

[*the*] *box's wood*

4.   Lastly, we illustrate briefly how the rules cope with SFs having two 'sp–ef' links from one node. Two examples are given in figs. 14 (i) and 14 (ii) below, both with two $\xrightarrow{\text{sp}}$(poss)$\xrightarrow{\text{ef}}$ links, but in fact almost any '(mod)' node could equally well appear in the links.

4.1. From the SF:

Fig. 14 (i)

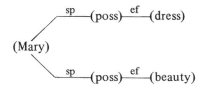

one linearisation, with '(dress)' at the end of a 'gl' link, is:

$$\xrightarrow{\text{gl}}[(\text{dress})\xrightarrow{\text{fe}}(\text{poss})\xrightarrow{\text{ps}}[(\text{Mary})\xrightarrow{\text{sp}}(\text{poss})\xrightarrow{\text{ef}}(\text{beauty})]\,]$$

fe   : $N^0(\text{dress}) \rightarrow A + N^0(\text{dress})$

ps   : $A(\text{poss}) \rightarrow \text{Ngen}$

(17)   [: $\text{Ngen} \rightarrow \text{NPgen}(\text{Ngen})$

(308)   sp   : $\text{Ngen}(\text{Mary}) \rightarrow X + \text{Ngen}(\text{Mary})$

ef   : $X(\text{poss}) \rightarrow \text{Adj}$

... beautiful Mary's dress

By rules illustrated already the reader can confirm that from the same linearisation can be realised *dress of* [*the*] *beautiful Mary*; *dress of Mary, who is beautiful*.

4.2. From the SF:

Fig. 14 (ii)

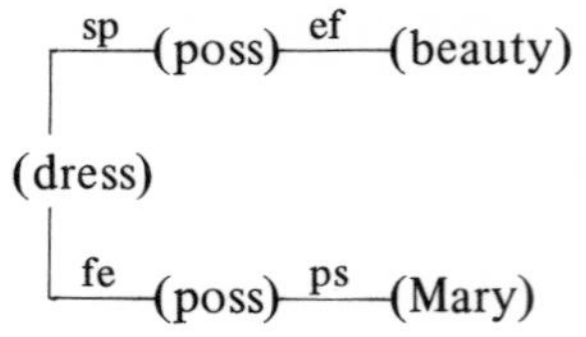

$$\begin{array}{l} \quad\quad\quad \overset{sp}{\rule{1.5em}{0.4pt}}(poss)\overset{ef}{\rule{1.5em}{0.4pt}}(beauty) \\ (dress) \\ \quad\quad\quad \overset{fe}{\rule{1.5em}{0.4pt}}(poss)\overset{ps}{\rule{1.5em}{0.4pt}}(Mary) \end{array}$$

one linearisation is:

$$\overset{gl}{\rightarrow}[(dress)\overset{fe}{\rule{1.5em}{0.4pt}}(poss)\overset{ps}{\rule{1.5em}{0.4pt}}(Mary)\quad b\quad (dress)\overset{sp}{\rule{1.5em}{0.4pt}}(poss)\overset{ef}{\rule{1.5em}{0.4pt}}(beauty)]$$

fe   : $N^0(dress) \rightarrow A + N^0(dress)$

ps   : $A(poss) \rightarrow Ngen$

sp   : $N^0(dress) \rightarrow X + N^0(dress)$

ef   : $X(poss) \rightarrow Adj$

Mary's beautiful dress

4.3. These examples clearly demonstrate that non-synonymous sentences must be realised from different SFs. Thus, we cannot derive *beautiful Mary's dress* from 14 (ii) nor can we derive *Mary's beautiful dress* from 14 (i) — the difference in 'sense' is reflected by the generation from different SFs.

V. PREPOSITIONS AND SUBORDINATE CLAUSES

A. Prepositions

A large number of prepositional constructions do not have any equivalent adjectival forms.

1. For example realisations of SFs containing '(about)'. From the SF:

$$(book) \xrightarrow{\text{sp}} (about) \xrightarrow{\text{ef}} (chemistry)$$

we can realise:

    sp : $NP(...) \rightarrow NP(...) + Y$

    sp : $N^0(book) \rightarrow N^0(book) + Wh(s) + Y$

(140) ef : $Y(about) \rightarrow V(be) + Pr(about) + N^0$

    book (which) is about chemistry

    sp : $N^0(book) \rightarrow N^0(book) + K$

(84) ef : $K(about) \rightarrow Pr(about) + N^0$

    book about chemistry

or: (85) ef : $K(about) \rightarrow Pr(on) + N^0$

    book on chemistry

Finally, there is a 'quasi-adjectival' realisation:

    sp : $N^0(book) \rightarrow X + N^0(book)$

(126) ef : $X(about) \rightarrow N^1$

    chemistry book

A true adjectival realisation is not possible: *chemical book* would not be acceptable as a synonym of *book about chemistry*. Also, unlike the 'adjectival' nodes, there is no inverse realisation by 'fe' and 'ps'. (The use of the superscript '1' with 'N' in rule (126) ensures that it may be modified only by adjectives (rule 303).)

2. However, many of the prepositional constructions are linked by 'ps' only to 'verbal' nodes and they rarely (if ever) have adjectival realisations. The following are two examples — more will be found in later chapters, particularly XI and XII.

2.1. The primary realisation of '(bene)' is the preposition *for* in the sense of *for the benefit of, for the sake of,* etc.

Fig. 15

$$(\text{John}) \xrightarrow{\text{agt}} (\text{buy}) \xrightarrow{\text{gl}} (\text{book})$$

$$\big\lfloor \xrightarrow{\text{sp}} (\text{bene}) \xrightarrow{\text{ef}} (\text{friend})$$

	agt	:	$NP(...) \rightarrow NP(...) + V$
	gl	:	$V(buy) \rightarrow V(buy) + NPt$
(328)	sp	:	$V(\Delta) \rightarrow V(\Delta) + W_{034}$
(110)	ef	:	$W_0(bene) \rightarrow Pr(for) + N^0$

John bought a book for a friend

2.2. The sememe '(instr)' is generally realised as the 'instrumental' *with*.

Fig. 16

$$(\text{John}) \xrightarrow{\text{agt}} (\text{break}) \xrightarrow{\text{gl}} (\text{window})$$

$$\big\lfloor \xrightarrow{\text{sp}} (\text{instr}) \xrightarrow{\text{ef}} (\text{hammer})$$

	sp	:	$V(\Delta) \rightarrow V(\Delta) + W_0$
(328)	sp	:	$V(\Delta) \rightarrow V(\Delta) + W_0$
(115)	ef	:	$W_0(instr) \rightarrow Pr(with) + N^0$

John broke a window with a hammer

B. Subordinate clauses

The close relationship between prepositions and subordinate conjunctions is reflected in the semolexemic rules by the generation of both through rule (328) and others producing the category 'W_0'. Subordinate constructions differ, however, from prepositional constructions in the rather more complex structures of their SFs.

1. The SF underlying a subordinate construction may be considered to consist of two SFs linked by a 'sp–ef' link between their 'verbal' nodes. For example, the two SFs

$$(\text{John})\xrightarrow{\text{agt}}(\text{steal})\xrightarrow{\text{gl}}(\text{car})$$

$$(\text{John})\xrightarrow{\text{sp}}(\text{mod}_2)\xrightarrow{\text{ef}}(\text{rich})$$

may be linked by '$\xrightarrow{\text{sp}}(\text{although})\xrightarrow{\text{ef}}$' to form the following:

Fig. 17 (i)

2. One linearisation of this SF is:

$$\text{decl}\longrightarrow[(\text{John})]\xrightarrow{\text{agt}}(\text{steal})\xrightarrow{\text{gl}}[(\text{car})]\,\text{b}\,(\text{steal})\xrightarrow{\text{sp}}(\text{although})—$$

$$\xrightarrow{\text{ef}}[(\text{mod}_2)\xrightarrow{\text{ps}}(\text{John})\,\text{b}\,(\text{mod}_2)\xrightarrow{\text{ef}}(\text{rich})]$$

	agt	:	$\text{NP}(...) \to \text{NP}(...) + \text{V}$
	gl	:	$\text{V}(\text{steal}) \to \text{V}(\text{steal}) + \text{NPt}$
	sp	:	$\text{V}(\Delta) \to \text{V}(\Delta) + \text{W}_0$
(106)	ef	:	$\text{W}_0(\text{although}) \to \text{Conj}(\text{although}) + \text{NPp}$
(29)	[	:	$\text{NPp} \to \text{NPp}(\text{Vrel}$

(286)   ps   : $Vrel(mod_2) \rightarrow N^0 + Y(mod_2)$

         ef   : $Y(mod_2) \rightarrow V(be) + Adj_2$

John stole a car although he was rich [5]

3. Instead of rule (106) we could have used rule (107) which operates on 'W$_0$(although)' to produce a prepositional realisation:

(107)   ef   : $W_0(although) \rightarrow Pr(in\ spite\ of) + NPc$

(22)   [: $NPc \rightarrow NPc(Vger$

(284)   ps   : $Vger(mod_2) \rightarrow Ngen + Yger(mod_2)$

(165)   ef   : $Yger(mod_2) \rightarrow Vger(be) + Adj_2$

John stole a car in spite of his being rich [5]

4. This capacity to generate either a prepositional or a subordinate conjunction construction from the same SF will be further illustrated in chapters XI and XIV. By using the category 'Vrel', already found after '(Conj(that)' earlier, we ensure that a subordinate conjunction is always followed by a clause; and by using 'Vger', we ensure that prepositions are not followed by clauses. This is also the effect of rules (110) and (115) in A.2 above, since if the sememe attached to 'N^0' is verbal, then a nominalisation with 'Nv' is realised after the preposition.

5. Instead of selecting '(John)' as theme when the pivot is '(steal)' we can choose '(although)'. (The rules in chapter II.C do not put any limitations on the kind of link which may occur between pivot and theme.) The effect of this choice is illustrated in fig. 17 (ii).

Fig. 17 (ii)

---

[5] We have assumed that the sememes '(John)' in fig. 17 (i) have the same referent. The treatment of anaphoric reference and the generation of *he* and *his* in these (and following) realisations will be described in the next chapter.

6. One linearisation is

$$decl \longrightarrow [(although) \xrightarrow{ef} [(mod_2) \xrightarrow{ps} (John) \, b \, (mod_2) \xrightarrow{ef} (rich)]]$$

$$\xrightarrow{ps} (steal) \xrightarrow{tga} [(John)] \, b \, (steal) \xrightarrow{gl} [(car)]$$

realised as:

(6)	decl	:	$S \rightarrow NPk$
(28)	[	:	$NPk \rightarrow NPk(W_0$
	ef	:	$W_0(although) \rightarrow Conj(although) + NPp$
	[	:	$NPp \rightarrow NPp(Vrel$
	ps	:	$Vrel(mod_2) \rightarrow N + Y(mod_2)$
	ef	:	$Y(mod_2) \rightarrow V(be) + Adj_2$
	]	:	$NPp(... \rightarrow NPp(...)$
	]	:	$NPk(... \rightarrow NPk(...)$
(283)	ps	:	$NPk(...) \rightarrow NP(...) + NPp$
	tga	:	$Vrel(steal) \rightarrow NP + V(steal)$
	gl	:	$V(steal) \rightarrow V(steal) + NPt$

although John was rich he stole a car

7. In this realisation we introduce three new rules, (6), (28) and (283), of considerable importance. With them and with other rules involving 'NPk' we are able to generate from many SFs sentences in which the subordinate clause, as in this case, or the prepositional phrase precede the main clause. As an example in which a preposition can head a sentence take the linearisation from the SF of fig. 16 (ii).

$$decl \longrightarrow [(instr) \xrightarrow{ef} (hammer)] \xrightarrow{ps} (break) \xrightarrow{tga} [(John)]$$

$$b \, (break) \xrightarrow{gl} [(window)]$$

This will be realised as:

(6)	decl	:	$S \rightarrow NPk$
(28)	[	:	$NPk \rightarrow NPk(W_0$

$$\text{ef} \quad : \quad W_0(\text{instr}) \to \text{Pr}(\text{with}) + N^0$$

(283)   ps   : $NPk(...) \to NP(...) + NPp$ etc.

with a hammer John broke a window

Other examples both of sentences headed by subordinate clauses and of sentences headed by prepositional phrases will be found later, particularly in chapter XI.

VI. ANAPHORIC REFERENCE

1.   Before proceeding further it is necessary to outline how anaphora is represented in SFs.

Reference back to previous statements made by either the speaker or his listener is an essential ingredient in the continuity and cohesiveness of any conversation. Indeed, it is difficult to conceive of any kind of communication without anaphora. It can be most easily illustrated by considering the use of pronouns.

(i)   *A man approached a policeman in the street. He was visiting the town and he asked for directions.*

The three lexemes, *man*, *he*, and *he*, all have the same referent. The assignment of the two pronouns to this particular referent is attributable to their anaphoric status. In themselves pronouns have a very large number of potential referents: *he* can denote any 'masculine' object. Through anaphora their referent is specified: in this case to *a man who approached a policeman in the street.*

An alternative way of putting (i) is to use *the man* instead of *he*:

(ii)   *A man approached a policeman in the street. The man was visiting the town.*

If the speaker had said *a man* the listener is likely to assume that another referent was intended. The use of the anaphoric *the* ensures that he knows that the speaker is continuing to talk about the *man* mentioned in the previous sentence.

If, however, the sentence in which *man* had been mentioned had occurred some time much earlier it may be necessary for the speaker to specify the referent more closely, e.g.

(iii) *A man approached a policeman in the street ...   The man who approached a policeman was visiting ...*

In this case we have an anaphoric *the* and a following relative clause which
restricts the range of referents to this particular 'man' — other 'men' may
have been talked about in the sentences between the two above. Relative
clauses following anaphoric *the* are nearly always 'restrictive' (section 6 below).

2.   In SFs anaphoric reference is indicated by a broken line from a node in
the SF to a node in another SF. (This follows a convention found in Tesnière
(1959).) The SFs underlying our examples are:

Fig. 18 (i)

$$(\text{man}) \xrightarrow{\text{agt}} (\text{approach}) \xrightarrow{\text{gl}} (\text{policeman})$$

$$(\text{man}) \xrightarrow{\text{agt}} (\text{visit}) \xrightarrow{\text{gl}} (\text{town})$$

When an anaphoric link, '-- ana --' is made between two nodes one of them is
replaced by '(pro)'. Thus, we can form the following SF:

Fig. 18 (ii)

$$(\text{pro}) \xrightarrow{\text{agt}} (\text{visit}) \xrightarrow{\text{gl}} (\text{town})$$
$$\overset{\text{ana}}{\vdots}$$
$$(\text{man}) \xrightarrow{\text{agt}} (\text{approach}) \xrightarrow{\text{gl}} (\text{policeman})$$

This is the SF underlying *The man who approached a policeman was visiting
the town* — semolexemic rules for the realisation will be given below. For the
SF of (i) and (ii) we need only remove the sememic structure underlying the
restrictive clause, i.e.

Fig. 18 (iii)

$$(\text{pro}) \xrightarrow{\text{agt}} (\text{visit}) \xrightarrow{\text{gl}} (\text{town})$$
$$\overset{\text{ana}}{\vdots}$$
$$(\text{man})$$

The formation of this SF may be considered to be a process involving the ex-
traction of the node '(man)' from the first SF in fig. 18 (i). Thus, in fig. 18
(iii) the speaker does not believe it is necessary to be as specific as in fig. 18
(ii), i.e. *he* or *the man* are sufficient for his purpose.

3.   We could replace '(policeman)' in fig. 18 (ii) by

$$(\text{pro})\overset{\text{ana}}{-\,-\,-}(\text{policeman})\overset{\text{agt}}{\rule{1.8cm}{0.4pt}}(\text{control})\overset{\text{gl}}{\rule{1.2cm}{0.4pt}}(\text{traffic})$$

from which a sentence with two anaphoric references can be derived: *The man who approached the policeman who was controlling traffic was visiting ...* Further, we might replace '(traffic)' by

$$(\text{pro})\overset{\text{ana}}{-\,-\,-}(\text{traffic})\overset{\text{agt}}{\rule{1.5cm}{0.4pt}}(\text{leave})\overset{\text{gl}}{\rule{1.2cm}{0.4pt}}(\text{market})$$

to produce a sentence with three anaphorae: *The man who approached the policeman who was controlling the traffic which was leaving the market was visiting ...* And so on.

In theory it seems anaphoric reference can extend backward almost ad infinitum, although no doubt limited by the embedding capacity of English (Yngve, 1960). Clearly it is a personal choice of any speaker or writer how much of previous SFs he incorporates anaphorically in his present SF: in fig. 18 (iii) it is just one node, in fig. 18 (ii) it is three nodes.

4. The rules connected with anaphora can be stated briefly.
(a) An 'ana' link is traced in linearisation always before any other link (and, being obligatory, no indication is made of 'branching').
(b) The semolexemic rules are:

$$(40) \quad \text{ana} \quad : \quad N^0(\text{pro}) \rightarrow \text{Pron}$$

$$(41) \quad \text{ana} \quad : \quad N^0(\text{pro}) \rightarrow D(\text{the}) + N^0$$

$$(43) \quad \text{ana} \quad : \quad V(\text{pro}) \rightarrow \text{Prov}$$

(c) The realisation of any links and nodes attached to '(pro)' by 'ana' is always completed before passing on to the rest of a linearisation.
(d) If any node at the end of an 'ana' link is normally bracketed in an independent SF (see chapter II.C.2) the brackets are retained, except when the 'ana' link is between two nodes of the same SF (as in the case of coordinate and subordinate constructions).

5. A partial linearisation and realisation of fig. 18 (ii) is:

$$\text{decl} \rightarrow [(\text{pro})\overset{\text{ana}}{-\,-\,\rightarrow}[(\text{man})]\overset{\text{agt}}{\rule{1cm}{0.4pt}}(\text{approach})\rule{1cm}{0.4pt}$$

$$\overset{\text{gl}}{\rule{1cm}{0.4pt}}\rightarrow[(\text{policeman})]\,]\overset{\text{agt}}{\rule{1cm}{0.4pt}}\rightarrow(\text{visit})\rightarrow$$

$$\begin{aligned}
\text{decl} \quad &: \quad S \to NPs \\
[\quad &: \quad NPs \to NP(N^0 \\
\text{ana} \quad &: \quad N^0(\text{pro}) \to D(\text{the}) + N^0 \\
[\quad &: \quad N^0 \to NPw(N^0 \\
\text{agt} \quad &: \quad NPw(...) \to NP(...) + Wh(s) + V
\end{aligned}$$

$$NP(D(\text{the}) + NP(N^0(\text{man})) + Wh(s) + V(\text{approach}) + NP(N^0(\text{policeman}))) + ...$$

the man who approached a policeman was visiting ...

In the case of a linearisation of fig. 18 (iii), rule (40) producing 'Pron' can be applied. [6] The graphemic realisation of 'Pron(man)' is *he* because the sememe '(man)' contains the semon '⟨male⟩', one of the few semons necessary for pronominal realisations.

6.   Relative clauses which are the result of anaphoric reference are always 'restrictive'. The other kind of relative clause — the 'non-restrictive' or 'descriptive' relative clause (Robbins, 1968) — is realised from SFs of a different form. The two SFs in fig. 18 (i) could be linked thus:

Fig. 19 (i)

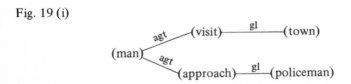

By semolexemic rules already illustrated in chapter III we can derive *A man who approached a policeman was visiting the town*. The relative clause here can be interpreted as either 'restrictive' or 'non-restrictive'. In its 'non-restrictive' interpretation the clause is not being used to specify the referent but to provide additional information about it. This usage is usually indicated by enclosing commas: *A man, who approached a policeman, was visiting the town*. In its 'restrictive' interpretation the clause is used to specify the referent of *man* (in the same way that *democracy* was specified by *as understood by Lenin* in chapter II.A) — normally this usage is indicated by an absence of enclosing commas.

Whereas in its 'non-restrictive' sense there is a synonymous realisation of

---

[6] By definition 'Pron' can be productive only when linked by 'ana' to a single sememe; therefore, '[' cannot (must not) operate on 'Pron'.

the SF with the contents of the relative and main clauses reversed, i.e. *A man, who was visiting the town, approached a policeman,* this is not the case when 'restrictive'. In order to ensure that the 'restricting' part of a SF is not detached from the sememe which it is specifying we enclose it in a box (or 'permanent' square bracket), thus:

Fig. 19 (ii)

$$\boxed{(\text{man})\xrightarrow{\text{agt}}(\text{approach})\xrightarrow{\text{gl}}(\text{policeman})}$$

$$\big|_{\text{agt}}$$
$$(\text{visit})$$
$$\big|_{\text{gl}}$$
$$(\text{town})$$

The effect of the boxing is to forbid in linarisation the tracing of the path from '(man)' to '(visit)' until after the path through '(approach)' to '(policeman)' has been traced. Thus, with the theme on '(man)' only one linearisation of fig. 19 (ii) is possible:

$$\text{decl} \longrightarrow [\,[(\text{man})]\xrightarrow{\text{agt}}(\text{approach})\xrightarrow{\text{gl}}[(\text{policeman})]\,]\!-\!\!-$$

$$\xrightarrow{\text{agt}}(\text{visit})\xrightarrow{\text{gl}}[(\text{town})]$$

7. It is possible to interpret the relative clause in *The man who approached a policeman was visiting the town* as being 'non-restrictive' if we consider that the only part of the underlying SF which is anaphoric is *the man*:

Fig. 19 (iii)

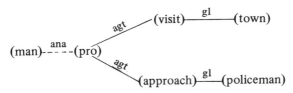

In this 'non-restrictive' sense there is, of course, a synonymous realisation *The man, who was visiting the town, approached a policeman.* We could box part of the SF in fig. 19 (iii) to make *who approached a policeman* 'restrictive' — as we did in fig. 19 (ii):

Fig. 19 (iv)

$$(man)\text{-}\underset{}{\overset{ana}{-\,-\,-}}\text{-}(pro)\underset{}{\overset{agt}{\rule{2cm}{0.4pt}}}(approach)\underset{}{\overset{gl}{\rule{2cm}{0.4pt}}}(policeman)$$

$$\overset{\overset{\big|\,agt}{}}{(visit)}$$

$$\overset{\overset{\big|\,gl}{}}{(town)}$$

The difference between this SF and that of fig. 18 (ii) is that here the only
anaphoric reference is to a single node '(man)' whereas in 18 (ii) the anaphora is to a previously mentioned phrase *A man approached a policeman*.
In 19 (iv) *who approached a policeman* has not been mentioned previously
(it is not anaphoric), but it is even so 'restrictive'. The distinction between
the two kinds of SF involving anaphora and 'restrictive' elements is possibly
unnecessary in practice; nevertheless it is believed that the distinction is a
valid one and it demonstrates the model's ability to deal with such nuances.

8. The question of anaphoric reference in relative pronouns (*who*, *which*,
etc.) has not been tackled. It would appear, however, that the kind of rules
required must be similar to those for the generation of pronouns (see section
5 above).

9. We are now in a position to deal with the occurrence of anaphora in subordinate clauses — a topic left over from the previous chapter. In the SF of
fig. 17 (i) the node '(John)' occurs twice. Replacing one node by '(pro)' and
making an 'ana' link to the other gives two alternative SFs:

Fig. 20 (i)

$$(pro)\underset{}{\overset{ana}{-\,-\,-\,-\,-\,-\,-\,-\,-\,-}}(John)$$

$$\overset{\big|\,agt}{(steal)}\underset{}{\overset{sp}{\rule{1.5cm}{0.4pt}}}(although)\underset{}{\overset{ef}{\rule{1.5cm}{0.4pt}}}(mod_2)$$

$$\overset{\big|\,gl}{(car)}\qquad\qquad\overset{\big|\,ef}{(rich)}$$

Fig. 20 (ii)

$$(John)\underset{}{\overset{ana}{-\,-\,-\,-\,-\,-\,-\,-\,-\,-}}(pro)$$

$$\overset{\big|\,agt}{(steal)}\underset{}{\overset{sp}{\rule{1.5cm}{0.4pt}}}(although)\underset{}{\overset{ef}{\rule{1.5cm}{0.4pt}}}(mod_2)$$

$$\overset{\big|\,gl}{(car)}\qquad\qquad\overset{\big|\,ef}{(rich)}$$

The SF in fig. 20 (ii) underlies the sentence *John stole a car although he was rich.* Its linearisation is:

$$\text{decl} \longrightarrow [(\text{John})] \xrightarrow{\text{agt}} (\text{steal}) \xrightarrow{\text{gl}} [(\text{car})] \, b \, (\text{steal}) \xrightarrow{\text{sp}} (\text{although}) \longrightarrow$$

$$\xrightarrow{\text{ef}} [(\text{mod}_2) \xrightarrow{\text{ps}} (\text{pro}) \, b \, (\text{mod}_2) \xrightarrow{\text{ef}} (\text{rich})]$$

Since the 'ana' link occurs between two nodes in the same SF, no account is made of the brackets enclosing '(John)' or of any nodes attached to it (see section 4 (d) above). In other words, when 'ana' links '(pro)' to another node in the same SF or linearisation the anaphoric reference is to a single sememe only. (The next chapter gives other examples with co-ordinate constructions.)

A partial realisation of the linearisation above would be, therefore:

$$\text{ef} \quad : \quad W_0(\text{although}) \rightarrow \text{Conj}(\text{although}) + \text{NPp}$$

$$\text{ps} \quad : \quad \text{Vrel}(\text{mod}_2) \rightarrow N^0 + Y(\text{mod}_2)$$

$$\text{ana} \quad : \quad N^0(\text{pro}) \rightarrow \text{Pron}$$

$$\text{ef} \quad : \quad Y(\text{mod}_2) \rightarrow V(\text{be}) + \text{Adj}_2$$

$$... + \text{Conj}(\text{although}) + \text{NPp}(\text{Pron}(\text{John}) + V(\text{be}) + \text{Adj}_2(\text{rich}))$$

10. From the linearisations of fig. 20 (ii) the reader will be able to confirm the realisation of:

(a) *John stole a car in spite of his being rich* (see chapter V.B.2 above)

(b) *Although he was rich John stole a car*

(c) *In spite of his being rich John stole a car*

From fig. 20 (i) we can obtain:

(d) *Although John was rich he stole a car* (see chapter V.B.6)

and also two unacceptable sentences:

(e) * *He stole a car although John was rich*

(f) * *He stole a car in spite of John's being rich* [7]

To account for the exclusion of sentences (e) and (f) we might postulate the general rule that '(pro)' may occur in a theme bracket if, but only if, the theme node itself is a sememe capable of prepositional or subordinate con-

---

[7] The sentences are, of course, acceptable if *he* does not have the same referent as *John*, i.e. when the underlying '(pro)' is linked anaphorically to a node outside the SF.

junction realisation. In (b) and (c) '(pro)' occurs in the theme bracket but the theme node is '(although)'; in (e) and (f), on the other hand, '(pro)' is itself the theme node. This rule would also exclude the passive forms of (e) and (f) — because the theme node would not be a 'prepositional' sememe:

(g) * *A car was stolen by him although John was rich*

(h) * *A car was stolen by him in spite of John's being rich*

VII. CO-ORDINATION

No attempt is made here to define co-ordination or to list and analyse those English words which may be considered co-ordinators, instead I shall merely sketch how the model can cope with certain — but by no means all — aspects of co-ordination. For illustration I employ the conjunctions *and* and *or*, on whose status as co-ordinators neither linguists nor philosophers (logicians) appear to have any doubts.

In co-ordinate constructions the members co-ordinated may be words, phrases, clauses or sentences. On the sememic stratum the situation is simpler: co-ordination is either between single sememes or between the linearisations of SFs.

A. Co-ordination of sememes

1. When the co-ordinating link for *and*, '$\xrightarrow{co}(\&)\xrightarrow{oc}$', joins two (or more) sememes, the node '(&)' occurs in the SF where otherwise a single sememe appears. For example in:

Fig. 21 (i)

$$(\text{John})\xrightarrow{\text{agt}}(\text{steal})\xrightarrow{\text{gl}}(\text{car})$$

we might replace '(John)' by '$(\text{John})\xrightarrow{co}(\&)\xrightarrow{oc}(\text{Peter})$', thus:

Fig. 21 (ii)

$$\begin{array}{c}\text{(John)}\\|\;{\scriptstyle 8}\\\text{(\&)}\xrightarrow{\quad\text{agt}\quad}\text{(steal)}\xrightarrow{\quad\text{gl}\quad}\text{(car)}\\|\;{\scriptstyle\text{oc}}\\\text{(Peter)}\end{array}$$

or '(steal)' by '(steal)$\xrightarrow{\text{co}}$(&)$\xrightarrow{\text{oc}}$(sell)':

Fig. 21 (iii)

$$\begin{array}{c}\text{(steal)}\\|\;{\scriptstyle 8}\\\text{(John)}\xrightarrow{\quad\text{agt}\quad}\text{(\&)}\xrightarrow{\quad\text{gl}\quad}\text{(car)}\\|\;{\scriptstyle 8}\\\text{(sell)}\end{array}$$

or '(car)' by '(car)$\xrightarrow{\text{co}}$(&)$\xrightarrow{\text{oc}}$(bicycle)':

Fig. 21 (iv)

$$\begin{array}{c}\text{(car)}\\|\;{\scriptstyle 8}\\\text{(John)}\xrightarrow{\quad\text{agt}\quad}\text{(steal)}\xrightarrow{\quad\text{gl}\quad}\text{(\&)}\\|\;{\scriptstyle 8}\\\text{(bicycle)}\end{array}$$

or all three nodes together:

Fig. 21 (v)

$$\begin{array}{ccc}\text{(John)} & \text{(steal)} & \text{(car)}\\|\;{\scriptstyle 8} & |\;{\scriptstyle 8} & |\;{\scriptstyle 8}\\\text{(\&)}\xrightarrow{\text{agt}}\text{(\&)}\xrightarrow{\text{gl}}\text{(\&)}\\|\;{\scriptstyle 8} & |\;{\scriptstyle 8} & |\;{\scriptstyle 8}\\\text{(Peter)} & \text{(sell)} & \text{(bicycle)}\end{array}$$

2. Similarly, adjectives and adverbs may be co-ordinated. From the SF of fig. 2 we can produce:

Fig. 21 (vi)

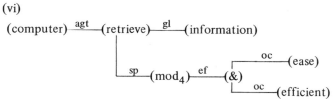

Only adjectives (and adverbs) belonging to the same adjective-class may be co-ordinated in this way (see chapter IV.A.1 above) since the node between 'sp' and 'ef' must be applicable to both sememes attached to '(&)'. [8]

3. Any number of sememes may be linked by 'co' to a node '(&)', e.g. the SF:

Fig. 22 (i)

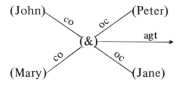

And any sememe linked to '(&)' may itself be an '(&)':

Fig. 22 (ii)

$$(John) \xrightarrow{co} (\&) \xrightarrow{oc} (Mary)$$
$$\Big\vert co$$
$$(\&) \xrightarrow{agt}$$
$$\Big\vert co$$
$$(Peter) \xrightarrow{co} (\&) \xrightarrow{oc} (Jane)$$

4. Instead of '(&)' in any of the SFs illustrated we could have the node '(vel)' realised as the conjunction *or*. The flexibility in this approach will be readily appreciated. The relationship between '(John)', '(Mary)', '(Peter)' and

---

[8] Co-ordination between adjectives (or adverbs) of different classes could be dealt with by optional operations on lexemic strings. For example, given a string such as 'Adj$_6$(v) + + Adj$_4$(w) + Adj$_3$(x) + Adj$_2$(y) + N(z)' (in which the order proposed by Vendler is followed) an optional rule might permit the insertion of 'Conj(and)' between 'Adj$_3$(x)' and 'Adj$_2$(y)'.

'(Jane)' in fig. 22 (i) is manifestly different from that in fig. 22 (ii) but both SFs can be realised (as we shall demonstrate below) by the phrase *John and Mary and Peter and Jane*. The ambiguity is well known to logicians. Just as in logic there are two possible formulae for *A and B or C*, namely '(A & B) v C' and 'A & (B v C)', there are two possible SFs:

5.   The semolexemic rules for co-ordination with '(&)' between single se-memes are as follows:

(225)   oc   : $C^0(\&) \rightarrow C^0 + C^1(\&)$

(226)   oc   : $C^1(\&) \rightarrow \text{Comma} + C^0 + C^1(\&)$

(228)   oc   : $C^1(\&) \rightarrow \text{Conj(and)} + C^0 + C^1(\&)$

(227)   oc   : $C^1(\&) \rightarrow \text{Conj(and)} + C^0$

where 'C' may be any of the categories 'N', 'V', 'Adj' or 'Adv'.

6.   With these rules we can generate co-ordinate constructions of both the 'emphatic' and 'non-emphatic' type (see Dik (1968a: 279)). One linearisation of fig. 22 (i) is:

6.1.   decl $\longrightarrow [(\&)\xrightarrow{\text{oc}}(\text{John})\,b\,(\&)\xrightarrow{\text{oc}}(\text{Mary})\,b\,(\&)\text{---}$

$\xrightarrow{\text{oc}}(\text{Peter})\,b\,(\&)\xrightarrow{\text{oc}}(\text{Jane})]\longrightarrow$

decl   : $S \rightarrow NPs$

(225)   oc   : $N^0(\&) \rightarrow N^0 + N^1(\&)$

(226)   oc   : $N^1(\&) \rightarrow \text{Comma} + N^0 + N^1(\&)$

(226)   oc   : $N^1(\&) \rightarrow \text{Comma} + N^0 + N^1(\&)$

(227)   oc   : $N^1(\&) \rightarrow \text{Conj(and)} + N^0$

John, Mary, Peter and Jane ['non-emphatic']

If in the last line rule (226) or rule (228) had been used then there would be no realisation because there is no graphic form for 'N(&)'.

6.2. An alternative realisation is:

$$(225) \quad \text{oc} \quad : \quad N^0(\&) \to N^0 + N^1(\&)$$

$$(228) \quad \text{oc} \quad : \quad N^1(\&) \to \text{Conj(and)} + N^0 + N^1(\&)$$

$$(228) \quad \text{oc} \quad : \quad N^1(\&) \to \text{Conj(and)} + N^0 + N^1(\&)$$

$$(227) \quad \text{oc} \quad : \quad N^1(\&) \to \text{Conj(and)} + N^0$$

John and Mary and Peter and Jane ['emphatic']

The choice between 'emphatic' and 'non-emphatic' is clearly one conditioned by a writer's contextual situation and stylistic habits. However, it is obviously important that the semolexemic rules allow for such variations.

6.3. As we mentioned above, this phrase (6.2) is also realised from the SF of fig. 22 (ii):

$$\text{decl} \longrightarrow [(\&) \xrightarrow{\text{oc}} [(\&) \xrightarrow{\text{oc}} (\text{John}) \, b \, (\&) \xrightarrow{\text{oc}} (\text{Mary})] \, b \, (\&) \longrightarrow$$

$$\xrightarrow{\text{oc}} [(\&) \xrightarrow{\text{oc}} (\text{Peter}) \, b \, (\&) \xrightarrow{\text{oc}} (\text{Jane})] \,] \longrightarrow$$

$$\text{oc} \quad : \quad N^0(\&) \to N^0 + N^1(\&)$$

$$[\quad : \quad N^0 \to \text{NPw}(N^0$$

$$\text{oc} \quad : \quad N^0(\&) \to N^0 + N^1(\&)$$

$$\text{oc} \quad : \quad N^1(\&) \to \text{Conj(and)} + N^0$$

$$] \quad : \quad \text{NPw}(... \to \text{NPw}(...)$$

$$\text{oc} \quad : \quad N^1(\&) \to \text{Conj(and)} + N^0; \text{etc. until:}$$

$$\text{NPs}(\text{NPw}(N^0(\text{John}) + \text{Conj(and)} + N^0(\text{Mary})) + \text{Conj(and)} + \text{NPw}(N^0(\text{Peter})$$
$$+ \text{Conj(and)} + N^0(\text{Jane})))$$

John and Mary and Peter and Jane ...

In this case, however, the phrase is not an instance of 'emphatic co-ordinations' since it is the only possible realisation of the linearisation.

7. The semolexemic rules for '(vel)' are similar to those for '(&)':

$$(229) \quad \text{oc} \quad : \quad C^0(\text{vel}) \to C^0 + C^1(\text{vel})$$

$$(230) \quad \text{oc} \quad : \quad C^0(\text{vel}) \to \text{Conj(either)} + C^0 + C^1(\text{vel})$$

$$(231) \quad \text{oc} \quad : \quad C^1(\text{vel}) \to \text{Comma} + C^0 + C^1(\text{vel})$$

$$(233) \quad oc \quad : \quad C^1(vel) \rightarrow Conj(or) + C^0 + C^1(vel)$$

$$(232) \quad oc \quad : \quad C^1(vel) \rightarrow Conj(or) + C^0$$

The presence of rule (230) enables four levels of emphasis to be distinguished, from 0 to 3 'emphatic' (in the terminology of Dik). Remembering that 'C(vel)' has no graphic form, the reader can confirm that the rules permit the following kinds of realisation:

John, Mary, Peter or Jane	[0 emphatic]
John or Mary or Peter or Jane	[1 emphatic]
Either John, Mary, Peter or Jane	[2 emphatic]
Either John or Mary or Peter or Jane	[3 emphatic]

B. Co-ordination of sememic formulae

1.   The links used to co-ordinate SFs are the same as those for the co-ordination of single sememes, namely ' $\xrightarrow{co}$(&)$\xrightarrow{oc}$ ' and ' $\xrightarrow{co}$(vel)$\xrightarrow{oc}$ '. However, when used in SF co-ordination the links are not introduced until after linearisation, i.e. after theme and pivot nodes have been selected.
1.1.   Thus, if we have two SFs: (a)$\xrightarrow{agt}$(b)$\xrightarrow{gl}$(c) and (d)$\xrightarrow{agt}$(e)$\xrightarrow{gl}$(f) they may be linearised:

$$decl \longrightarrow [(a)] \xrightarrow{agt} (b) \xrightarrow{gl} [(c)]$$

and

$$decl \longrightarrow [(d)] \xrightarrow{agt} (e) \xrightarrow{gl} [(f)]$$

and then co-ordinated:

$$decl \longrightarrow [(a)] \xrightarrow{agt} (b) \xrightarrow{gl} [(c)] \xrightarrow{co} (\&) \xrightarrow{oc} [(d)] \xrightarrow{agt} (e) \xrightarrow{gl} [(f)]$$

The co-ordinating link connects the end of one linearisation with the beginning of the other. This treatment can be justified by the observation (made by Dik (1968a: 165 ff.) and others) that there is frequently no reason, other than stylistic, why a particular expression occurs as two juxtaposed sentences or as one co-ordinated sentence:

(i) *She died. We buried her*
(ii) *She died and we buried her*

1.2. It should further be noticed that the order in which the two sentences occur in (i) and the order in which the two co-ordinated parts occur in (ii) are significant. A quite different sense is indicated by

(iii) *We buried her. She died*

The same semantic value must be attached to the change of (ii) to:

(iv) *We buried her and she died*

The significance of order in both juxtaposed sentences and co-ordinated sentences lends support to the view that co-ordination is optional and that it takes place after the SFs have been linearised, i.e. after a speaker has decided on what he wants to express first and which elements (nodes) are to be thematic (cf. chapter II.C above).

2. Just as anaphoric reference can be made from one sentence back to an earlier one it is clear that anaphora can occur between parts of a co-ordinated sentence. For example, suppose that in our two SFs the node '(d)' has the same referent as node '(a)'. As an independent sentence $(d)\xrightarrow{agt}(e)\xrightarrow{gl}(f)$ could appear (linearised) as: decl $\longrightarrow[(pro)\text{-}\xrightarrow{ana}\text{-}(a)]\xrightarrow{agt}(e)\xrightarrow{gl}[(f)]$. When linked by '$\xrightarrow{co}(\&)\xrightarrow{oc}$' to a linearisation of $(a)\xrightarrow{agt}(b)\xrightarrow{gl}(c)$ the 'ana' link would be made thus:

$$decl \longrightarrow [(a)]\xrightarrow{agt}(b)\xrightarrow{gl}[(c)]\xrightarrow{co}(\&)\xrightarrow{oc}[(pro)]\xrightarrow{agt}(e)\xrightarrow{gl}[(f)]$$

As in the case with rather similar linearisations involving subordinate conjunctions (VI.9), the 'ana' link goes direct to the node and does not consider any enclosing brackets.

2.1. An example of the linearisation above could be:

$$decl \longrightarrow [(John)\xrightarrow{agt}(sell)\xrightarrow{gl}[(car)]\xrightarrow{co}(\&)\xrightarrow{oc}[(pro)]\longrightarrow$$

$$\xrightarrow{agt}(buy)\xrightarrow{gl}[(bicycle)]$$

John sold a car and he bought a bicycle

Underlying this are the SFs:

$(John)\xrightarrow{\text{agt}}(sell)\xrightarrow{\text{gl}}(car)$

$(John)\xrightarrow{\text{agt}}(buy)\xrightarrow{\text{gl}}(bicycle)$

which could be equally realised as the independent (juxtaposed) sentences:

$decl\longrightarrow[(John)]\xrightarrow{\text{agt}}(sell)\xrightarrow{\text{gl}}[(car)]$

$decl\longrightarrow[(pro)\xdashrightarrow{\text{ana}}(John)]\xrightarrow{\text{agt}}(buy)\xrightarrow{\text{gl}}[(bicycle)]$

John sold a car. He bought a bicycle

2.2. The following two examples illustrate anaphoric links between nodes in different positions in co-ordinated linearisations:

2.21 $decl\longrightarrow[(John)]\xrightarrow{\text{agt}}(sell)\text{---}$

John sold a car and Bill bought it

2.22 $decl\longrightarrow[(John)]\xrightarrow{\text{agt}}(sell)\xrightarrow{\text{gl}}[(car)]\xrightarrow{\text{co}}(\&)\xrightarrow{\text{oc}}[(pro)]\text{---}$

$\xrightarrow{\text{lg}}(buy)\xrightarrow{\text{tga}}[(Bill)]$

John sold a car and it was bought by Bill

3.   For the realisation of these linearisations we need the semolexemic rules:

(61)   co   :   NP(...) → NP(...) + L

(234)   oc   :   L(&) → Conj(and) + NPs

Thus, the realisation of 2.1 proceeds:

agt   :   NP(...) → NP(...) + V

gl   :   V(sell) → V(sell) + NPt

co   :   NP(...) → NP(...) + L

oc   :   L(&) → Conj(and) + NPs

$$[\quad : \quad NPs \to NP(N^0$$

$$ana \quad : \quad N^0(pro) \to Pron$$

$$agt \quad : \quad NP(...) \to NP(...) + V$$

$$gl \quad : \quad V(buy) \to V(buy) + NPt$$

$NP(N^0(John)) + V(sell) + NP(N^0(car)) + Conj(and) + NP(Pron(John))$

$\quad + V(buy) + NP(N^0(bicycle))$

4. Perhaps rather more common than *John sold a car and he bought a bicycle* is the (synonymous) sentence *John sold a car and bought a bicycle* in which the anaphoric pronoun *he* is omitted. To account for this we might postulate that an alternative graphemic realisation of 'Pron(John)' is G/Δ. However, this solution would obviously cause complications in cases when only G/he is acceptable (e.g. in non-co-ordinated sentences).

4.1. Therefore, we suggest that the linearisation in 2.1 has a synonymous form:

$$decl \longrightarrow [(John)] \xrightarrow{agt} (sell) \xrightarrow{gl} [(car)] \xrightarrow{co} (\&) \xrightarrow{oc} (buy) \xrightarrow{gl} [(bicycle)]$$

4.2. For *John sold and Bill bought a car*, closely related to the sentence in 2.21 above, we can therefore propose the similar linearisation:

$$decl \longrightarrow [(John)] \xrightarrow{agt} (sell) \xrightarrow{co} (\&) \xrightarrow{oc} [(Bill)] \xrightarrow{agt} (buy) \xrightarrow{gl} [(car)]$$

5. To account for the realisations of these linearisations we need two more semolexemic rules:

$$(62) \quad co \quad : \quad V(x) \to V(x) + L$$

$$(235) \quad oc \quad : \quad L(\&) \to Conj(and) + V$$

5.1. Part of the realisation of *John sold a car and bought a bicycle* would be:

$$(61) \quad co \quad : \quad NP(...) \to NP(...) + L$$

$$(235) \quad oc \quad : \quad L(\&) \to Conj(and) + V$$

$$gl \quad : \quad V(buy) \to V(buy) + NPt$$

Note that rule (234) would be unproductive because 'gl' cannot operate on 'NPs'.

5.2. In the case of *John sold and Bill bought a car* part of the realisation would proceed:

$$\text{agt} \quad : \quad \text{NP}(...) \rightarrow \text{NP}(...) + \text{V}$$

(62) $\text{co} \quad : \quad \text{V}(\text{sell}) \rightarrow \text{V}(\text{sell}) + \text{L}$

(234) $\text{oc} \quad : \quad \text{L}(\&) \rightarrow \text{Conj}(\text{and}) + \text{NPs}$

$$\text{agt} \quad : \quad \text{NP}(...) \rightarrow \text{NP}(...) + \text{V}$$

Rule (235) would be unproductive because '[' cannot operate on 'V'.

6.   We are now in a position to attempt a formalisation of the processes by which the linearisations in 2 and 4 above may be derived from a linearisation such as that in 1.1, viz.

$$\text{decl} \longrightarrow [(a)] \xrightarrow{\text{agt}} (b) \xrightarrow{\text{gl}} [(c)] \xrightarrow{\text{co}} (\&) \xrightarrow{\text{oc}} [(d)] \xrightarrow{\text{agt}} (e) \xrightarrow{\text{gl}} [(f)]$$

6.1. If nodes '(a)' and '(d)' have the same sememe and referent

  (i) node '(d)' may be replaced by '(pro)' and an 'ana' link made to '(a)': example 2.1 *John sold a car and he bought a bicycle.*

 (ii) node '(d)' together with its enclosing square brackets and the 'agt' link may be eliminated: example 4.1 *John sold a car and bought a bicycle.*

6.2. If nodes '(c)' and '(f)' have the same sememe and referent

(iii) node '(f)' may be replaced by '(pro)' and an 'ana' link made to '(c)': example 2.21 *John sold a car and Bill bought it.*

(iv) node '(c)' together with its enclosing square brackets and the 'gl' link may be eliminated: example 4.2 *John sold and Bill bought a car* [9]

7.1. The synonymy of some of the above realisations with sentences having relative clauses is worth noting. For example *John sold a car and Bill bought it* (2.21) or *John sold a car and it was bought by Bill* (2.22) have the synonym *John sold a car which was bought by Bill.* The latter would be derived

---

[9] Instead of rules (ii) and (iv) eliminating sememes we could introduce 'dummies':
   (ii′) node '(d)' may be replaced by '(Δ)': thus

$$\text{decl} \longrightarrow [(a)] \xrightarrow{\text{agt}} (b) \xrightarrow{\text{gl}} [(c)] \xrightarrow{\text{co}} (\&) \xrightarrow{\text{oc}} [(Δ)] \xrightarrow{\text{agt}} (e) \xrightarrow{\text{gl}} [(f)]$$

   (iv′) node '(c)' may be replaced by '(Δ)': thus

$$\text{decl} \longrightarrow [(a)] \xrightarrow{\text{agt}} (b) \xrightarrow{\text{gl}} [(Δ)] \xrightarrow{\text{co}} (\&) \xrightarrow{\text{oc}} [(d)] \xrightarrow{\text{agt}} (e) \xrightarrow{\text{gl}} [(f)]$$

This procedure would be obviously simpler and would obviate the need for rules (62) and (235). However, for chiefly theoretical reasons I am very reluctant to admit dummy sememes in either SFs or linearisations (chapter XIII).

from the linearisation:

$$\text{decl} \longrightarrow [(\text{John})] \xrightarrow{\text{agt}} (\text{sell}) \xrightarrow{\text{gl}} [\,[(\text{car})] \xrightarrow{\text{lg}} (\text{buy}) \xrightarrow{\text{tga}} [(\text{Bill})]\,]$$

which in turn is obtained from the SF:

$$(\text{John}) \xrightarrow{\text{agt}} (\text{sell}) \xrightarrow{\text{gl}} (\text{car}) \xrightarrow{\text{lg}} (\text{buy}) \xrightarrow{\text{tga}} (\text{Bill})$$

From this SF, by rules already adequately illustrated, the following sentences can also be derived: *Bill bought a car which John sold, A car which John sold was bought by Bill, A car which Bill bought was sold by John,* etc. The relative clauses are clearly 'non-restrictive' (VI.6.).

7.2. It would seem, therefore, that if we have two SFs

$$(a) \xrightarrow{\text{agt}} (b) \xrightarrow{\text{gl}} (c)$$

$$(d) \xrightarrow{\text{agt}} (e) \xrightarrow{\text{gl}} (f)$$

and nodes '(c)' and '(f)' the same sememe and referent (as in 6.2), then we may derive the SF: $(a) \xrightarrow{\text{agt}} (b) \xrightarrow{\text{gl}} (c) \xrightarrow{\text{lg}} (e) \xrightarrow{\text{tga}} (d)$ from which, of course, various linearisations are possible.

8. To what extent are we justified in asserting the synonymy of such a variety of linearisations and realisations as those presented in the previous paragraphs? It would seem to be beyond doubt that as far as the speaker (or writer) is concerned the following sentences are all expressions of the reference of the SFs:

$$(\text{John}) \xrightarrow{\text{agt}} (\text{sell}) \xrightarrow{\text{gl}} (\text{car})$$

$$(\text{Bill}) \xrightarrow{\text{agt}} (\text{buy}) \xrightarrow{\text{gl}} (\text{car})$$

when the two sememes '(car)' have the same referent:

(a) *John sold a car. Bill bought it*
(b) *John sold a car. It was bought by Bill*
(c) *John sold a car and Bill bought it* (= 2.21)
(d) *John sold a car, and it was bought by Bill* (= 2.22)
(e) *John sold and Bill bought a car* (= 4.2)
(f) *John sold a car which was bought by Bill* (= 7.1)

From the listener's (or reader's) point of view, however, the position is not quite so clear. Whereas in (a)−(d) and (f) he is unlikely to assume that the object sold by John was different from that bought by Bill, this is not the case in (e). Indeed, the probable interpretation of *John sold and Bill bought a car* is that two different cars are in question. For this reason, speakers (and writers) are likely to avoid this expression as it is liable to misinterpretation and in consequence it is quite likely that most users of English will say that (e) is not always synonymous with (c), (d) or (f). Just as there are lexemes with two or more sememes, we must recognise that some linearisations are also homonymous since they may be derived from two or more SFs. By one reading, then, (e) is a synonym of (c), (d) and (f) but by another reading it is synonymous with *John sold a car and Bill bought a [= another] car*.

C. Relationships between co-ordinate constructions

Let us now pass on to the consideration of two SFs which are to be co-ordinated but which have two nodes with the same referents.

1. For example, the SF:

Fig. 23 (i)

$$(\text{John}) \xrightarrow{\text{agt}} (\text{own}) \xrightarrow{\text{gl}} (\text{car})$$

$$(\text{John}) \xrightarrow{\text{agt}} (\text{drive}) \xrightarrow{\text{gl}} (\text{car})$$

If the two sememes '(John)' have the same referent and the two sememes '(car)' have the same referent, it may be linearised with two 'ana' links:

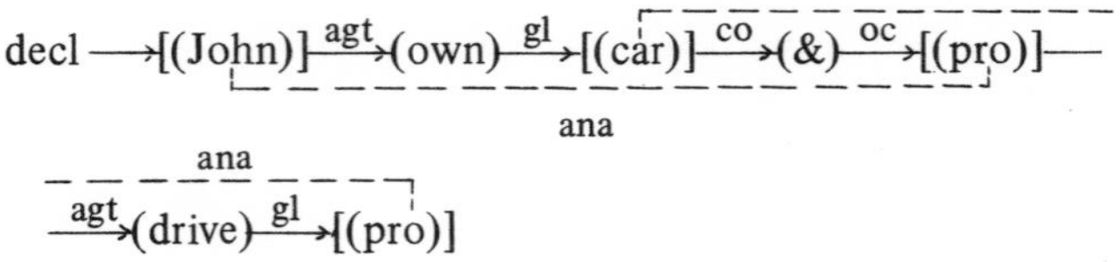

$$\text{decl} \longrightarrow [(\text{John})] \xrightarrow{\text{agt}} (\text{own}) \xrightarrow{\text{gl}} [(\text{car})] \xrightarrow{\text{co}} (\&) \xrightarrow{\text{oc}} [(\text{pro})] —$$

ana

$$\xrightarrow{\text{ana}}$$

$$\xrightarrow{\text{agt}} (\text{drive}) \xrightarrow{\text{gl}} [(\text{pro})]$$

giving the realisation *John owns a car and he drives it*. This sentence, however, has clearly a synonym derived from a single SF with a co-ordinated 'verbal' node:

Fig. 23 (ii)

$$(John) \xrightarrow{\text{agt}} (\&) \xrightarrow{\text{gl}} (car)$$

with (own) connected above $(\&)$ by oc, and (drive) connected below $(\&)$ by oc.

$$\text{decl} \longrightarrow [(John)] \xrightarrow{\text{agt}} (\&) \xrightarrow{\text{oc}} (own)\ b\ (\&) \xrightarrow{\text{oc}} (drive)\ b\ (\&) \xrightarrow{\text{gl}} [(car)]$$

John owns and drives a car

2. Similarly, the co-ordination of

Fig. 23 (iii)

$$(John) \xrightarrow{\text{agt}} (buy) \xrightarrow{\text{gl}} (car)$$

$$(John) \xrightarrow{\text{agt}} (buy) \xrightarrow{\text{gl}} (house)$$

which may be realised as *John bought a car and he bought a house* (note that the verb is not subject to anaphoric replacement by a pro-verb) has a synonymous realisation from

Fig. 23 (iv)

$$(John) \xrightarrow{\text{agt}} (buy) \xrightarrow{\text{gl}} (\&)$$

with (car) connected above $(\&)$ by oc, and (house) connected below $(\&)$ by oc.

John bought a car and a house

3. However, if we co-ordinate

Fig. 23 (v)

$$(John) \xrightarrow{\text{agt}} (play) \xrightarrow{\text{gl}} (chess)$$

$$(Bill) \xrightarrow{\text{agt}} (play) \xrightarrow{\text{gl}} (chess)$$

we can obtain *John played chess and Bill played chess*, while from

Fig. 23 (vi)

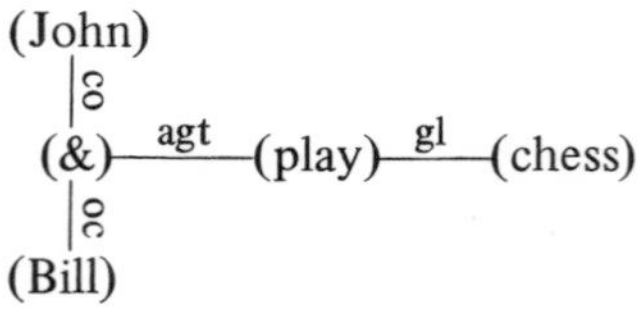

$$
\begin{array}{c}
\text{(John)} \\
\Big|\ \text{c} \\
\text{(\&)}\underline{\quad \text{agt}\quad}\text{(play)}\underline{\quad \text{gl}\quad}\text{(chess)} \\
\Big|\ \text{c} \\
\text{(Bill)}
\end{array}
$$

we have *John and Bill played chess.* It is undoubtedly true that in some contexts the two sentences are synonymous, but generally in the interpretation
of the first two different events will be assumed, i.e. *John* was playing against
a different opponent from *Bill*, whereas in the second there is one event, i.e.
John was playing against *Bill*. The consequence of this is that we would be
wrong to assume that fig. 23 (v) and fig. 23 (vi) are synonymous.

4.   In the case of figs. 23 (iii) and 23 (iv) on most occasions *John bought a
house and he bought a car* would be considered synonymous with *John
bought a house and a car.* However, the latter asserts that the house and car
were bought at the same time whereas the former makes no such assertion.
We might say, therefore, that given *John bought a house and a car* we may
derive *John bought a house and he bought a car* but not vice versa. With *John
owns and drives a car* and *John owns a car and he drives it*, however, it seems
that the two sentences are synonymous by all interpretations. Therefore we
can derive either one of the underlying SFs from the other underlying SF.

5.   It appears then, that two co-ordinated SFs

$$
\text{(a)}\underline{\quad\text{agt}\quad}\text{(b)}\underline{\quad\text{gl}\quad}\text{(c)} \qquad \text{and} \qquad \text{(d)}\underline{\quad\text{agt}\quad}\text{(e)}\underline{\quad\text{gl}\quad}\text{(f)}
$$

with (i) nodes '(a)' and '(d)' having the same sememe and referent and '(b)'
and '(e)' having the same sememe and referent; or (ii) nodes '(a)' and '(d)'
having the same sememe and referent and '(c)' and '(f)' having the same
sememe and referent; or (iii) nodes '(b)' and '(e)' having the same sememe
and referent and '(c)' and '(f)' having the same sememe and referent, may be
equivalent in some circumstances to the SFs

$$\text{(i)} \quad (a)\overset{agt}{\underline{\quad}}(b)\overset{gl}{\underline{\quad}}(\&)\begin{smallmatrix}(c)\\ |\,\text{co}\\ \\ |\,\text{co}\\(f)\end{smallmatrix} \qquad \text{(ii)} \quad (a)\overset{agt}{\underline{\quad}}(\&)\overset{gl}{\underline{\quad}}(c)\begin{smallmatrix}(b)\\ |\,\text{co}\\ \\ |\,\text{co}\\(e)\end{smallmatrix} \quad \text{or} \quad \text{(iii)} \quad (\&)\overset{agt}{\underline{\quad}}(b)\overset{gl}{\underline{\quad}}(c)\begin{smallmatrix}(a)\\ |\,\text{co}\\ \\ |\,\text{co}\\(d)\end{smallmatrix}$$

respectively or they may not. Whether the equivalence holds seems to depend on the sememic constitution of the SFs concerned. In our particular examples we found that fig. 23 (i) was equivalent to fig. 23 (ii) — an instance of (ii) above — fig. 23 (iii) was partially equivalent to fig. 23 (iv) — an instance of (i) — and fig. 23 (v) was not equivalent to fig. 23 (vi). However, undoubtedly other examples could be found in which SFs conforming to (ii) were not equivalent and SFs conforming to (iii) were equivalent. Similarly, we can probably find many other examples, like 23 (iii) and 23 (iv), where one SF implies the other but not vice versa.

6.   Furthermore, there are many SFs with co-ordinated sememes which cannot under any circumstances be "broken down" into independent (co-ordinated) SFs. As the following examples show it would be wrong to attempt to derive all types of co-ordination from co-ordinated SFs. (Dik (1968a: 75—92) among others has demonstrated the fallacy of certain transformational grammars in asserting that all co-ordinate structures must be derived in this way.)

6.1. *John and Mary are a couple ← * John is a couple and Mary is a couple. The team is composed of John, Paul and Peter ← * The team is composed of John and it is composed of Paul and ...*
*He combined oxygen and hydrogen ← * He combined oxygen and he combined hydrogen.*
*The book and the manuscript were compared ← * The book was compared and the manuscript was compared.*

6.2.   Hence, there are many cases in which, for example, a SF of the form

$$(a)\overset{agt}{\underline{\quad}}(b)\overset{gl}{\underline{\quad}}(\&)\begin{smallmatrix}(c)\\ |\,\text{co}\\ \\ |\,\text{co}\\(f)\end{smallmatrix}$$

is not equivalent to the co-ordination of $(a)\overset{agt}{\underline{\quad}}(b)\overset{gl}{\underline{\quad}}(c)$ and $(a)\overset{agt}{\underline{\quad}}(b)\overset{gl}{\underline{\quad}}(f)$. However, in the case of fig. 23 (iv) and fig. 23 (iii) above we found that the former does imply the latter. By "implication", or rather more exactly 'sememic implication' since the process takes place at the sememic level, we mean that given a realisation from one form of SF we are justified in deriving synonymous realisations from the other SF (or combination of SFs).

6.3. Clearly, then, whereas fig. 23 (iv) does 'sememically imply' fig. 23 (iii), the relationship of 'sememic implication' does not exist for our examples in 6.1 above. It would appear to be forbidden by the sememes present in their SFs.

7.   The situation is further complicated by the existence of what is generally known as 'comitative co-ordination' (e.g. Fillmore, 1968). Synonymous with *John and Bill played chess*, which refers to one event, we find *John played chess with Bill*. This can be derived from:

Fig. 24 (i)

$$\text{(John)} \overset{\text{agt}}{\searrow}$$
$$\text{(Bill)} \overset{\text{agt}}{\nearrow} \text{(play)} \overset{\text{gl}}{---} \text{(chess)}$$

$$\text{decl} \longrightarrow [(\text{John})] \overset{\text{agt}}{\longrightarrow} (\text{play}) \overset{\text{gl}}{\longrightarrow} [(\text{chess})] \quad b \quad (\text{play}) \overset{\text{tga}}{\longrightarrow} [(\text{Bill})]$$

using the new rule

(366)   tga : $V(\Delta) \rightarrow V(\Delta) + Pr(\text{with}) + NP$.

There is no risk that in using this rule we might generate incorrect sentences because this rule and rule (365), which operates on 'V(x)', are the only ones in which 'tga' is productive with 'V'.

    Similarly, 'comitative co-ordination' occurs with 'gl' links. Synonymous with *The book and the manuscript were compared* is the sentence *The book was compared with the manuscript*.

Fig. 24 (ii)

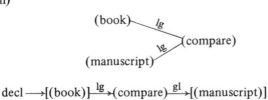

$$\text{decl} \longrightarrow [(\text{book})] \overset{\text{lg}}{\longrightarrow} (\text{compare}) \overset{\text{gl}}{\longrightarrow} [(\text{manuscript})]$$

$$\text{lg} \quad : \quad NP(...) \rightarrow NP(...) + V(be) + Vpp^0$$

(210) $\quad$ gl $\quad : \quad Vpp^0(\text{compare}) \rightarrow Vpp^0(\text{compare}) + Pr(\text{with}) + NP$

As with the 'tga' rules there is no risk of incorrect realisations from this rule
or the other 'gl' rule (211).

8. Thus, the SF in fig. 23 (vi) which underlies *John and Bill played chess* is
equivalent to the SF in fig. 24 (i), and the SF underlying *The book and the
manuscript were compared* is equivalent to the SF in fig. 24 (ii). However,
there are many sentences derived from SFs with two co-ordinated sememes
which are not equivalent to two 'comitatively co-ordinated' sentences. For
example:
John and Mary are a couple → * *John is a couple with Mary.*
The team is composed of John, Paul and Peter → * *The team is composed of
John with Paul ...*
John bought a car and a house → * *John bought a car with a house* (this sentence is only acceptable in a different 'sense').
The SFs with co-ordinated sememes underlying the sentences on the left do
not imply the SFs with 'comitative co-ordination' underlying the sentences
on the right. It would appear, then, that although a 'comitative' SF, as in
fig. 24 (i), always implies a SF with co-ordinated sememes, as in fig. 23 (vi),
the reverse 'sememic implication' is not necessarily true.

Other instances of 'sememic implication' will be illustrated in later sections, but none are as complex as those obtaining between the various kinds
of co-ordinate structures. Later chapters will also illustrate 'sememic equivalence', i.e. when one form of SF implies and is implied by another form of
SF, and a general discussion of the relationships between SFs will be found in
chapter XV in a wider context.

VIII. ARTICLES, QUANTIFIERS AND NUMERALS

A. General

I have dealt so far with no articles other than anaphoric *the*. Even a cursory examination would show that anaphora cannot account for all uses of the definite article — for an extensive and detailed investigation of the subject see Robbins (1968).

1. In sentences such as
    The horse is an animal
    The cheetah attains great speeds
    The marten is a close relative of the sable
the referent of *horse, cheetah*, etc. is the whole genus and not one specific member. Constructions with the generic *the* (as Robbins calls this usage) have synonyms with constructions containing unmarked plurals:
    Horses are animals
    Cheetahs attain great speeds
    Martens are close relatives of sables
It is perhaps open to question whether we are fully justified in deriving both forms from the same sememe, i.e. (horse, pl) = ^{G}/the horse and ^{G}/horses; (cheetah, pl) = ^{G}/the cheetah and ^{G}/cheetahs. What is quite clear, however, is that generic *the* cannot have the same sememic representation as anaphoric *the*.

Similarly, the definite articles in the following phrases cannot be derived from anaphoric representations since they have full synonyms in 'unmarked' forms:

the progress of science → scientific progress
the retrieval of information → information retrieval

2. The English indefinite article *a/an* has two basic meanings: in one, *a* can be replaced by *a certain*, *a particular*; and in the other, it can be replaced by *any*. Thus a sentence such as *John would like a book on chemistry* may indicate either that one particular referent is desired or that any item fitting the description would be acceptable.

For the first usage, as *a certain*, I follow Greenberg (1966) in treating it as a realisation of an 'unmarked' sememe. Thus, (boy) = ^{G}/a boy, (book) = ^{G}/a book. In the plural an 'unmarked' sememe is realised with no article: (boy, pl) = ^{G}/boys, (book, pl) = ^{G}/books.

For the second usage the indefinite article is treated as a variant of the quantifier *any*: thus *a (= any) boy* is derived from

$$(\text{boy}) \xrightarrow{\text{sp}} (\text{quant}) \xrightarrow{\text{ef}} (\text{any})$$

This use of *any* must be kept distinct from its occurrence in negated sentences when it has quite different origins (see X.A.2).

3. There are a number of words which may be grouped together as 'quantifiers'. Apart from *any* we find *some*, *several*, *many*, *all*, *few*, *every* and the negatives *no* and *none*. (The latter I shall leave until the other aspects of negation have been treated.)

The semantic structure of quantifiers from the paradigmatic point of view will not be investigated here, but for an interesting examination I may refer to Vater (1963).

Numerals, both ordinal and cardinal, have many similarities with the quantifiers and I shall treat them together.

4. Both quantifiers and numerals are linked to another sememe, which may be '(pro)', by a 'sp—ef' link incorporating '(quant)' and '(num)' respectively. For example:

Fig. 25

$$(\text{book, pl}) \xrightarrow{\text{sp}} (\text{quant}) \xrightarrow{\text{ef}} (\text{some})$$
$$(\text{book, pl}) \xrightarrow{\text{sp}} (\text{quant}) \xrightarrow{\text{ef}} (\text{many})$$
$$(\text{book, pl}) \xrightarrow{\text{sp}} (\text{quant}) \xrightarrow{\text{ef}} (\text{any})$$
$$(\text{book, pl}) \xrightarrow{\text{sp}} (\text{num}) \xrightarrow{\text{ef}} (\text{three})$$
$$(\text{book}) \xrightarrow{\text{sp}} (\text{quant}) \xrightarrow{\text{ef}} (\text{any})$$
$$(\text{book}) \xrightarrow{\text{sp}} (\text{num}) \xrightarrow{\text{ef}} (\text{one})$$
$$(\text{pro}) \xrightarrow{\text{sp}} (\text{quant}) \xrightarrow{\text{ef}} (\text{some})$$
$$(\text{pro}) \xrightarrow{\text{sp}} (\text{quant}) \xrightarrow{\text{ef}} (\text{any})$$
$$(\text{pro}) \xrightarrow{\text{sp}} (\text{num}) \xrightarrow{\text{ef}} (\text{three})$$
$$(\text{pro}) \xrightarrow{\text{sp}} (\text{num}) \xrightarrow{\text{ef}} (\text{one})$$

Most quantifiers and numerals can be linked only with sememes containing the '⟨pl⟩' semon, a few can be linked only with 'singular' sememes, e.g. '(one)', '(every)', '(each)'; others, e.g. '(any)' and '(non)', can be linked with either.

B. Adjectival realisations

1. 'As one would expect from the 'sp–ef' representation one kind of realisation for quantifiers and numerals is 'adjectival'. Adjective realisations of the SFs in fig. 25 are: *some books, many books, any books, three books*, etc. The semolexemic rules required are:

(301)	sp	:	$N^0(x) \to X + N^0(x)$
(134)	ef	:	$X(\text{quant}) \to \text{Adj}$
(127)	ef	:	$X(\text{num}) \to \text{Adj}$

and the lexographemic transformations: $\text{Adj}(\text{some}) = \text{G}/\text{some}$, $\text{Adj}(\text{many}) = \text{G}/\text{many}$, etc.

2. For quantifiers the use of rules (299), (300) and (316) is unproductive because 'ef' cannot operate on 'K(quant)' or 'Y(quant)'. Thus we do not find * *books of/with some*, * *books (which) are some*, * *books of/with many*, * *books (which) are many* (cf. IV.D.1).

With numerals 'ef' may operate on 'Y(num)' using rule (147) viz.:

ef   :   Y(num) → V(be) + Adj + Pr(in) + N(number)

Sentences such as *books (which) are three in number* occur, however, only under certain conditions which need to be examined. As with quantifiers, rule (299) is unproductive; 'ef' cannot operate on 'K(num)': we do not have * *books of/with three*, etc.

3. Just as there are rules concerning the order of adjective-classes (IV.A.1 above), it is evident that any quantifier always precedes any numeral: *all three books, every third book, any four books*, etc. We find never * *three all books*, * *two any books*, etc.

   Like adjectives and adverbs in the same class, two or more quantifiers are co-ordinated

Fig. 26 (i)

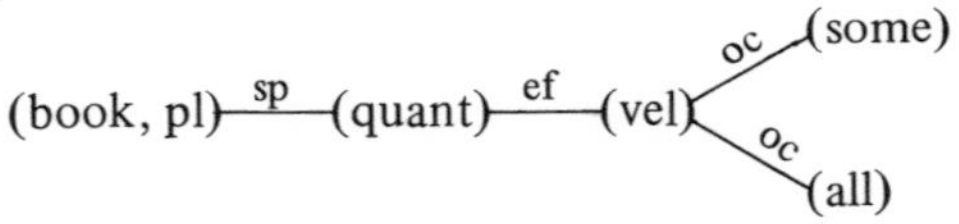

some or all books

and two or more numerals are co-ordinated

Fig. 26 (ii)

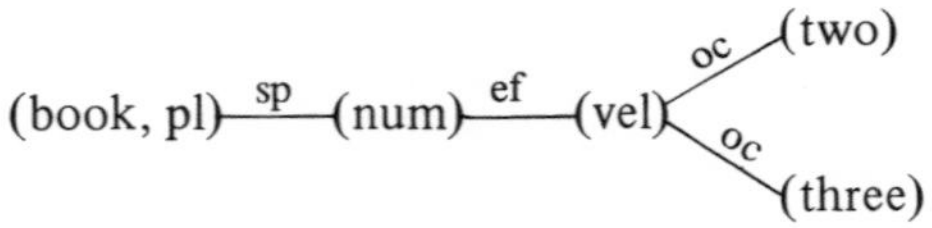

two or three books

In the case of numerals, the lower number usually precedes the higher: *three or four boys* and not * *four or three boys*. (With quantifiers the rules of precedence are more complex.)

C. Partitive realisations

Quantifiers and numerals have 'partitive' realisations with the operations of 'fe' and 'ps'. The quantifier or numeral stands as the 'theme' or 'tail' node of a SF, and at the end of 'ps' is always found a '(pro)' sememe linked anaphorically to another sememe or SF:

Fig. 27 (i)

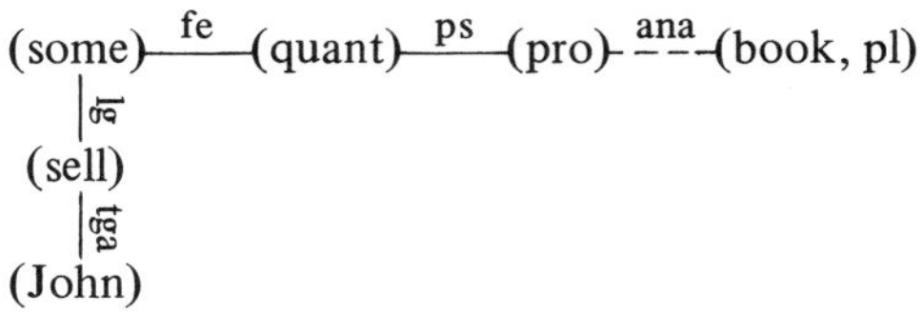

$$(\text{some}) \xrightarrow{\text{fe}} (\text{quant}) \xrightarrow{\text{ps}} (\text{pro}) \xrightarrow{\text{ana}} (\text{book, pl})$$

$$\Big|\text{lg}$$

$$(\text{sell})$$

$$\Big|\text{tga}$$

$$(\text{John})$$

Linearised as:

$$\text{decl} \longrightarrow [(\text{some}) \xrightarrow{\text{fe}} (\text{quant}) \xrightarrow{\text{ps}} (\text{pro}) \dashrightarrow (\text{book, pl})] \longrightarrow$$

$$\xrightarrow{\text{lg}} (\text{sell}) \xrightarrow{\text{tga}} [(\text{John})]$$

we obtain fe : $N^0(\text{some}) \rightarrow N^0(\text{some}) + B$

(260) ps : $B(\text{quant}) \rightarrow Pr(\text{of}) + N^0$

ana : $N^0(\text{pro}) \rightarrow D(\text{the}) + N^0$

some of the books were sold by John

Similarly for a numeral:

fe : $N^0(\text{three}) \rightarrow N^0(\text{three}) + B$

(253) ps : $B(\text{num}) \rightarrow Pr(\text{of}) + N^0$

three of the books were sold by John

2. For neither quantifiers nor numerals are rules (181), (183) or (187) productive since 'ps' does not operate on 'A(quant)', 'A(num)', 'J(quant)' or 'J(num)': thus, we do not find * *some (which) are the books*', * *three (which) are the books*', * *the some books*, etc. (cf. again chapter IV).

3. As in the 'adjectival' realisations, quantifiers and numerals may be coordinated:

Fig. 27 (ii)

$$(\text{some}) \overset{co}{\diagdown} \quad \overset{fe}{\diagup} (\text{quant}) \overset{ps}{---} (\text{pro}) \overset{ana}{---} (\text{book, pl})$$
$$(\text{vel}) \overset{oc}{\diagdown}$$
$$\downarrow \qquad (\text{all})$$

some or all of the books ...

4. In fig. 27 (iii) is given a SF in which the anaphoric link is to more than a single sememe

Fig. 27 (iii)

$$(\text{some}) \overset{fe}{---} (\text{quant}) \overset{ps}{---} (\text{pro}) \overset{ana}{---} (\text{book, pl}) \overset{sp}{---} (\text{quant}) \overset{ef}{---} (\text{many})$$
$$\big|\,{}^{lg} \qquad\qquad\qquad\qquad\qquad \big|\,{}^{lg}$$
$$(\text{sell}) \qquad\qquad\qquad\qquad\qquad\qquad (\text{buy})$$
$$\big|\,{}^{tga} \qquad\qquad\qquad\qquad\qquad \big|\,{}^{tga}$$
$$(\text{John}) \qquad\qquad\qquad\qquad\qquad\quad (\text{Bill})$$

Some of the many books which Bill bought were sold by John

or

John sold some of the many books bought by Bill

In the realisations of these sentences it is evident that the relative clause which is introduced is 'restrictive'. When '(some)' is the theme or tail we do not find a (correct) linearisation which traces through 'lg' and 'tga' to '(John)' before passing through '(quant)' to '(pro)', i.e. * *some, which were sold by John, of the many books bought by Bill ...* We must postulate, therefore, a 'permanent' boxing (see VI.6) of the part of the SF containing the '(quant)' node.

Our postulation is further justified when we look at the relative clause realisations with 'adjectival' quantifiers and numerals.

Fig. 28 (i)

$$(\text{all}) \overset{fe}{---} (\text{quant}) \overset{ps}{---} (\text{man, pl}) \overset{sp}{---} (\text{mod}_2) \overset{ef}{---} (\text{rich})$$
$$\big|\overset{sp}{\underline{\quad}} (\text{mod}_3) \overset{ef}{---} (\text{happy})$$

From this SF we could derive *All men who are rich are happy* or *All men who are happy are rich.* But these two sentences are by no means synonymous. Therefore, in order to prevent their derivation from the same SF we must place part of the SF in a 'permanent' box — and this box always contains the '(quant)' node.

As other examples, consider *some men who are rich are happy*, *many men who are rich are happy* and *any man who is rich is happy*. In each case the presence of a quantifier requires that the relative clause is 'restrictive'.

5. In the last example *any* has a variant in *a*, thus: *a man who is rich is happy*. It would seem (Robbins 1968) that whenever *a + N* is followed by a 'restrictive' relative clause then the indefinite article is a variant of the quantifier *any*.

Fig. 28 (ii)

$$(\text{any}) \xrightarrow{\text{fe}} (\text{quant}) \xrightarrow{\text{ps}} (\text{number}) \xrightarrow{\text{sp}} (\text{mod}_1) \xrightarrow{\text{ef}} (\text{even})$$

$$\Big|_{\text{ga}}$$

$$(\text{divide}) \xrightarrow{\text{sp}} (\text{mod}_7) \xrightarrow{\text{ef}} (\text{pot})$$

$$\Big|_{\text{ga}}$$

$$(\text{two})$$

From this SF can be derived:

> *Any number which is even is divisible by two*
> *A number which is even is divisible by two*
> *Any even number is divisible by two*
> *An even number is divisible by two*

The details of these realisations I leave to the reader. (The derivation of the 'passive' adjective *divisible* is explained below in X.D.2.)

D. Collectives

To conclude this chapter I would like to illustrate some realisations of nouns which while they are not strictly quantifiers can be accounted for by the rules operating on '(quant)'. The nouns in question are many (perhaps all) of the collectives *herd*, *flock*, *shoal*, etc. and weights and measures *ounce*, *pound*, *acre*, *pint*, etc.

1. These nouns have no 'adjectival' realisations. From:

Fig. 29 (i)

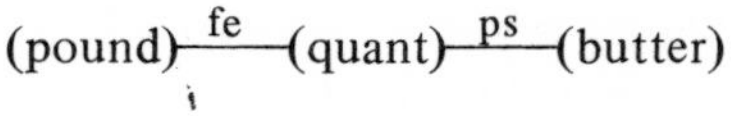

$$(\text{pound}) \xrightarrow{\quad \text{fe} \quad} (\text{quant}) \xrightarrow{\quad \text{ps} \quad} (\text{butter})$$

We can derive only:

fe   : $N^0(\text{pound}) \rightarrow N^0(\text{pound}) + B$

ps   : $B(\text{quant}) \rightarrow Pr(\text{of}) + N^0$

a pound of butter

No operations involving 'sp' and 'ef' are productive.

2.   As this example shows, the sememe at the end of 'ps' does not necessarily have to be '(pro)' (cf. section C.1 above). But, when it is, the same semolexemic rules can be used:

Fig. 29 (ii)

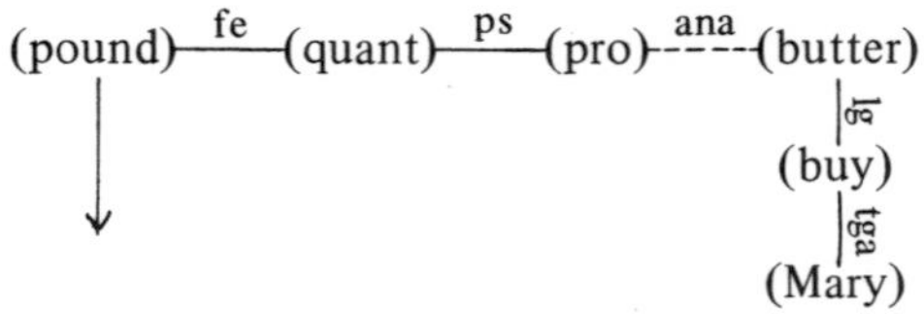

$$(\text{pound}) \xrightarrow{\quad \text{fe} \quad} (\text{quant}) \xrightarrow{\quad \text{ps} \quad} (\text{pro}) \xdashrightarrow{\quad \text{ana} \quad} (\text{butter})$$

(buy)

(Mary)

a pound of the butter which Mary bought ...

3.   One essential difference from the quantifiers is that this class of noun may be modified by numerals and true quantifiers: *three pounds of butter*, *some pints of milk*; by quantifiers and numerals together: *all three pounds of butter, some four pints of milk*; and by co-ordinated quantifiers or numerals: *three or four pounds of butter, each and every pint of milk*.

4.   Like the quantifiers and numerals, however, all relative clauses which are realised are 'restrictive'. Thus, beside *A pint of milk which Mary bought was drunk by John* we do not have * *A pint which was drunk by John was of milk which Mary bought* (cf. section C.5 above).

5.   One interesting point must not go unremarked. The sememes occurring at the end of 'ps' in SFs containing these nouns are always either 'plural' nouns or 'mass' nouns (*butter* and *milk*) for example. We find, therefore, both *The hunter saw a herd of elephants* and *The hunter saw a herd of elephant*.

In the second sentence the referent is considered as a group (or 'en masse') and in the first as individuals. It would seem that we have here again a partial synonymy in English of 'singular' and 'plural' forms. In A.1 above *the horse* was tentatively derived from '(horse, pl)'. Can we also postulate that 'mass' nouns are derived from 'plural' sememes, i.e. '(fish, pl)' is the source for both *fishes* and *fish*? And in those cases where no singular form exists, e.g. for *milk* and *butter*, can we assume that a '⟨pl⟩' semon is present implicitly in their sememes?

In subsequent sections, e.g. in that on negation, it will be found that the substitution of 'mass' nouns for 'plurals' does not invalidate any of the semo-lexemic rules. On the other hand 'mass' nouns must always be followed by singular verb forms (see next chapter for rules of concord). It seems that we must continue to derive 'mass' nouns and 'generic' nouns like *horse* and *fish* from 'singular' sememes, but perhaps we may posit a relationship of 'sememic implication' between the singular and plural forms of a certain restricted set of sememes (to include '(horse)' and '(horse, pl)' etc.) and treat 'mass' nouns on occasions *as if* they were 'plural'.

IX. TENSE, MODALITY AND CONCORD

1. English verbs are modified by certain features (realised graphically as adjuncts or suffixes) for the indication of past or future tense, perfective or imperfective action, 'continuous' (or 'progressive') movement, negation, etc. Some of these modifications are 'sentential' in the sense that the features apply to whichever verb happens to be in the main clause. For example, compare the sentences:

(a) *The computer retrieved information easily*
(b) *Information was retrieved easily by computer*
(c) *It was easy to retrieve information by computer*
(d) *For the computer to retrieve information was easy*

In each of these synonymous sentences (derived from the same SF, see chapter III.A), the action is placed in the past. However, the feature '⟨past⟩' does not modify the same lexeme in every case but whichever appears as the main verb, i.e. in (a) *retrieved* and in (b), (c) and (d) *was*.

2. In this model the main verb is closely connected with the selection of pivot node. It has been found that 'sentential' modifications can be accounted for if verbal features are attached to the pivot node of SFs. The sememes (or semons) representing these features are collected together and form part of the SF but they are not attached to it until a pivot node has been selected.

A collection of sememes representing verbal features for a given SF is placed within a pair of braces — called 'verbal modification braces' or, for the sake of brevity, VM. For each feature there is a unique Greek letter to which its sememe is attached in any VM. Thus, the VM containing the 'sentential' features '⟨past⟩', '⟨perfective⟩' and '⟨negative⟩' is represented by:

$$\{\gamma(\text{perf}), \ \epsilon(\text{past}), \ \zeta(\text{non})\} \ .$$

The present tense has no sememe (or semon) — I follow Greenberg (1966) in considering it 'unmarked'.

As we shall see, the purpose of the Greek letters is to ensure that features are applied in the correct order during verbal modification — for this order I have assumed that the one given by Chomsky (1957: 61–64) is substantially accurate.

3.   The pivot and theme nodes are selected during the preliminary stages of linearisation (see II.C.2). The VM is attached to the pivot by a 'π' link before the next stages of SF linearisation. At the same time, from the theme node are extracted those semons indicating number and person which are needed for 'subject-verb' concord and they are added to the sememes already present in the VM. The singular and the third person are considered 'unmarked' (again following Greenberg), the plural is represented by '⟨pl⟩' and the first and second persons by '⟨1⟩' and '⟨2⟩' respectively. If any of these semons are found in the theme node they are attached in the VM to the Greek letter η. For example, our VM above might be amended to:

$$\{\gamma(\text{perf}), \ \epsilon(\text{past}), \ \zeta(\text{non}), \ \eta(1, \text{pl})\} \ .$$

Note that '⟨pl⟩' will also be added to the VM if the theme node is one of the co-ordinating sememes, '(&)' or '(vel)'.

4.   The rules for linearisation and realisation can be stated briefly:

(a)   The 'π' link is traced always before any other link: thus, like the 'ana' link where a similar principle applies (see VI.4(a)), it is represented by a broken line.

(b)   As a semolexemic rule, 'π' operates on the last full verb form, i.e. on the last 'V(x)' and never on 'Vpp(x)', 'Vger(x)', 'Vinf(x)', etc.

(c)   The braces of VMs are ignored in realisations: they serve merely to keep together the verbal features applicable in one SF.

(d)   Sememes in VMs are applied strictly according to the order of their letters in the Greek alphabet (i.e. 'δ(x)' always precedes 'ϵ(x)'), and like 'π' they operate only on the last full verb form.

A full list of VM semolexemic rules is found in appendix C. It will be noticed that among them is included a rule for the generation of the modal *can, could, be able,* etc. Other modals, such as *may, might, must, ought,* may perhaps be attached to the same Greek letter α. However, it seems that most, if not all (and including *can, be able,* etc.), may be attached to 'δ' in place of '(fut)' — compare *He will be doing it, He could be doing it, He might be doing it*. But in this study I have refrained from going into the details of modal modification of verbs, since my purpose (as ever) is to expound the model and not to present a working system in full detail. In any case we need to know far more about the paradigmatic structure of modals, probably on the lines of Boyd and Thorne (1969) and Leech (1969).

5. VM semolexemic rules are illustrated by realisations of fig. 30.

Fig. 30

$$\text{SF: (John)} \xrightarrow{\text{agt}} \text{(sell)} \xrightarrow{\text{gl}} \text{(car, pl)}$$
$$\downarrow \text{sp} \; (\text{mod}_4) \xrightarrow{\text{ef}} \text{(ease)}$$

$$\text{VM: } \{\gamma(\text{perf}), \; \delta(\text{fut}), \; \zeta(\text{non})\}$$

5.1. Having selected '(John)' as the theme and '(sell)' as the pivot and after attaching the VM to '(sell)' by a 'π' link we can obtain, as one linearisation, the following:

$$\text{decl} \longrightarrow [(\text{John})] \xrightarrow{\text{agt}} (\text{sell}) \xdashrightarrow{\pi} \{\gamma(\text{perf}), \delta(\text{fut}), \zeta(\text{non})\}$$
$$\xrightarrow{\text{gl}} [(\text{car, pl})] \, \text{b (sell)} \xrightarrow{\text{sp}} (\text{mod}_4) \xrightarrow{\text{ef}} (\text{ease})$$

This is realised:

	agt	: $\text{NP}(...) \rightarrow \text{NP}(...) + \text{V}$
(400)	π	: $\text{V}(\text{sell}) \rightarrow \text{V}^1(\text{sell})$
(404)	$\gamma(\text{perf})$:	$\text{V}^1(\text{sell}) \rightarrow \text{V}^2(\text{have}) + \text{Vpp}^2(\text{sell})$
(407)	$\delta(\text{fut})$:	$\text{V}^2(\text{have}) \rightarrow \text{V}^2(\text{will}) + \text{Vnt}^0(\text{have})$
(414)	$\zeta(\text{non})$:	$\text{V}^2(\text{will}) \rightarrow \text{V}^2(\text{will}) + \text{Adv}(\text{non})$
(212)	gl	: $\text{Vpp}^2(\text{sell}) \rightarrow \text{Vpp}^0(\text{sell}) + \text{NPt}$
	sp	: $\text{Vpp}^0(\Delta) \rightarrow \text{Vpp}^0(\Delta) + \text{Z}_{034}$

$$\text{NP}(\text{N}^0(\text{John})) + \text{V}^2(\text{will}) + \text{Adv}(\text{non}) + \text{Vnt}^0(\text{have}) + \text{Vpp}^0(\text{sell})$$
$$+ \text{NP}(\text{N}^0(\text{car, pl})) + \text{Adv}_4(\text{ease})$$

John will not have sold cars easily

Two points about this realisation need comment. Firstly, as 'γ(perf)' produces a 'Vpp' we must ensure that the application of 'gl' gives no incorrect realisation — we cannot, for example, permit 'comitative co-ordination' (rule (210)).

Therefore we distinguish this perfective 'Vpp' by the superscript '2'. (Note that the insertion of adverbs before the past participle – *John will not have easily sold cars* – is permitted by rule (349).) Secondly, we have introduced a new category 'Vnt' to indicate an infinitive without a preceding *to*. [10] Later sections will illustrate its use more extensively.

5.2. When '(car, pl)' is chosen as theme node, the VM absorbs the '$\langle$pl$\rangle$' semon. With '(sell)' still pivot, we can have the linearisation:

$$\text{decl} \longrightarrow [(\text{car, pl})] \xrightarrow{\text{lg}} (\text{sell}) \xrightarrow{\pi} \{\gamma(\text{perf}), \delta(\text{fut}), \zeta(\text{non}), \eta(\text{pl})\}$$

$$\xrightarrow{\text{sp}} (\text{mod}_4) \xrightarrow{\text{ef}} (\text{ease}) \text{b (sell)} \xrightarrow{\text{tga}} [(\text{John})]$$

	lg	:	$NP(...) \rightarrow NP(...) + V(\text{be}) + Vpp^0$
	π	:	$V(\text{be}) \rightarrow V^1(\text{be})$
	$\gamma(\text{perf})$:	$V^1(\text{be}) \rightarrow V^2(\text{have}) + Vpp^2(\text{be})$
	$\delta(\text{fut})$	:	$V^2(\text{have}) \rightarrow V^2(\text{will}) + Vnt^0(\text{have})$
	$\zeta(\text{non})$	:	$V^2(\text{will}) \rightarrow V^2(\text{will}) + Adv(\text{non})$
(417)	$\eta(\text{pl})$	:	$V^2(\text{will}) \rightarrow V^2(\text{pl, will})$
(346)	sp	:	$Vpp^0(\text{sell}) \rightarrow Z_{3469} + Vpp^0(\text{sell})$, etc.

Cars will not have been easily sold by John

The rationale for allowing 'π' to operate only on the last full verb is seen clearly. However, since *will* is the realisation of both 'V(will)' and 'V(pl, will)' we have still to show the effect of the '$\langle$pl$\rangle$' semon. Suppose we substitute the VM $\{\gamma(\text{perf}), \eta(\text{pl})\}$ in the above linearisation. This will give us:

$$\pi \quad : \quad V(\text{be}) \rightarrow V^1(\text{be})$$
$$\gamma(\text{perf}): \quad V^1(\text{be}) \rightarrow V^2(\text{have}) + Vpp^2(\text{be})$$
$$\eta(\text{pl}) \quad : \quad V^2(\text{have}) \rightarrow V^2(\text{pl, have})$$

Cars have been easily sold by John

The graphic realisation of 'V(have)' is *has*, that of 'V(pl, have)' is *have*.
5.3. Finally, when '(mod$_4$)' is the pivot and the VM is attached to it we have as one linearisation:

---

[10] In theory it is probably unnecessary to distinguish between the two 'infinitive' categories 'Vinf' and 'Vnt'. But in practice it seems that rather simpler semolexemic rules can be formulated if the distinction is kept.

$$\text{decl} \longrightarrow [(\text{ease})] \xrightarrow{\text{fe}} (\text{mod}_4) \xrightarrow{\pi} \{\gamma(\text{perf}), \delta(\text{fut}), \zeta(\text{non})\}$$

$$\xrightarrow{\text{ps}} [(\text{sell}) \xrightarrow{\text{tga}} [(\text{John})] \ b(\text{sell}) \xrightarrow{\text{gl}} [(\text{car}, \text{pl})]]]$$

decl : $S \to \text{Pron(it)} + \text{V(be)} + \text{AJ}$

fe : $\text{AJ}(...) \to \text{AJ}(...) + G$

π : $\text{V(be)} \to \text{V}^1(\text{be})$

$\gamma(\text{perf})$: $\text{V}^1(\text{be}) \to \text{V}^2(\text{have}) + \text{Vpp}^2(\text{be})$

$\delta(\text{fut})$: $\text{V}^2(\text{have}) \to \text{V}^2(\text{will}) + \text{Vnt}^0(\text{have})$

$\zeta(\text{non})$: $\text{V}^2(\text{will}) \to \text{V}^2(\text{will}) + \text{Adv(non)}$

ps : $G(\text{mod}_4) \to \text{NPe}$, etc.

it will not have been easy for John to sell cars

6. In order to illustrate other VM semolexemic rules we will use the same SF of fig. 30 and the linearisation of 5.1, but attach different VMs.

6.1. With the VM $\{\epsilon(\text{past}), \zeta(\text{non})\}$ we can show the realisation of the verb *do*:

π : $\text{V(sell)} \to \text{V}^1(\text{sell})$

(410) $\epsilon(\text{past})$: $\text{V}^1(\text{sell}) \to \text{V}^1(\text{past}, \text{sell})$

(413) $\zeta(\text{non})$: $\text{V}^1(\text{past}, \text{sell}) \to \text{V}^1(\text{past}, \text{do}) + \text{Adv(non)}$
$+ \text{Vnt}^0(\text{sell})$

(206) gl : $\text{Vnt}^0(\text{sell}) \to \text{Vnt}^0(\text{sell}) + \text{NPt}$

John did not sell cars easily

6.2. To illustrate the 'continuous' verb form, the VM $\{\beta(\text{cont}), \epsilon(\text{past})\}$

(402) $\beta(\text{cont})$: $\text{V}^1(\text{sell}) \to \text{V}^2(\text{be}) + \text{Vger(sell)}$

(411) $\epsilon(\text{past})$: $\text{V}^2(\text{be}) \to \text{V}^2(\text{past}, \text{be})$

(202) gl : $\text{Vger(sell)} \to \text{Vger(sell)} + \text{NPt}$

John was selling cars easily

6.3. One of the modals can be illustrated with VM $\{\alpha(\text{pot}), \gamma(\text{perf})\}$

(401) $\alpha(\text{pot})$: $\text{V}^1(\text{sell}) \to \text{V}^2(\text{pot}) + \text{Vnt}^0(\text{sell})$

(405) $\gamma(\text{perf})$: $\text{V}^2(\text{pot}) \to \text{V}^2(\text{have}) + \text{Vpp}^2(\text{pot})$

John has been able to sell cars easily

with the VM $\{\alpha(\text{pot}), \delta(\text{fut})\}$

$$\alpha(\text{pot}):\quad V^1(\text{sell}) \to V^2(\text{pot}) + Vnt^0(\text{sell})$$

(407) $\delta(\text{fut}):\quad V^2(\text{pot}) \to V^2(\text{will}) + Vnt^0(\text{pot})$

John will be able to sell cars easily

and with the VM $\{\gamma(\text{perf}), \delta(\text{pot}), \epsilon(\text{past})\}$

$$\gamma(\text{perf}):\quad V^1(\text{sell}) \to V^2(\text{have}) + Vpp^2(\text{sell})$$

(409) $\delta(\text{pot}):\quad V^2(\text{have}) \to V^2(\text{pot}) + Vnt^0(\text{have})$

(411) $\epsilon(\text{past}):\quad V^2(\text{pot}) \to V^2(\text{past, pot})$

John could have sold cars easily

The graphic forms are: V (past, pot) = ^{G}/could; Vnt(pot) = ^{G}/be able to; Vpp(pot) = ^{G}/been able to.

7.   From an earlier chapter it will be recalled that Vendler's class A_7 includes *possible* and *impossible*. There is clearly a close connection between these adjectives and the modal verbs *can*, *could*, etc. and their negated forms *cannot*, *could not*, etc.

  (i) *John can sell cars easily*
  (ii) *John can not sell cars easily*
  (iii) *It is possible for John to sell cars easily*
  (iv) *It is impossible for John to sell cars easily*

Sentence (iii) seems to be a synonym of (i) and sentence (iv) a synonym of (ii). Whereas the adjectives *possible* and *impossible* are derived from nodes linked by ' $\xrightarrow{\text{sp}}(\text{mod}_7)\xrightarrow{\text{ef}}$ ' to the sememe '(sell)', the modals *can* and *cannot* are derived from sememes in a VM attached to '(sell)' by a 'π' link.

    We appear to have here an instance of 'sememic equivalence', i.e. one form of SF both implies and is implied by another form of SF (see VII.C.8). In this case, a SF containing a node '(x)' linked by ' $\xrightarrow{\text{sp}}(\text{mod}_7)\xrightarrow{\text{ef}}$ ' to a node '(pot)' or nodes '(pot)$\xrightarrow{\text{sp}}$(quant)$\xrightarrow{\text{ef}}$(non)' implies and is implied by a SF with a VM containing '$\alpha(\text{pot})$' or '$\alpha(\text{pot}), \zeta(\text{non})$' respectively.

    Whether the VM may contain the sememe '(pot)' attached to 'δ' instead of 'α' is open to question. To a certain extent it depends on whether the sentence *John could not have sold cars* is considered synonymous with *It had been impossible for John to sell cars*. If this synonymy is allowed then the sentence must also be synonymous with *John had not been able to sell cars*. I do not believe that this is acceptable under any reading and so I presume that '(pot)' may be attached only to 'α' for the relationship of 'sememic equivalence' with SFs containing '(mod$_7$)' to be valid.

X. NEGATION AND SOME ADJECTIVAL AND ADVERBIAL MODIFICATIONS

A. Negation of nouns and sentences

Linguists generally recognise two basic kinds of negation: sentence-negation and negation of sentence elements (Klima, 1964; Jackendoff, 1969). The first has been treated in the previous section as one sememe introduced 'sententially' into a SF from a VM. The negation of an individual sentence constituent is represented in an SF by a 'quantifier' link to a '(non)' sememe (cf. VIII.A.4 above), i.e.

$$(x) \xrightarrow{\text{sp}} (\text{quant}) \xrightarrow{\text{ef}} (\text{non}) \;.$$

1. The semolexemic rules decribed for quantifiers are used, therefore, also in sememe-negation.

1.1. Fig. 31 (i)

$$(\text{John}) \xrightarrow{\text{agt}} (\text{sell}) \xrightarrow{\text{gl}} (\text{book, pl})$$
$$\qquad\qquad\qquad\qquad\qquad \Big\downarrow \xrightarrow{\text{sp}} (\text{quant}) \xrightarrow{\text{ef}} (\text{non})$$

$$\begin{aligned}
\text{sp} \quad &: \quad N^0(\text{books}) \to X + N^0(\text{books}) \\
\text{ef} \quad &: \quad X(\text{quant}) \to \text{Adj}
\end{aligned}$$

John sold no books $\text{Adj}(\text{non}) = {}^{G}/\text{no}$

105

1.2. Fig. 31 (ii)

$$(\text{John})\xrightarrow{\text{agt}}(\text{sell})\xrightarrow{\text{gl}}(\text{non})$$

$$\downarrow \text{fe}$$

$$(\text{quant})\xrightarrow{\text{ps}}(\text{pro})\xrightarrow{\text{ana}}(\text{book, pl})$$

fe   : $N^0(\text{non}) + B$

ps   : $B(\text{quant}) \rightarrow Pr(\text{of}) + N^0$

John sold none of the books $N(\text{non}) = {}^G/\text{none}$

1.3. The same restrictions obtain for SFs and realisations with '(non)' as for other quantifier sememes (cf. VIII.B.3, C.5 and D.3).

(a) As a quantifier, *no* always precedes any numeral: *no three books.*

(b) It occurs only with 'restrictive' relative clauses: *no men who are rich are happy, none of the men who are rich are happy.*

(c) It may modify collectives, weights and measures: *no pints of milk, none of the pints of milk.*

2. Synonymous with the realisations of fig. 31 (i) and 31 (ii) above, *John sold no books* and *John sold none of the books*, we find sentences involving sentence-negation: *John did not sell any books* and *John did not sell any of the books*. The lexeme *any* occurring in this case is clearly not derived from the quantifier link $(x)\xrightarrow{\text{sp}}(\text{quant})\xrightarrow{\text{ef}}(\text{any})$ but rather it is a modification introduced under the influence of the 'sentential' negative '$\zeta(\text{non})$' in the VM.

2.1. In order to account for its appearance, we posit a link between the '(non)' sememe in a VM and the 'tail' sememe of a linearisation. For example in the following SF '(John)' is the theme node, '(sell)' the pivot node and '(books)' the tail node:

Fig. 31 (iii)

$$(\text{John})\xrightarrow{\text{agt}}(\text{sell})\xrightarrow{\text{gl}}(\text{books})$$

$$\vdots \pi$$

$$\left\{\begin{array}{l}\epsilon(\text{past})\\\zeta(\text{non})\end{array}\right\} \text{---}$$

In addition to the 'π' link we have added another broken-line, a 'tp' link (= 'tail to pivot' link). This SF would be linearised:

$$\text{decl}\longrightarrow[(\text{John})]\xrightarrow{\text{agt}}(\text{sell})\text{-}^{\pi}\text{-}\!\!\rightarrow\{\epsilon(\text{past}), \zeta(\text{non})\}\xrightarrow{\text{gl}}[(\text{books})\text{-}^{\text{tp}}\!\!\rightarrow(\text{non})$$

As with 'ana' links the 'tp' link takes no account of any kind of bracketing around the nodes it connects; also it is traced before other links. The linearisation is realised as follows:

$$\text{agt} \quad : \quad NP(...) \to NP(...) + V$$

$$(400) \quad \pi \quad : \quad V(\text{sell}) \to V^1(\text{sell})$$

$$(410) \quad \epsilon(\text{past}): \quad V^1(\text{sell}) \to V^1(\text{past, sell})$$

$$(413) \quad \zeta(\text{non}): \quad V^1(\text{past, sell}) \to V^1(\text{past, do}) + Adv(\text{non}) + Vnt^0(\text{sell})$$

$$\text{gl} \quad : \quad Vnt^0(\text{sell}) \to Vnt^0(\text{sell}) + NPt$$

$$[\quad : \quad NPt \to NP(N^0$$

$$(390) \quad \text{tp} \quad : \quad N^0(\text{books}) \to \overline{Adj} + N^0(\text{books})$$

With the graphemic realisation of $\overline{Adj}(\text{non})$ as *any* we derive:

John did not sell any books

2.2. The comparable SF to that of fig. 31 (iii) for the sentence including *... any of the ...* is:

Fig. 31 (iv)

From the linearisation:

$$\text{decl} \longrightarrow [(\text{John})] \xrightarrow{\text{agt}} (\text{sell}) \xrightarrow{\pi} \{\epsilon(\text{past}), \zeta(\text{non})\} \xrightarrow{\text{gl}} [(\text{pro}) - - -$$

$$- - \xrightarrow{\text{tp}} (\text{non}) b\, (\text{pro}) \xrightarrow{\text{ana}} (\text{books})]$$

the realisation parallels the one above until:

$$[\quad : \quad NPt \to NP(N^0$$

$$(391) \quad \text{tp} \quad : \quad N^0(\text{pro}) \to \overline{N} + Pr(of) + N^0(\text{pro})$$

$$\text{ana} \quad : \quad N^0(\text{pro}) \to D(\text{the}) + N^0$$

With the graphemic realisation: $\overline{N}(\text{non}) = {}^G/\text{any}$, we have:

John did not sell any of the books

3. The semolexemic rules for 'tp' are just these two:

(390)   tp   : $N^0(x) \rightarrow \overline{Adj} + N^0(x)$

(391)   tp   : $N^0(pro) \rightarrow \overline{N} + Pr(of) + N^0(pro)$

As the second example shows, the 'tp' link must be traced before the 'ana' link for a correct realisation. From the linearisation:

$$\xrightarrow{\;gl\;}[(pro)\xrightarrow{ana}(books)b\ (pro)\xrightarrow{tp}(non)]$$

ana   : $N^0(pro) \rightarrow D(the) + N^0$

tp   : $N^0(books) \rightarrow \overline{Adj} + N^0(books)$

we would have * *the any books*. To exclude such a realisation, therefore, we formulate the rule that the 'tp' link is traced in linearisations always before any other link (including any 'ana' link).

4. It seems to be true that SF of the form in figs. 31 (i) and 31 (ii) are always synonymous with SFs of the form in figs. 31 (iii) and 31 (iv) respectively. We have then another instance of 'sememic equivalence': the SF in 31 (i) implies and is implied by the SF in fig. 31 (iii).

5. A SF containing a quantifier link may be subjected to both SF-negation and sememe-negation. The sentences *John sold every book*, *John sold many books* and *John sold some books* can be negated either as *John did not sell every book*, *John did not sell many books* and *John did not sell some books* (SF-negation), or as *John sold not every book*, *John sold not many books* and *John sold not some books [but all of them]* (sememe-negation).

5.1. SF-negation is perfectly straightforward. Rules for the derivation of *John did not sell many books* from the following SF have been illustrated already:

Fig. 32 (i)

$$(John)\xrightarrow{agt}(sell)\xrightarrow{gl}(books)\xrightarrow{sp}(quant)\xrightarrow{ef}(many)$$

$$\Big\downarrow \pi$$

$$\{\epsilon(past),\ \zeta(non)\}$$

5.2. In the case of sememe-negation, the node negated must be always the quantifier itself and never the node modified by the quantifier. We do not find sentences such as * *John sold no every book*, * *John sold no many books* or * *John sold no some books*, so we cannot permit SFs such as:

Fig. 32 (ii)

$$(\text{John})\xrightarrow{\text{agt}}(\text{sell})\xrightarrow{\text{gl}}(\text{books})\xrightarrow{\text{sp}}(\text{quant})\xrightarrow{\text{ef}}(\text{many})$$

with π link to $\{\epsilon(\text{past})\}$ and sp link to (quant), ef link to (non)

For this reason we do not find the kind of SF in fig. 31 (iii) with a 'tp' link when the tail node is modified by a quantifier. Sentences such as * *John did not sell any every book*, * *John did not sell any many books* and * *John did not sell any some books* are quite unacceptable. Therefore, only SFs of the following kind are followed

Fig. 32 (iii)

$$(\text{John})\xrightarrow{\text{agt}}(\text{sell})\xrightarrow{\text{gl}}(\text{books})\xrightarrow{\text{sp}}(\text{quant})\xrightarrow{\text{ef}}(\text{many})$$

with π link to $\{\epsilon(\text{past})\}$ and sp link to (quant), ef link to (non)

John sold not many books

B. Negation of adjectives and adverbs

To realise the SF in fig. 32 (iii) we must turn now to the rules dealing with the negation of the categories 'Adj' and 'Adv'.

There are basically two ways in which adjectives and adverbs are negated: one is by the simple preposing of the adverbial *not* and the other involves the prefixing of *un-*, *in-*, *non-*, etc. Both methods are illustrated with the partial SF:

Fig. 33 (i)

$$(\text{x})\xrightarrow{\text{sp}}(\text{mod}_4)\xrightarrow{\text{ef}}(\text{ease})\xrightarrow{\text{sp}}(\text{quant})\xrightarrow{\text{ef}}(\text{non})$$

linearised as: $\rightarrow(\text{x})\xrightarrow{\text{sp}}(\text{mod}_4)\xrightarrow{\text{ef}}[(\text{ease})\xrightarrow{\text{sp}}(\text{quant})\xrightarrow{\text{ef}}(\text{non})]$.

1. The first realisation proceeds:

$$\text{sp} \quad : \quad N^0(x) \to X + N^0(x)$$

$$\text{ef} \quad : \quad X(\text{mod}_4) \to \text{Adj}_4$$

$$[\quad : \quad \text{Adj}_4 \to \text{AJ}(\text{Adj}_4$$

(295) $\quad$ sp $\quad : \quad \text{Adj}_4(\text{ease}) \to Z_0 + \text{Adj}_4(\text{ease})$

(168) $\quad$ ef $\quad : \quad Z_0(\text{quant}) \to \text{Adv}$

$$\dots + \text{AJ}(\text{Adv}(\text{non}) + \text{Adj}_4(\text{ease})) + N^0(x) \dots$$

... not easy ...

This realisation is obviously used for the derivation of *not many*, *not every*, *not some* (A.5 above) since quantifiers are assigned the category 'Adj'. The negation of adverbs follows a similar pattern with the relevant rule being:

(297) $\quad$ sp $\quad : \quad \text{Adv}_4(\text{ease}) \to Z_0 + \text{Adv}_4(\text{ease})$ $\quad$ *not easily*

2. Although this is the simplest kind of negation it is not the one found most frequently — probably because *not* is used almost exclusively for sentence-negation (Klima, 1964). Therefore, we find far more often a realisation in which two sememes are merged for the derivation of a single lexeme:

$$\text{sp} \quad : \quad N^0(x) \to X + N^0(x)$$

$$\text{ef} \quad : \quad X(\text{mod}_4) \to \text{Adj}_4$$

$$[\quad : \quad \text{Adj}_4 \to \text{AJ}(\text{Adj}_4$$

(296) $\quad$ sp $\quad : \quad \text{Adj}_4(\text{ease}) \to \text{Adj}_4(\text{ease}, Z_8)$

(169) $\quad$ ef $\quad : \quad Z_8(\text{quant}) \to \zeta$

$$\dots + \text{AJ}(\text{Adj}_4(\text{ease}, \zeta(\text{non}))) + N^0(x) \dots$$

The graphemic realisation of $\text{Adj}_4(\text{ease}, \zeta(\text{non}))$ is *uneasy*. This realisation introduces 'Z_8' which can never produce an adverb from '(mod_8)' (see IV.B.3). Here it is used only in combination with '(quant)' for the derivation of 'ζ' to which may be attached the sememe '(non)' — as in VMs.

In the case of quantifiers, the "merged" lexeme is not a prefix form * *unmany* but has a different root, e.g. *few*. (Whether *few* is a true negative of *many* is perhaps doubtful — it involves questions of paradigmatic structure (see Vater, 1963).)

The parallel realisation for adverbs proceeds:

(298)   sp   : $Adv_4(ease) \rightarrow Adv_4(ease, Z_8)$

         ef   : $Z_8(quant) \rightarrow \zeta$

with the graphemic realisation of $Adv_4(ease, \zeta(non))$ as *uneasily*.

C. Comparatives and superlatives

The rules we have introduced can also be used in the modification of adjectives and adverbs other than in negation.

1. By replacing '(non)' by '(comp)' in the SF of fig. 33 (i) we can derive comparative forms of adjectives and adverbs:

Fig. 33 (ii)

$$(x)\xrightarrow{sp}(mod_4)\xrightarrow{ef}(ease)\xrightarrow{sp}(quant)\xrightarrow{ef}(comp)$$

As in the case of negation there are two kinds of realisation: one is the preposing of *more* and the other involves the addition of the suffix *-er*.

From the linearisation:

$$\rightarrow(x)\xrightarrow{sp}(mod_4)\xrightarrow{ef}[(ease)\xrightarrow{sp}(quant)\xrightarrow{ef}(comp)]$$

1.1. We can realise by:

     sp   : $Adj_4(ease) \rightarrow Z_0 + Adj_4(ease)$

     ef   : $Z_0(quant) \rightarrow Adv$

         ... $+ AJ(Adv(comp) + Adj_4(ease))$ ...

            ... *more easy* ...

or: sp   : $Adj_4(ease) \rightarrow Adj_4(ease, Z_8)$

          ef   : $Z_8(quant) \rightarrow \zeta$

         ... $+ AJ(Adj_4(ease, \zeta(comp)))$ ...

            ... *easier* ...

(where the graphemic realisation is $Adj_4(ease, \zeta(comp)) = $ G/easier).

1.2. In the case of adverbs we have:

     sp   : $Adv_4(ease) \rightarrow Z_0 + Adv_4(ease)$

to produce *more easily*; but they have no suffix form: * *easierly* is unacceptable. Hence there is no graphemic realisation of $Adv_4(ease, \zeta(comp))$.

2. In a similar manner we can derive superlative forms of adjectives and adverbs. Replacing '(non)' in fig. 33 (i) by '(sup)' gives:

Fig. 33 (iii)

$$(x)\overset{sp}{\rule{1cm}{0.4pt}}(mod_4)\overset{ef}{\rule{1cm}{0.4pt}}(ease)\overset{sp}{\rule{1cm}{0.4pt}}(quant)\overset{ef}{\rule{1cm}{0.4pt}}(sup)$$

From which we can realise:

$$sp \quad : \quad Adj_4(ease) \rightarrow Z_0 + Adj_4(ease)$$
$$ef \quad : \quad Z_0(quant) \rightarrow Adv$$
$$... most\ easy\ ...$$

and the suffix form:

$$sp \quad : \quad Adj_4(ease) \rightarrow Adj_4(ease, Z_8)$$
$$ef \quad : \quad Z_8(quant) \rightarrow \zeta$$
$$... easiest\ ...$$

As with the comparative, adverbs have only one realisation:

$$sp \quad : \quad Adv_4(ease) \rightarrow Z_0 + Adv_4(ease)$$
$$... most\ easily\ ...$$

3. There is no theoretical reason why sememes other than '(non)' should not be attached to 'ζ'. In the case of '(comp)' and '(sup)' they are always embedded to form '$Adj_4(ease, \zeta(comp))$', etc. and they are never likely to occur in VMs: in English at least, there are no comparative or superlative modifications of verbs.

I shall not go into the problem of how comparative constructions such as *John sold cars more easily than Bill* should be formulated in SFs, since this would entail a rather more detailed analysis of conjunction in general than I am able to pursue in this study.

4. Finally, as well as '(comp)' and '(sup)', the node '(non)' in 33 (i) can be replaced by the sememe '(very)' – representing the adverb *very*, which can only modify other adjectives or adverbs and cannot stand alone.

Fig. 33 (iv)

$$(x)\xrightarrow{\text{sp}}(\text{mod}_4)\xrightarrow{\text{ef}}(\text{ease})\xrightarrow{\text{sp}}(\text{quant})\xrightarrow{\text{ef}}(\text{very})$$

$$\text{sp} \quad : \quad \text{Adj}_4(\text{ease}) \to Z_0 + \text{Adj}_4(\text{ease})$$

$$\text{ef} \quad : \quad Z_0(\text{quant}) \to \text{Adv}$$

$$... \; very \; easy \; ...$$

Similarly for the adverbial *very easily*. There is no suffix form parallel with the comparatives and superlatives: therefore we find no graphemic realisation for any lexeme containing 'ζ(very)'.

It is interesting to note that certain languages, e.g. Russian, have modified forms of the adjective which can be translated in English as either a superlative or as a *very*-construction. Indeed, even in English the use of the superlative instead of *very* is not unusual: *it was a most interesting experience*. The evident closeness between the forms suggests that our parallel treatment is justified.

D. 'Passive' adjectives

From an earlier section it will be recalled that sentences such as *information is impossible to retrieve by computer* and *clothes are impossible to wash by machine* were derived from SFs containing '(mod_7)', and were realised with the rule

$$(345) \quad \text{sp} \quad : \quad \text{Vpp}^0(x) \to X_{478} + \text{Vinf}^1(x) \, .$$

As we pointed out in IX.7 the adjective must be derived from '$(\text{pot})\xrightarrow{\text{sp}}(\text{quant})\xrightarrow{\text{ef}}(\text{non})$'. Only now, however, are we able to give the realisation in detail.

1. Fig. 33 (v)

$$(\text{machine})\xrightarrow{\text{agt}}(\text{wash})\xrightarrow{\text{gl}}(\text{clothes})$$
$$\xrightarrow{\text{sp}}(\text{mod}_7)\xrightarrow{\text{ef}}(\text{pot})\xrightarrow{\text{sp}}(\text{quant})\xrightarrow{\text{ef}}(\text{non})$$

The SF may be linearised:

$$\text{decl} \longrightarrow [(\text{clothes})] \xrightarrow{\text{lg}} (\text{wash}) \xrightarrow{\text{sp}} (\text{mod}_7) \xrightarrow{\text{ef}} [(\text{pot}) \xrightarrow{\text{sp}} (\text{quant})]$$

$$\xrightarrow{\text{ef}} (\text{non})] \quad b \quad (\text{wash}) \xrightarrow{\text{tga}} [(\text{machine})]$$

	lg	:	$NP(...) \rightarrow NP(...) + V(be) + Vpp^0$
(345)	sp	:	$Vpp^0(\text{wash}) \rightarrow X_{478} + Vinf^1(\text{wash})$
	ef	:	$X_7(\text{mod}_7) \rightarrow Adj_7$
	[	:	$Adj_7 \rightarrow AJ(Adj_7$
(296)	sp	:	$Adj_7(\text{pot}) \rightarrow Adj_7(\text{pot}, Z_8)$
	ef	:	$Z_8(\text{quant}) \rightarrow \zeta$
	tga	:	$Vinf^1(\text{wash}) \rightarrow Vinf^0(\text{wash}) + Pr(\text{by}) + NP$

and with the graphemic realisation of $Adj_7(\text{pot}, \zeta(\text{non}))$ as *impossible*:

> *clothes are impossible to wash by machine*

2.   An interesting variant of this sentence is one containing a 'passive' adjective (Vendler's class A_l):

> *clothes are unwashable by machine*

One possible method of deriving this from the same SF in 33 (v) is by extending the principle of "sememe merging" one stage further:

	lg	:	$NP(...) \rightarrow NP(,..) + V(be) + Vpp^0$
(344)	sp	:	$Vpp^0(\text{wash}) \rightarrow Vpp^0(\text{wash}, X_7)$
	ef	:	$X_7(\text{mod}_7) \rightarrow Adj_7$
	[	:	$Adj_7 \rightarrow AJ(Adj_7$
	sp	:	$Adj_7(\text{pot}) \rightarrow Adj_7(\text{pot}, Z_8)$
	ef	:	$Z_8(\text{quant}) \rightarrow \zeta$
	tga	:	$Vpp^0(...) \rightarrow Vpp^0(...) + Pr(\text{by}) + NP$

$NP(N^0(\text{clothes})) + V(be) + Vpp^0(\text{wash}, AJ(Adj_7(\text{pot}, \zeta(\text{non})))) + Pr(\text{by})$
$+ NP(N^0(\text{machine}))$

The somewhat monstrous looking '$Vpp^0(\text{wash}, AJ(Adj_7(\text{pot}, \zeta(\text{non}))))$' is transformed into *unwashable*, firstly, by removing the 'non-terminal' AJ and its brackets, all superscripts and all subscripts to form '$Vpp(\text{wash}, Adj(\text{pot}, \zeta(\text{non})))$' and then by a lexographemic rule to ^{G}/unwashable.

In the same way other 'passive' adjectives, both negated and not, e.g. *solvable, unsolvable, divisible* (see VIII.C.5), *indivisible, retrievable, irretrievable*, can be derived from SFs containing the nodes '(mod_7)' and '(pot)'.

XI. EXPRESSIONS OF SPACE AND TIME

A. General

1. In English spatiotemporal relationships can be expressed in a variety of different ways: through adverbial or prepositional constructions, through conjunctions or verbs and, of course, as we have seen, through the tenses of verbs (for expressing temporal situations). Other languages may have recourse also to the case system of nouns, particularly for spatial relationships (Lyons, 1968: 299 ff.). The richness of the means available to languages is not surprising when we remember that every language-utterance, whether spoken or written, is made in a particular place and at a particular time. I cannot hope to cover here all the various options available in English, so I shall concentrate on a limited number of sememes and illustrate some of their various realisations.

2. Leech (1969: 97–201) has made a valuable detailed study of the paradigmatic structure of English in this area. For my purposes, however, a simplification is preferable since my main aim is to illustrate how the model deals with spatiotemporal relationships and what semolexemic rules are required. A useful classification of the prepositions of space and time, largely in accord with the views of many linguists (Lyons, 1968: 300; Fillmore, 1966; Dik, 1968b), divides them into three basic groups:

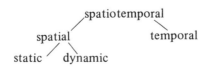

3. The sememes I shall deal with here are listed in the following table
grouped according to this tripartite classification. Against each sememe is
given its usual prepositional realisation(s), as a rough indication of its denota-
tion.

temporal	*dynamic*	*static*
(temp) *at, on*		
(ad) *to, until*	(to) *to, towards*	(pos, from) *from*
(ab) *from*	(from) *from, out of*	(pos, pre) *in front of*
(ante) *before*	(pre) *in front of, before*	(pos, inter) *between*
	(inter) *between*	(pos, sub) *under*
	(sub) *under*	(pos, in) *in*
	(in) *into*	(pos, on) *on*
	(on) *onto*	

These sememes occur in SFs only between 'sp' and 'ef' links. Although in
theory the node at the end of 'ps' or 'ef' could be either a 'verbal' or a
'nominal' sememe it seems in practice that only with sememes in the static
class is this the case. We find that sememes in the temporal and dynamic
classes are attached only to 'verbal' sememes.

B. Temporal expressions

Firstly, sememes in the temporal class.

1. The action, event, etc. denoted by the 'verbal' sememe in a SF is specified
to a particular point of time by using the sememe '(temp)' to attach either a
single sememe indicating clock time, a day of the week or a date, or another
'verbal' node linked to other sememes.
1.1. In the following SF '(temp)' is found with a sememe '(Thursday)' indicating a day of the week:

Fig. 34 (i)

This may be realised:

$$\text{sp} \quad : \quad V(\Delta) \to V(\Delta) + W_0$$
$$(123) \quad \text{ef} \quad : \quad W_0(\text{temp}) \to \text{Pr(on)} + N_\theta^0$$

John read a book on Thursday

The subscript 'θ' ensures that the 'N' is only a "day of the week". For clock time the preposition is *at* (e.g. *at six o'clock*) and for months and years *in* (e.g. *in 1968, in May*).

1.2. A SF in which '(temp)' links two 'verbal' sememes is:

Fig. 34 (ii)

$$\text{sp} \quad : \quad V(\Delta) \to V(\Delta) + W_0$$
$$(122) \quad \text{ef} \quad : \quad W_0(\text{temp}) \to \text{Conj(while)} + \text{NPp}$$

John read a book while Bill wrote a letter

2. The sememes '(ab)' and '(ad)' indicate the commencement and conclusion of actions at specified points of time. They are frequently found together attached to the same node in SFs, e.g.:

Fig. 34 (iii)

$$\text{sp} \quad : \quad V(\Delta) \to V(\Delta) + W_0$$
$$(103) \quad \text{ef} \quad : \quad W_0(\text{ab}) \to \text{Pr(from)} + N^0$$
$$\text{sp} \quad : \quad V(\Delta) \to V(\Delta) + W_0$$
$$(104) \quad \text{ef} \quad : \quad W_0(\text{ad}) \to \text{Pr(to)} + N^0$$

John read a book from dawn to dusk

As this realisation illustrates, we need rules rather like those for '(mod)' nodes to ensure that a 'sp–ef' link containing '(ab)' is traced in linearisations before one containing '(ad)'. It seems that there is no limit to the number of temporal links to any one node — we can, for example, add '——$\underline{\text{sp}}$—(temp)——— ——$\underline{\text{ef}}$—(Thursday)' to the SF of 34 (iii) and realise *John read a book from dawn to dusk on Thursday.*

3. The sememe '(ante)' is used to indicate that the referent of the 'verbal' sememe precedes a particular point of time or the referent of another 'verbal' sememe.

3.1. Substituting '(ante)' for '(temp)' in the SF of fig. 34 (i) we obtain:

Fig. 35 (i)

$$(\text{John})\xrightarrow{\text{agt}}(\text{read})\xrightarrow{\text{gl}}(\text{book})$$
$$\big|_{\text{sp}}(\text{ante})\xrightarrow{\text{ef}}(\text{Thursday})$$

and with the rule

(109)   ef   : $W_0(\text{ante}) \rightarrow \text{Pr(before)} + N^0$

John read a book before Thursday

3.2. Similarly in the SF of fig. 34 (ii):

Fig. 35 (ii)

$$(\text{John})\xrightarrow{\text{agt}}(\text{read})\xrightarrow{\text{gl}}(\text{book})$$
$$\big|_{\text{sp}}$$
$$(\text{ante})$$
$$\big|_{\text{ps}}$$
$$(\text{Bill})\xrightarrow{\text{agt}}(\text{write})\xrightarrow{\text{gl}}(\text{letter})$$

realised, via rule

(108)   ef   : $W_0(\text{ante}) \rightarrow \text{Conj(before)} + NPp$

as: *John read a book before Bill wrote a letter*

3.3. The link '——$\underline{\text{fe}}$—(ante)—$\underline{\text{ps}}$——', being the inverse of the 'sp–ef' link in the above SFs, produces the antonym of *before*: the preposition and conjunction *after.*

Fig. 35 (iii)

$$(\text{John}) \xrightarrow{\text{agt}} (\text{read}) \xrightarrow{\text{gl}} (\text{book})$$

$$(\text{ante}) \xrightarrow{\text{ps}} (\text{Thursday})$$

fe : $V(\Delta) \to V(\Delta) + W_0$

(288) ps : $W_0(\text{ante}) \to \text{Pr(after)} + N^0$

John read a book after Thursday

3.4. Similarly, from a linearisation of 35 (ii) with '(write)' as pivot instead of '(read)' we can realise, using the rule:

(287) ps : $W_0(\text{ante}) \to \text{Conj(after)} + \text{NPp}$

Bill wrote a letter after John read a book

4. From the section on subordinate conjunctions, it will be recalled that a sememe between 'sp' and 'ef' can be chosen as theme node, thus permitting the realisation of sentences with a preposition or subordinate conjunction at the head.

4.1. The rules given enable us to realise sentences headed by temporal conjunctions. From the SF of fig. 34 (ii) we can derive *While Bill wrote a letter John read a book*. From the SF of fig. 35 (ii) can be realised *Before Bill wrote a letter John read a book* and *After John read a book Bill wrote a letter* (the latter using rule (100) viz.

ef : $\text{NPk}(...) \to \text{NP}(...) + \text{NPp}$

4.2. They also enable the derivation of sentences headed by temporal prepositional phrases. Thus from a linearisation of fig. 34 (i) with '(ante)' as theme and '(read)' as pivot:

$$\text{decl} \longrightarrow [(\text{temp}) \xrightarrow{\text{ef}} (\text{Thursday})] \xrightarrow{\text{ps}} [(\text{read}) \xrightarrow{\text{tga}} [(\text{John})]$$

$$b(\text{read}) \xrightarrow{\text{gl}} [(\text{book})]]$$

decl : $S \to \text{NPk}$

[: $\text{NPk} \to \text{NPk}(W_0$

ef : $W_0(\text{temp}) \to \text{Pr(on)} + N^0_\theta$

ps : $\text{NPk}(...) \to \text{NP}(...) + \text{NPp}$

$$\text{tga} \quad : \quad \text{Vrel(read)} \rightarrow \text{NP} + \text{V(read)}$$

$$\text{gl} \quad : \quad \text{V(read)} \rightarrow \text{V(read)} + \text{NPt}$$

On Thursday John read a book

In this way we can derive from the SF of fig. 35 (i) *Before Thursday John read a book* and from the SF of fig. 35 (iii) *After Thursday John read a book*.

5. There are also verbal realisations of 'temporal' sememes — as an example consider '(ante)' in the SF of fig. 35 (ii) above.

5.1. With '(ante)' as the pivot node and '(read)' as the theme, we can produce as one linearisation:

$$\text{decl} \longrightarrow [(\text{read}) \xrightarrow{\text{tga}} [(\text{John})] \quad \text{b} \quad (\text{read}) \xrightarrow{\text{gl}} [(\text{book})]] \xrightarrow{\text{sp}} (\text{ante})\text{---}$$

$$\xrightarrow{\text{ef}} [(\text{write}) \xrightarrow{\text{tga}} [(\text{Bill})] \quad \text{b} \quad (\text{write}) \xrightarrow{\text{gl}} [(\text{letter})]]$$

which can be realised:

$$\text{decl} \quad : \quad \text{S} \rightarrow \text{NPs}$$

$$\text{tga} \quad : \quad \text{Nv}^0(\text{read}) \rightarrow \text{NPgen} + \text{Nv}^1(\text{read})$$

$$\text{gl} \quad : \quad \text{Nv}^1(\text{read}) \rightarrow \text{Nv}^2(\text{read}) + \text{Pr(of)} + \text{NP}$$

$$\text{sp} \quad : \quad \text{NP(...)} \rightarrow \text{NP(...)} + \text{Y}$$

$$(142) \quad \text{ef} \quad : \quad \text{Y(ante)} \rightarrow \text{V(precede)} + \text{N}^0$$

$$[\quad : \quad \text{N}^0 \rightarrow \text{NP(N}^0$$

$$\text{tga} \quad : \quad \text{Nv}^0(\text{write}) \rightarrow \text{NPgen} + \text{Nv}^1(\text{write})$$

$$\text{gl} \quad : \quad \text{Nv}^1(\text{write}) \xrightarrow{\cdot} \text{Nv}^2(\text{write}) + \text{Pr(of)} + \text{NP}$$

John's reading of a book preceded Bill's writing of a letter

Instead of rule (142) we could have selected

$$(141) \quad \text{ef} \quad : \quad \text{Y(ante)} \rightarrow \text{V(be)} + \text{Vpp(follow)} + \text{Pr(by)} + \text{N}^0$$

by which a passive construction is formed with the antonym of *precede*: *John's reading of a book was followed by Bill's writing of a letter.*

5.2. Choosing '(write)' as the theme instead of '(read)' we can realise: *Bill's writing of a letter followed John's reading of a book* and *Bill's writing of a letter was preceded by John's reading of a book.* For these we need the semolexemic rules:

(270) ps : $J(ante) \rightarrow V(follow) + N^0$

(269) ps : $J(ante) \rightarrow V(be) + Vpp(precede) + Pr(by) + N^0$

5.3. These sentences are stylistically awkward and seem rather forced. However, the reader will readily find examples which must be derived from SFs containing '$\underline{\quad sp \quad}$(ante)$\underline{\quad ef \quad}$' and which are perfectly acceptable. Sentences such as:

The fierce fighting was followed by a temporary cessation of hostilities
A full confession of his crime followed the man's arrest by the police
The accumulation of relevant data should always precede important policy decisions.

5.4. Since '(ante)' has verbal realisations it is not surprising that it also has realisations as verbal nouns ('Nv'), e.g. *precedence* and *succession*. I will not go into the details of their derivation as the principles have been already amply illustrated.

C. Dynamic spatial expressions

The realisation of the dynamic sememes can be accommodated by rules parallel to those given for the temporal sememes.

1. From the SF:

Fig. 36 (i)

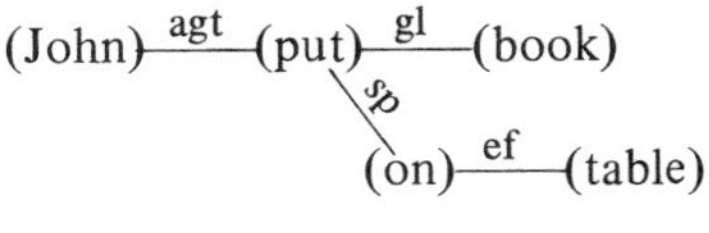

$$(John)\underline{\quad agt \quad}(put)\underline{\quad gl \quad}(book)$$
$$\searrow sp$$
$$(on)\underline{\quad ef \quad}(table)$$

1.1. with '(John)' as theme node and '(put)' as pivot, we can realise:

$\qquad$ sp : $V(\Delta) \rightarrow V(\Delta) + W_0$

(117) ef : $W_0(on) \rightarrow Pr(onto) + N^0$

$\qquad$ *John put a book onto a table*

1.2. and with '(on)' as theme and '(put)' as pivot:

$\qquad$ decl : $S \rightarrow NPk$

$\qquad$ ef : $W_0(on) \rightarrow Pr(onto) + N^0$

ps   :   NPk(...) → NP(...) + NPp

Onto a table John put a book

1.3. Examples of realisations of other dynamic sememes are:

(from)   :   *John took a bottle out of a cupboard*
               Out of a cupboard John took a bottle
(sub)   :   *Mary put a letter under the mat*
               Under the mat Mary put a letter
(pre)   :   *Bill parked the car in front of the school*
               In front of the school Bill parked the car

1.4. Just as the realisation of '$\xrightarrow{\text{fe}}$(ante)$\xrightarrow{\text{ps}}$' produces the antonym of *before*, we can realise *over* and *behind* from '$\xrightarrow{\text{fe}}$(sub)$\xrightarrow{\text{ps}}$' and '$\xrightarrow{\text{fe}}$(pre)$\xrightarrow{\text{ps}}$':

Mary put the mat over the stain
Bill put the letter behind the clock

2. In the case of '(inter)' the node at the end of 'ef' must be either a sememe containing the semon '⟨pl⟩' or the node '(&)':

Fig. 36 (ii)

$$(\text{John})\xrightarrow{\text{agt}}(\text{put})\xrightarrow{\text{gl}}(\text{chair})$$
$$\downarrow_{\text{ps}}$$
$$(\text{inter})$$
$$\downarrow_{\text{ef}}$$
$$(\text{bed})\xrightarrow{\text{co}}(\&)\xrightarrow{\text{oc}}(\text{table})$$

(116)   ef   : $W_0(\text{inter}) \to \text{Pr(between)} + N^0$

         [: $N^0 \to NP(N^0$

         oc   : $N^0(\&) \to N^0 + N^1(\&)$

         oc   : $N^1(\&) \to \text{Conj(and)} + N^0$

John put the chair between the bed and the table

3. It seems that few (perhaps none?) of the dynamic sememes can be realised as conjunctions — if such a realisation is found, then the kind of rules outlined for the temporal sememes will suffice.

   Similarly, it seems that verbal realisations are very rare among the dynamic sememes. Of the sememes given in the table in section A.3 above perhaps only '(to)' has a possible verbal form: *approach* (?) Again, for any verbal realisations that may be needed, the rules for temporal sememes can be followed.

D. Static spatial expressions

With static sememes we find the greatest variety of possible realisations. This is because they may be attached to 'nominal' sememes as well as 'verbal' sememes and because they have adjectival realisations in addition to realisations as prepositions, conjunctions and verbs.

1. In fig. 37 (i) we have a SF with a static sememe attached to a 'verbal' node:

Fig. 37 (i)

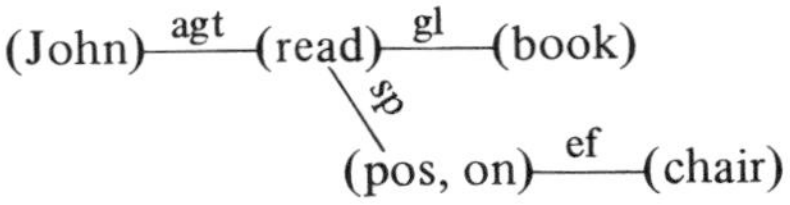

$$(John) \xrightarrow{\text{agt}} (read) \xrightarrow{\text{gl}} (book)$$
$$(pos, on) \xrightarrow{\text{ef}} (chair)$$

Its realisations follow the pattern found for the temporal and dynamic sememes.

1.1. Thus, with '(read)' as pivot and '(John)' as theme and employing the rule

(118)   ef   : $W_0(pos, on) \rightarrow Pr(on) + N^0$

we can derive:

John read a book on a chair

1.2. With '(read)' as pivot and '(pos, on)' as theme we obtain a sentence headed by the prepositional phrase:

On a chair John read a book

2. In the SF of fig. 37 (ii) the same sememes occur but this time '(pos, on)' is attached to the 'nominal' sememe '(book)':

Fig. 37 (ii)

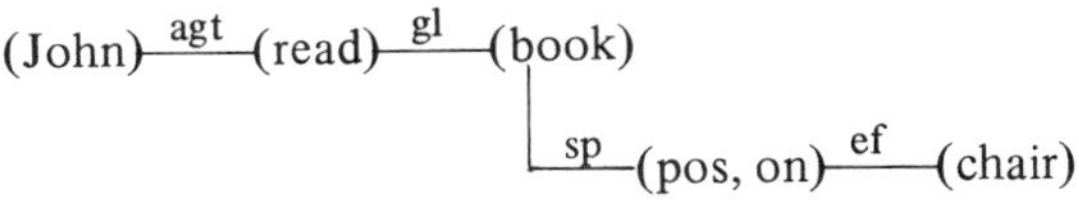

$$(John) \xrightarrow{\text{agt}} (read) \xrightarrow{\text{gl}} (book)$$
$$\xrightarrow{\text{sp}} (pos, on) \xrightarrow{\text{ef}} (chair)$$

With '(read)' as pivot and '(John)' as theme, two realisations are possible:

2.1.   gl   :   V(read) → V(read) + NPt

                        [:   NPt → NP(N^0

                        sp   :   N^0(book) → N^0(book) + Wh(s) + Y

(151)   ef   :   Y(pos, on) → V(be) + Pr(on) + N^0

John read a book which was on a chair

2.2. or: sp   :   N^0(book) → N^0(book) + K

(91)   ef   :   K(pos, on) → Pr(on) + N^0

John read a book on a chair

2.3. The surface form of this last realisation is the same as that in section 1 above. However, as the SFs from which they are derived and their synonyms show, they differ considerably in meaning: in the former (1.1) it is the action of reading which takes place on a chair whereas in the last example (2.2) it is the object read which is (or was found) on a chair.

3. As the derivation of 2.1 shows, static sememes are capable of 'verbal' realisations.

3.1. From the SF of 37 (ii) with the pivot on '(pos, on)' and with '(book)' as the theme node we can derive a sentence containing a relative clause (which may be either 'restrictive' or 'non-restrictive' — see chapter VI.6 above):

$$\text{decl} \longrightarrow [\,[(\text{book})] \xrightarrow{\text{lg}} (\text{read}) \xrightarrow{\text{tga}} [(\text{John})]\,] \xrightarrow{\text{sp}} (\text{pos, on}) \xrightarrow{\text{ef}} (\text{chair})$$

                        lg   :   NPw(...) → NP(...) + Wh(s) + Vrel

                        tga   :   Vrel(read) → NP + V(read)

                        sp   :   NP(...) → NP(...) + Y

                        ef   :   Y(pos, on) → V(be) + Pr(on) + N^0

A book which John read was on a chair

3.2. From the SF of fig. 37 (i) with '(pos, on)' as pivot and '(read)' as theme, the possible realisations include:

John's reading of a book was on a chair

The unlikeliness of such a sentence occurring does not entail that its realisation should be forbidden: it may be stylistically awkward but it is not nonsense.

4. Like the temporal and dynamic sememes, static sememes have realisations from 'fe—ps' linearisations which are antonymous to realisations from 'fe—ef' linearisations. Alongside:

4.1. *The book (is) under the newspaper*   via $\xrightarrow{sp}$(pos, sub)$\xrightarrow{ef}$
The house (is) in front of the church   via $\xrightarrow{sp}$(pos, pre)$\xrightarrow{ef}$

we have:

The newspaper (is) over the book   via $\xrightarrow{fe}$(pos, sub)$\xrightarrow{ps}$
The church (is) behind the house   via $\xrightarrow{fe}$(pos, pre)$\xrightarrow{ps}$

4.2. For the inverse 'verbal' realisation of '(pos, on)' we might suppose *support*, derived by a rule

$$ps \quad : \quad J(pos, on) \to V(support) + N^0$$

This would permit *A chair supported a book which was read by John.* In itself, this sentence shows how dubious the realisation must be: the doubts are underlined when we consider that this rule would also permit. *A chair supported the reading by John of a book,* etc. (!)

4.3. Rather firmer, it seems, is the inverse 'verbal' realisation of '(pos, in)'. From the SF:

Fig. 37 (iii)   (water)$\xrightarrow{sp}$(pos, in)$\xrightarrow{ef}$(bottle)

we may derive, by rules

$$(150) \quad ef \quad : \quad Y(pos, in) \to V(be) + Pr(in) + N^0$$

and $$(90) \quad ef \quad : \quad K(pos, in) \to Pr(in) + N^0$$

Water is in the bottle and *Water in the bottle*

and also, by rule

$$(278) \quad ps \quad : \quad J(pos, in) \to V(contain) + N^0$$

The bottle contains water

5. The close relationship between the "possessives" and the "locatives" (or static spatial prepositions) has been noted by many linguists, e.g. Lyons (1968: 390 ff.) and Fillmore (1966). It is recognised here by the presence of "pos" in the notations adopted for the static sememes.

5.1. Synonymous with *The bottle contains water* derived from the SF of 37 (iii) we find *The bottle has water in it* and, as a prepositional realisation from 'ps' on 'K', *The bottle with water in it.*

Similar realisations containing *have* or *with* are possible for other static sememes, e.g.

$\xrightarrow{\text{sp}}$(pos, sub)$\xrightarrow{\text{ef}}$ *The book has the newspaper over it*
                                       The book with the newspaper over it
$\xrightarrow{\text{fe}}$(pos, sub)$\xrightarrow{\text{ps}}$ *The newspaper has the book under it*
                                       The newspaper with the book under it
$\xrightarrow{\text{sp}}$(pos, pre)$\xrightarrow{\text{ef}}$ *The house has the church behind it*
                                       The house with the church behind it
$\xrightarrow{\text{fe}}$(pos, pre)$\xrightarrow{\text{ps}}$ *The church has the house in front of it*
                                       The church with the house in front of it

(Compare these realisations with those of 4.1 above.)

$\xrightarrow{\text{fe}}$(pos, on)$\xrightarrow{\text{ps}}$ *The chair has a book on it*
                                       The chair with a book on it
$\xrightarrow{\text{fe}}$(pos, inter)$\xrightarrow{\text{ps}}$ *The bed and the table have a chair between them*

The lexeme *it* (and in the last example *them*) refers back anaphorically to the 'subject' of *have* or the noun modified by *with*. Since an accurate formulation of the necessary semolexemic rules has not yet been established, the rules for the derivation of these sentences will not be found in the appendix.

5.2. SFs containing '(poss)', '(posq)' and '(posh)' all had realisations involving *have* and *with* (the lexemes generally considered to indicate 'possession' of some kind or other), e.g. from chapter IV.D above:

> *Mary has beauty, ... Mary with beauty*
> *Star has much light, ... star with much light*
> *Table has the shape of a rectangle,   ... table with the shape of a rectangle*

The same SFs had 'adjectival' realisations from the operation of 'ef' upon 'X(poss)', 'X(posq)' and 'X(posh)': *beautiful Mary*, *luminous star* and *rectangular table*.

In certain cases 'adjectival' realisations are possible with the static sememes. One example is:

$$(\text{town})\xrightarrow{\text{sp}}(\text{pos, in})\xrightarrow{\text{ef}}(\text{England})$$

(130)   sp : $N^0(\text{town}) \to X + N^0(\text{town})$
        ef : $X(\text{pos, in}) \to \text{Adj}$

        English town

Another example, this time with the sememe '(pos, from)' is:

$$(\text{ship})\xrightarrow{\text{sp}}(\text{pos, from})\xrightarrow{\text{ef}}(\text{France})$$

(129) ef : X(pos, from) → Adj

French ship

For most static sememes, however, 'adjectival' realisations are not found because the sememes usually occurring at the end of 'ef' do not have adjectival forms. This is the case with '(bottle)' in the SF of fig. 37 (iii). For certain static sememes we must presume, in addition, that 'ef' is not productive when they are attached to 'X' — this would appear to be so for '(pos, sub)', '(pos, pre)' and '(pos, inter)', but this can only be confirmed by an exhaustive examination of the paradigmatic structure of the "locatives".

E. Relationships between dynamic and static expressions

1. As we remarked earlier, dynamic sememes may be attached only to 'verbal' sememes whereas static sememes may be attached either to 'verbal' sememes or to 'nominal' sememes. Also it may be noted that certain 'verbal' sememes may have linked to them only a restricted set of dynamic sememes and will admit no static sememes. For example, '(put)' seems to demand the presence of '(onto)', '(into)', '(inter)' etc. but rejects '(pos, on)', '(pos, in)' and '(pos, inter)'.

We may account for these facts in two ways. We might say that certain sememes are incompatible with each other when linked in a specified way in a SF. Thus, all dynamic sememes are incompatible with 'nominal' sememes attached to them by 'ps', and '(put)' is incompatible with '(pos, on)', etc. On the other hand, we might say that these sememes do not occur in SFs linked in this way simply because there are no extralinguistic 'events' to which such combinations of sememes may refer. By the first explanation, 'sememic incompatibility', we would deny the co-occurrence of certain sememes in SFs; whereas by the second, 'referential implausibility', we would allow them to co-occur while asserting that it is extremely unlikely that they would in fact ever do so. In chapter XV I return to this point and come to certain conclusions about which explanation should be adopted.

2. A rather interesting relationship can be discerned between SFs containing dynamic sememes and SFs containing static sememes. From the SF of fig. 36 (i), viz.

$$(John) \xrightarrow{\text{agt}} (put) \xrightarrow{\text{gl}} (book)$$
$$\big\downarrow \text{sp} \; (on) \xrightarrow{\text{ef}} (table)$$

John puts a book on the table

may be 'inferred' the following SF:

$$(book) \xrightarrow{\text{sp}} (pos, on) \xrightarrow{\text{ef}} (table)$$

The book is on the table

By 'inference' is meant the following: the existence (or occurrence) of the extralinguistic event of a SF is assumed to follow necessarily from the existence (or occurrence) of the event referred to by another SF. In this case, after the book has been put on the table by John a listener can rightly assume that the book is now on the table. The relationship is one obtaining not between the SFs themselves (nor indeed between their realisations) but between the events (or states) they refer to. It is thus a relationship essentially different from those of 'sememic implication' and 'sememic equivalence'. However, even though the relationship is between what the SFs refer to and not between SFs themselves it appears to be possible to formulate rules for inference on the sememic stratum, thus paralleling some of the rules of propositional calculus (see chapter XV below).

XII. THE COPULA AND EXPRESSIONS
OF SIMILARITY AND DIFFERENCE

A. Copula

Earlier chapters have illustrated many realisations which include the verb *be* but so far no explanation has been provided for the generation of the simple copula-sentence *A is B* where both *A* and *B* are nouns. Logicians have long recognised that the relationship between *A* and *B* can be of three kinds:
  (i) both have the same referent, i.e. they are equivalent (A = B),
  (ii) the referent of *A* is a member of the class *B* (A $\in$ B),
  (iii) the referents of *A* (the class *A*) are included in the class *B* (A $\subset$ B).
In the 'equivalence' relationship (i) the referents of both *A* and *B* are specified exactly; in 'class-membership' (ii) only *A* is specific since *B* has a number of potential referents; and in 'class-inclusion' (iii) neither *A* nor *B* are specific.

1.   In this model a referent is specific if it is expressed by a sememe representing a proper name or it may be made specific by the anaphoric process, i.e. expressed by '(pro)' linked to a sememe or group of sememes which specify it (see chapter VI above). The 'equivalence' relationship is represented by the sememe '(cop)', 'class-membership' by '(cop, mem)' and 'class-inclusion' by '(cop, sb)'. All these sememes occur only within 'sp–ef' links in SFs. In the case of the link '$\xrightarrow{\text{sp}}$(cop)$\xrightarrow{\text{ef}}$', therefore, the nodes at the end of 'ps' and of 'ef' are both specific, i.e. either the '(pro)' sememe or a 'proper name' sememe. With '(cop, mem)' only one node, that at the end of 'ef', is specific, and with '(cop, sb)' neither node is specific.
    As the following semolexemic rules show, the only realisations of these

'copula' sememes are verbal, except for '(cop, mem)' which has a quasi-adjectival realisation.

(144)   ef   : $Y(cop) \rightarrow V(be) + N^0$

(238)   ps   : $A(cop, mem) \rightarrow N^1$

(274)   ps   : $J(cop) \rightarrow V(be) + N^0$

(275)   ps   : $J(cop, mem) \rightarrow V(be) + N^0$

(277)   ps   : $J(cop, sb) \rightarrow V(be) + N^0$

2.   Only the sememe '(cop)' has realisations with *be* in both directions – as we should expect in an 'equivalence' relationship.

2.1.   An example with two '(pro)' sememes is:

$$(\text{woman})-\overset{ana}{=}-(\text{pro})\overset{sp}{-}(\text{cop})\overset{ef}{-}(\text{pro})-\overset{ana}{=}-(\text{doctor})$$

realised as: ana   : $N^0(pro) \rightarrow D(the) + N^0$

                        sp   : $NP(...) \rightarrow NP(...) + Y$

(144)   ef   : $Y(cop) \rightarrow V(be) + N^0$

                        ana   : $N^0(pro) \rightarrow D(the) + N^0$

                        the woman is the doctor

and as: ana   : $N^0(pro) \rightarrow D(the) + N^0$

                        fe   : $NP(...) \rightarrow NP(...) + J$

(274)   ps   : $J(cop) \rightarrow V(be) + N^0$

                        ana   : $N^0(pro) \rightarrow D(the) + N^0$

                        the doctor is the woman

The SF and its realisations make it quite clear that an identity between the two referents of *the woman* and *the doctor* is being asserted.

2.2.   Two examples of a SF including a 'proper name' sememe with '(cop)':

$$(\text{Mary})\overset{sp}{-}(\text{cop})\overset{ef}{-}(\text{pro})-\overset{ana}{=}-(\text{doctor})$$

realised as: *Mary is the doctor* and as *the doctor is Mary*

$$(\text{woman})-\overset{ana}{=}-(\text{pro})\overset{sp}{-}(\text{cop})\overset{ef}{-}(\text{Mary})$$

realised as: *the woman is Mary* and *Mary is the woman.*

2.3. Examples with two 'proper names' are in practice rare but not impossible: *Bonaparte is Napoleon, Paris is France* (i.e. everything which is typically French can be found in Paris).

3. In the 'class-membership' relationship, '(cop, mem)', the copula is realised only in one direction. For example:

3.1. $\quad$ (doctor)$\xrightarrow{\text{ana}}$(pro)$\xrightarrow{\text{fe}}$(cop, mem)$\xrightarrow{\text{ps}}$(woman)

is realised as: $\quad$ ana $\quad$: $\quad$ N^0(pro) $\to$ D(the) + N^0

$\qquad\qquad\qquad$ fe $\quad$: $\quad$ NP(...) $\to$ NP(...) + J

$\quad$ (275) $\quad$ ps $\quad$: $\quad$ J(cop, mem) $\to$ V(be) + N^0

$\qquad\qquad\qquad\qquad$ *the doctor is a woman*

Except perhaps in rather strained and affected speech, * *a woman is the doctor* seems unacceptable. (If it were argued that such a structure is acceptable then we need only add one rule, i.e.

$\qquad\qquad$ ef $\quad$: $\quad$ Y(cop, mem) $\to$ V(be) + N^0.)

3.2. An example with a 'proper name' sememe is:

$\qquad$ (Brown)$\xrightarrow{\text{fe}}$(cop, mem)$\xrightarrow{\text{ps}}$(doctor)

$\qquad\qquad\qquad$ *Brown is a doctor*

3.3. Both these SFs have realisations with a noun in a quasi-adjectival function. Thus from:

$\qquad$ (doctor)$\xrightarrow{\text{ana}}$(pro)$\xrightarrow{\text{fe}}$(cop, mem)$\xrightarrow{\text{ps}}$(woman)

is realised: $\quad$ ana $\quad$: $\quad$ N^0(pro) $\to$ D(the) + N^0

$\qquad\qquad\qquad$ fe $\quad$: $\quad$ N^0(doctor) $\to$ A + N^0(doctor)

$\quad$ (238) $\quad$ ps $\quad$: $\quad$ A(cop, mem) $\to$ N^1

$\qquad\qquad\qquad\qquad$ *the woman doctor ...*

The use of the superscript '1' ensures that only adjectives may modify 'N' (rule (303)).

Similarly from: $(Brown) \xrightarrow{\text{fe}} (cop, mem) \xrightarrow{\text{ps}} (doctor)$ we can derive
Doctor Brown.

3.4. Although the realisation of quasi-adjectival nouns is not infrequent — as
we saw in the sections on nominalisations and adjectives other sources for
their derivation exist — it seems that this source has severe restrictions attached to it. Beside *The boy is a thief* and *The policeman is a driver* we do not
find * *The thief boy* or * *The driver policeman*. On the other hand we do
have both *The thief is a boy* and *The boy thief* and also *The king is a warrior*
and *The warrior king*.

4. For the 'class-inclusion' relationship with '(cop, sb)' there is a realisation
in only one direction. From the SF:

$$(horse, pl) \xrightarrow{\text{fe}} (cop, sb) \xrightarrow{\text{ps}} (animal, pl)$$

we can derive: fe   : $NP(...) \rightarrow NP(...) + J$

(277)   ps   : $J(cop, sb) \rightarrow V(be) + N^0$

Horses are animals

or with generic *the* (see VIII.A.1 above): *The horse is an animal*. The presence
of '⟨sb⟩' in '(cop, sb)' indicates that the sememe at the end of 'ps', '(animal)',
consists of a set of semons which are a *subset* of the set of semons making up
the sememe at the end of 'ef', '(horse)'. This is the reason why the converse
* *Animals are horses* is unacceptable: the class of animals is not included in
the class of horses.

4.1. Closely related to *Horses are animals* (and logically implied by it) is the
statement *Any horse is an animal*. This can be derived from:

$$(horse) \xrightarrow{\text{fe}} (cop, sb) \xrightarrow{\text{ps}} (animal)$$
$$\Big|\text{ds}$$
$$(quant)$$
$$\Big|\text{a}$$
$$(any)$$

As we have seen (VIII.C.5) this is also the origin of *A horse is an animal*.
Again, the 'subset' relationship obtains between '(horse)' and '(animal)' and
in consequence the converse copula-statement * *An animal is a (= any) horse*
cannot be permitted.

4.2. Whenever a copula-statement is made in which neither referents are
specific there is the implicit assumption that a 'subset' relationship exists

between them. Thus, if we have the sentence *Whales are fish* (or *The whale is a fish*) then we have an assertion that the class of *whales* is included in the class of *fish*, i.e. the SF:

$$(\text{whale, pl}) \xrightarrow{\text{fe}} (\text{cop, sb}) \xrightarrow{\text{ps}} (\text{fish, pl})$$

The truth or falsity of the assertion can be tested only by reference to the extralinguistic world. In other words, the SF itself is neutral regarding the legitimacy of the presence of '⟨sb⟩' in the formula (see chapter XV below).

B. Apposition

1.   Rather similar to the quasi-adjectival realisation in 3.3 above, *The woman doctor* ... , is one of apposition, viz. *The doctor, a woman* ... . The latter can be derived from the same SF:

$$(\text{doctor}) \xrightarrow{\text{ana}} (\text{pro}) \xrightarrow{\text{fe}} (\text{cop, mem}) \xrightarrow{\text{ps}} (\text{woman})$$

in the following way:

	ana	:	$N^0(\text{pro}) \rightarrow D(\text{the}) + N^0$
(184)	fe	:	$N^0(\text{doctor}) \rightarrow N^0(\text{doctor}) + \text{Comma} + \text{Ap} + \text{Comma}$
(245)	ps	:	$\text{Ap}(\text{cop, mem}) \rightarrow N^0$
			the doctor, a woman, ...

2.   To illustrate further these rules involving the 'non-terminal' category 'Ap' consider the SF:

Fig. 37

$$(\text{John}) \xrightarrow{\text{agt}} (\text{buy}) \xrightarrow{\text{gl}} (\text{car})$$
$$\Big|\, \text{fe}$$
$$(\text{cop, mem})$$
$$\Big|\, \text{ps}$$
$$(\text{friend}) \xrightarrow{\text{fe}} (\text{poss}) \xrightarrow{\text{ps}} (\text{pro}) \xrightarrow{\text{ana}} (\text{soldier})$$

One realisation of this would be a 'non-restrictive' relative clause with *be*:

John, who is a friend of the soldier, bought a car (the rules for which can be found in earlier sections). Another is an appositive phrase:

fe   : $N^0(John) \rightarrow N^0(John) + Comma + Ap + Comma$

ps   : $Ap(cop, mem) \rightarrow N^0$

[: $N^0 \rightarrow NP(N^0$

fe   : $N^0(friend) \rightarrow N^0(friend) + B$

ps   : $B(poss) \rightarrow Pr(of) + N^0$

John, a friend of the soldier, bought a car

3.   Since apposition may also occur with other '(cop)' nodes we must extend the rules to include:

(302)   sp   : $N^0(x) \rightarrow N^0(x) + Comma + Ap + Comma$

(80)   ef   : $Ap(cop) \rightarrow N^0$

(244)   ps   : $Ap(cop) \rightarrow N^0$

thus allowing for *The woman, the doctor, ...* ; *Brown, the doctor, ...* ; *The doctor, the woman, ...* ; and *The doctor, Brown ...* .
And also rule

(246)   ps   : $Ap(cop, sb) \rightarrow N^0$

to permit the realisation of *The whale, a mammal, ...* , etc.

4.   Apposition is also found with adjectives following the noun they modify:
    The child, poor, unhappy and abandoned, wept
    The soldier, hungry and tired, knocked on the door
For these we need a further semolexemic rule:

(81)   ef   : $Ap(mod_n) \rightarrow Comma + Adj_n + Comma$

C. Similarity

Expressions of similarity are derived from SFs with certain features in common with those underlying copula sentences. There are two 'similarity' sememes '(sim)' and '(sim, sb)' occurring in 'sp–ef' links.

1.   An example of a SF containing a '(sim, sb)' link is:

$$(\text{metal}) \xrightarrow{\text{sp}} (\text{sim, sb}) \xrightarrow{\text{ef}} (\text{silver})$$

This has the realisations:

	sp	:	$NP(...) \rightarrow NP(...) + Y$
	sp	:	$N^0(\text{metal}) \rightarrow N^0(\text{metal}) + Wh(s) + Y$
(164)	ef	:	$Y(\text{sim, sb}) \rightarrow V(\text{be}) + Pr(\text{like}) + N^0$

metal (which) is like silver

and

	sp	:	$N^0(\text{metal}) \rightarrow N^0(\text{metal}) + K$
(99)	ef	:	$K(\text{sim, sb}) \rightarrow Pr(\text{like}) + N^0$

metal like silver

It has also adjectival realisations:

	sp	:	$N^0(\text{metal}) \rightarrow X + N^0(\text{metal})$
(136)	ef	:	$X(\text{sim, sb}) \rightarrow Adj$

silvery metal

	sp	:	$N^0(\text{metal}) \rightarrow N^0(\text{metal}) + Wh(s) + Y$
(163)	ef	:	$Y(\text{sim, sb}) \rightarrow V(\text{be}) + Adj$

metal which is silvery

The adjective-class here is Vendler's A_b or A_c and it includes also *metallic, wooden, silken, steely, catlike, human, canine,* etc. The presence of '(sb)' indicates, as in the case of '(cop, sb)', that the sememe at the end of 'ps' is a subset of the sememe at the end of 'ef'. Any statement of the form *A is like B* implies, therefore, the assumption that the class of *B* is included in that of *A*: but regarding the truth or falsity of the assumption the SF is neutral.

2. The sememe '(sim)' occurs when there is no implied 'subset' relationship. It can be illustrated with the SFs:

$$(\text{surface}) \xrightarrow{\text{sp}} (\text{sim}) \xrightarrow{\text{ef}} (\text{metal})$$
$$(\text{face}) \xrightarrow{\text{sp}} (\text{sim}) \xrightarrow{\text{ef}} (\text{lion})$$
$$(\text{face}) \xrightarrow{\text{sp}} (\text{sim}) \xrightarrow{\text{ef}} (\text{child})$$

Some realisations, in brief, are:

(162)   ef   : $Y(sim) \rightarrow V(be) + Pr(like) + Pron(that)$
$+ Pr(of) + N^0$

surface (which) is like that of metal

(161)   ef   : $Y(sim) \rightarrow V(be) + Pr(like) + Ngen$

face (which) is like a lion's

(98)   ef   : $K(sim) \rightarrow Pr(like) + Pron(that) + Pr(of) + N^0$

surface like that of metal
face like that of a child

(97)   ef   : $K(sim) \rightarrow Pr(like) + Ngen$

face like a child's

Realisations with adjectives (in the same classes A_b and A_c as above) are:

(135)   ef   : $X(sim) \rightarrow Adj$

metallic surface, leonine face, childlike face

(160)   ef   : $Y(sim) \rightarrow V(be) + Adj$

surface (which) is metallic, etc.

3.   The sememe '(sim)', but not apparently ever '(sim, sb)', may be attached to a 'verbal' node and may therefore be realised adverbially or by a prepositional phrase.

From the SFs: $(talk) \underline{\quad sp \quad} (sim) \underline{\quad ef \quad} (fool)$

$(act) \underline{\quad sp \quad} (sim) \underline{\quad ef \quad} (child)$

we can realise

(120)   ef   : $W_0(sim) \rightarrow Pr(like) + N^0$

talk like a fool, act like a child

or: (170)   ef   : $Z_0(sim) \rightarrow Adv$

talk foolishly, act childishly

Note that the suffix attached to the realisation of '(child)' is *-like* when it modifies a 'nominal' sememe and *-ish* when it modifies a 'verbal' sememe. This factor could be dealt with by adding subscripts in the appropriate rules.

4.   However, the sememes '(sim)' and '(sim, sb)' cannot account for all ex-

pressions including *like*. The sentence *Tigers are like lions* cannot be derived from the SF

$$(\text{tigers})\xrightarrow{\text{sp}}(\text{sim, sb})\xrightarrow{\text{ef}}(\text{lions})$$

since this would permit the derivation of the unacceptable * *leonine tigers* and * *tigers like lions*.

4.1. What the sentence asserts is that the two referents are similar in the sense that they share common features. A paraphrase of *Tigers are like lions* might be *Tigers are animals which are like lions*, i.e. both tigers and lions are animals which share features putting them in a separate class (e.g. "felines"). The SF for *Tigers are animals which are like lions* reveals two 'subset' relationships: one of '(cop, sb)' between '(tigers)' and '(animals)' and one of '(sim, sb)' between '(lions)' and '(animals)':

Fig. 38 (i)

$$(\text{tigers})\xrightarrow{\text{fe}}(\text{cop, sb})\xrightarrow{\text{ps}}(\text{animals})\xrightarrow{\text{sp}}(\text{sim, sb})\xrightarrow{\text{ef}}(\text{lions})$$

For the SF from which we derive *Tigers are like lions* we hypothesise a contraction of this SF, thus:

Fig. 38 (ii)

$$(\text{tigers})\xrightarrow{\text{fe}}(\text{cop, sim, sb})\xrightarrow{\text{ef}}(\text{lions})$$

The sememe '(cop, sim, sb)' indicates that the two nodes at the ends of the 'ef' links are similar in some sense and that they are also both included in a larger but unspecified class.

4.2. The realisation of the SF in fig. 38 (ii) proceeds:

	fe	:	$NP(...) \rightarrow NP(...) + J$
	fe	:	$N^0(\text{tigers}) \rightarrow N^0(\text{tigers}) + Wh(s) + J$
(83)	ef	:	$J(\text{cop, sim, sb}) \rightarrow V(\text{be}) + Pr(\text{like}) + N^0$
			tigers (which) are like lions

and in the reverse direction:

	fe	:	$N^0(\text{lions}) \rightarrow N^0(\text{lions}) + Wh(s) + J$
	ef	:	$J(\text{cop, sim, sb}) \rightarrow V(\text{be}) + Pr(\text{like}) + N^0$
			lions (which) are like tigers

For the reason given already there are obviously no adjectival or prepositional realisations.

4.3. Between the two SFs in fig. 38 we have clearly an instance of 'sememic implication': fig. 38 (i) implies fig. 38 (ii). But equally clearly the relationship is not reciprocal: fig. 38 (ii) does not imply fig. 38 (i) for the simple reason that the class in which both sememes are included is not necessarily unique. Apart from '(animals)' and '(felines)' which we have already mentioned, other classes which may include both '(tigers)' and '(lions)' are for example '(creatures)', '(predators)' and '(cats)'.

4.4. A synonym of *Tigers are like lions* is the sentence *Tigers and lions are alike.* We can derive the latter from the SF:

Fig. 38 (iii)

$$
\begin{array}{c}
\text{(tigers)} \\
\Big| \, \infty \\
\text{(\&)} \overline{\quad\quad}^{\text{lg}}\overline{\quad\quad}\text{(cop, sim, sb)} \\
\Big| \, \infty \\
\text{(lions)}
\end{array}
$$

using the rule   lg   : $NP(...) \rightarrow NP(...) + V(be) + Vpp^0$

and the graphemic realisation of 'Vpp(cop, sim, sb)' as *alike*. It appears that SFs of the form in fig. 38 (ii) are always synonymous with SFs of the form in fig. 38 (iii) and the converse is always the case. We have, therefore, an instance of 'sememic equivalence' in which two SFs — 38 (ii) and 38 (iii) — imply and are implied by each other. (We may contrast this with the relationship between the SFs for comitative co-ordination — 24 (i) or 24 (ii) — and co-ordinated constituents — 23 (vi) — which are superficially similar in form to the SFs in figs. 38 (ii) and 38 (iii) respectively. There, however, the relationship was quite definitely not one of 'sememic equivalence' (see VII.C.8).)

D. Difference

Expressions of 'difference' can be derived from the SFs containing the nodes '(diff)', '(diff, sb)' and '(cop, diff, sb)' with rules analogous to those outlined for 'similarity' constructions.

1. $\quad$ (metal)$\xrightarrow{\text{sp}}$(diff, sb)$\xrightarrow{\text{ef}}$(silver)

$\quad$ (146) $\quad$ ef $\quad$: $\quad$ Y(diff, sb) $\rightarrow$ V(be) + Adj(different)
$$+ \text{Pr(from)} + N^0$$

metal (which) is different from silver

$\quad\quad$ (87) $\quad$ ef $\quad$: $\quad$ K(diff, sb) $\rightarrow$ Adj(different) + Pr(from) + N^0

metal different from silver

2. $\quad$ (behave)$\xrightarrow{\text{sp}}$(diff)$\xrightarrow{\text{ef}}$(lawyer)

$\quad$ (145) $\quad$ ef $\quad$: $\quad$ Y(diff) $\rightarrow$ V(be) + Adj(different) + Pr(from)
$$+ \text{Pron(that)} + \text{Pr(of)} + N^0$$

behaviour (which) is different from that of a lawyer

$\quad\quad$ (86) $\quad$ ef $\quad$: $\quad$ K(diff) $\rightarrow$ Adj(different) + Pr(from) + Pron(that)
$$+ \text{Pr(of)} + N^0$$

behaviour different from that of a lawyer

$\quad\quad$ (113) $\quad$ ef $\quad$: $\quad$ W_0(diff) $\rightarrow$ Adv(different) + Pr(from) + N^0

... behave differently from a lawyer

3. $\quad$ (gold)$\xrightarrow{\text{fe}}$(cop, diff, sb)$\xrightarrow{\text{ef}}$(silver)

$\quad\quad$ (82) $\quad$ ef $\quad$: $\quad$ J(cop, diff, sb) $\rightarrow$ V(be) + Adj(different)
$$+ \text{Pr(from)} + N^0$$

gold is different from silver

and from a SF like that in 38 (iii):

$\quad\quad\quad\quad$ lg $\quad$: $\quad$ NP(...) $\rightarrow$ NP(...) + V(be) + Vpp

$\quad\quad\quad\quad\quad\quad$ Vpp (cop, diff, sb) = ^{G}/different

gold and silver are different [11]

---

[11] The synonym of this, *Gold and silver differ*, can be derived from the same SF using a rule for the derivation of 'ergative' verbs, which are discussed in the next chapter. The lexeme *differ* is thus found to be a realisation of 'Verg(cop, diff, sb)'.

4.   Although there are no direct adjectival realisations from '(diff)' and
'(diff, sb)' we do find realisations including the negative forms of adjectives
derivable from '(like)' and '(like, sb)', i.e. Vendler's classes A_b and A_c: *un-
lawyerlike behaviour.* This seems to support the common view of *different* as
the antonym of *like* and, therefore, an interpretation of '(diff)' as shorthand
for '(like)——^{sp}——(quant)——^{ef}——(non)'.

XIII. OTHER KINDS OF VERB

Except for those verbs realised from the operations of 'sp', 'ef', 'fe' and 'ps', the verbs used in the examples have been all transitives with a single object. Not only have the intransitives, reflexives and 'two-object' verbs been neglected but the kind of transitives considered has been restricted.

A. Other transitives

1. The class of transitive verb which has been illustrated is probably the one most frequently found in English, namely that in which a sentence of the form N + V + N has a nominalisation Nv + *of* + N + *by* + N, e.g.
computer retrieves information → retrieval of information by computer.
Examples of sentences with the same pattern, N + V + N, which have different kinds of nominalisations are not difficult to find:

    (i) *smoking affects health*   → *effect of smoking on health*
    (ii) *old people need assistance* → *need of old people for assistance*
    (iii) *science interests Bill*   → *interest of Bill in science*

2. For the sentences on the left-hand side we need no additional semo-lexemic rules to derive them from SFs of the form $(a)\underline{\quad^{agt}\quad}(b)\underline{\quad^{gl}\quad}(c)$. However, it is clear that the rules operating on 'Nv(x)' must be expanded. The easiest way in which this can be done is to introduce a classification of verbal sememes as V_1, V_2, V_3, etc. Thus, suppose that '(affect)' belonged to class 'V_2' then the realisation of the nominalisation in example (i) could be:

$$(\text{smoking})\xrightarrow{\text{agt}}(\text{affect})\xrightarrow{\text{gl}}(\text{health})$$

$$\rightarrow[(\text{affect})\xrightarrow{\text{tga}}[(\text{smoking})]\,b\,(\text{affect})\xrightarrow{\text{gl}}[(\text{health})]\,]$$

[: $\text{NPt} \rightarrow \text{NP}(\text{N}^0$

category modification $N(v_2, \text{affect}) \Rightarrow Nv_2(\text{affect})$
(II.C.4.9)

tga   : $Nv_2(\text{affect}) \rightarrow Nv_2(\text{affect}) + \text{Pr}(\text{of}) + \text{NP}$

gl   : $Nv_2(\Delta) \rightarrow Nv_2(\Delta) + \text{Pr}(\text{ɔn}) + \text{NP}$

effect of smoking on health

3. The postulation of different verb classes enables us to include as transitives those verbs which require the insertion of a preposition before their object, e.g.

John waited for the train   (cf. *John awaited the train*)
Bill gazed at the reflection (cf. *Bill contemplated the reflection*)

In other words we can derive such sentences from the basic SF form
$(\text{a})\xrightarrow{\text{agt}}(\text{b})\xrightarrow{\text{gl}}(\text{c})$ by means of rules such as

gl   : $V_4(x) \rightarrow V_4(x) + \text{Pr}(\text{at}) + \text{NPt}$

4. Verbs commonly having adjectival 'objects', e.g.

John felt sick
John became rich

might also be derived from the basic SF with 'agt' and 'gl' links, cf.

John felt a pain
John became president

On the other hand, they could be derived from SFs with 'sp' and 'ef' links which are, as we have seen, the origin of 'N + *be* + Adj' realisations. Thus *John became rich* might be generated from

$$(\text{John})\xrightarrow{\text{sp}}(\text{become})\xrightarrow{\text{ef}}(\text{rich})$$

by a rule such as ef   : $Y(\text{become}) \rightarrow V(\text{become}) + \text{Adj}$

This would permit the easy formulation of a rule for the 'inference' from *John became rich* to *John is rich*. The latter sentence would be generated from

$$(\text{John})\xrightarrow{\text{sp}}(\text{mod}_2)\xrightarrow{\text{ef}}(\text{rich})$$

If we were to posit in the sememe for '(become)' the presence of all the semons in '(mod_2)' plus a semon '⟨inceptive⟩' (following a suggestion by Leech (1969: 57—59)), we could say: a SF containing '(mod_2)' can be inferred from a SF containing '(become)' by the elimination of the semon '⟨inceptive⟩'. [12]

5. A classification of verb-classes would entail a detailed examination of the paradigmatic structure of the English verb-system and would lead far beyond the immediate aim of this monograph. My assumption that all other transitives can be accommodated in the basic SF structure cannot in consequence be supported by any demonstration in detail.

B. Intransitives and ergatives

There are many occasions when speakers do not or cannot specify the agent or object of an action. Examples are:
  (i) *John ate at five o'clock*
 (ii) *Tea was eaten at five o'clock*
(iii) *John ran to school*
 (iv) *Mathematics was taught at school*
In (ii) and (iv) the 'agent' is not specified by the speaker, either by choice or because the agent is not known. In (i) the object, e.g. *tea*, has not been specified. In (iii) there is no conceivable object of *ran*: it is an example of a true intransitive verb. The verb *eat* is, in contrast, a 'pseudo-intransitive', i.e. it may be transitive or intransitive according to circumstances.

1. There is no need to provide additional semolexemic rules to account for 'agent-less' and 'object-less' sentences. Thus intransitives and 'pseudo-intransitives' are derived from SFs of the form:

$$(a)\xrightarrow{\text{agt}}(b)$$

As in the examples (i) and (iii) above 'sp—ef' links may be attached to the verbal node '(b)' and may be realised as adverbs or as prepositional phrases.

[12] It seems, therefore, that verbs such as *feel* and *become* are found between 'agt' and 'gl' links when their 'object' is a noun and between 'sp' and 'ef' links when their 'object' is an adjective. This treatment must, however, be considered extremely tentative at present.

Similarly, 'agent-less' sentences are derived from SFs of the form

$$(c)\underline{\quad \text{lg} \quad}(b)$$

Again any 'sp–ef' link may be attached to the verbal node, to produce sentences such as (ii) and (iv) above.

2. There is no reason to posit in the case of 'non-agentive' SFs the presence of a 'dummy' sememe attached to '(b)' by 'agt', e.g.

$$(c)\underline{\quad \text{lg} \quad}(b)\underline{\quad \text{tga} \quad}(\Delta)$$

which is a method sometimes adopted by transformational grammarians. Indeed there are sound objections to such a procedure, as far as this model is concerned. Firstly, since every sememe in a SF refers to (or expresses) a percept, a concept or a relationship between percepts or concepts, i.e. has sense, it is contradictory to have a sememe with no referent or sense. Secondly, unless the link were also 'dummy', false realisations would result. From a SF such as (information)$\underline{\quad \text{lg} \quad}$(retrieve)$\underline{\quad \text{tga} \quad}(\Delta)$ the semolexemic rules would derive *Information was retrieved by* Δ. In order to obtain the correct form, further rules would have to be devised to eliminate '*by* Δ' and the like. It is clear that, even ignoring the theoretical objection against 'dummy' sememes, it is easier in practice to avoid this complication by simply omitting the 'agt' link if no 'agent' is specified.

3. There are a number of verbs in English which may occur as either transitives or intransitives but which are unlike the 'pseudo-intransitives' in a number of ways. Consider the examples:
   (i) *The stone moved*
   (ii) *John moved*
   (iii) *John moved the stone*
In (i) and (ii) *moved* is intransitive and in (iii) transitive. However, there is an important relationship between (i) and (iii). If presented with sentence (i) we might ask 'Who moved it?', i.e. 'Who was the 'agent' responsible for the movement?', and the answer contained in (iii) is 'John did'. The subject of the intransitive *moved* in (i) appears as the object of the transitive *moved* in (iii). The intransitive form is, moreover, a true intransitive and not a 'pseudo-intransitive' like *eat* in 1 (i) above where the object is merely unspecified. Following Lyons (1968: 350 ff.) and others, e.g. Anderson (1969), Fillmore (1968), we may call these verbs 'ergatives'. Apart from *move*, we find *change, grow, open, close, start, stop*, etc.

4. Ergative verbs have subjects which are either 'agentive' or 'non-agentive'. In the former case, they can be derived like normal transitives and intransitives, e.g.

$$(\text{John}) \underline{}^{\text{agt}} \underline{} (\text{move}) \qquad\qquad \textit{John moved}$$

$$(\text{John}) \underline{}^{\text{agt}} \underline{} (\text{move}) \underline{}^{\text{gl}} \underline{} (\text{stone}) \qquad \textit{John moved the stone}$$

In the latter case, it is proposed that they are derived from a 'lg' link. Thus the SF:

$$(\text{stone}) \underline{}^{\text{lg}} \underline{} (\text{move})$$

may be realised:

(217)   lg   :   NP(...) $\rightarrow$ NP(...) + Verg

with the graphemic rule Verg(move) = ^{G}/move *The stone moved.*

From the same SF we may, of course, generate a passive sentence, namely *The stone was moved.* The two sentences are synonymous although, as Halliday (1967: 47) has pointed out, the emphasis is different: *The stone moved* is "process-oriented" whereas *The stone was moved* is "agent-oriented". [13] An analogous difference is that between sentences realised from the same SF but differing in the choice of theme node.

5. A sentence such as *John moved* containing an animate noun as 'subject' and a verb which can be either ergative or intransitive is, therefore, ambiguous. By one interpretation John is 'agentive', i.e. the sentence is derived from (John) $\underline{}^{\text{agt}}\underline{}$ (move), and by the other *John* is 'non-agentive', i.e. derived from (John) $\underline{}^{\text{lg}}\underline{}$ (move). (Is this ambiguity the source of much philosophical argument over questions of prime causes and free will?)

---

[13] Obviously whenever the 'agent' is specified, only the passive construction may be realised, i.e. *The stone was moved by John* and not * *The stone moved (by) John.* Hence 'tga' cannot operate on 'Verg(x)'.

It is the potentiality of the passive construction to specify an agent (if necessary) which would appear to underlie Halliday's choice of terminology. The ergative construction does not have this potentiality, hence it is "process-oriented" as opposed to "agent-oriented".

C. Reflexives

When the agent and patient of an action are the same, it is expressed in sentences including a reflexive pronoun. Thus, from the SF

Fig. 39

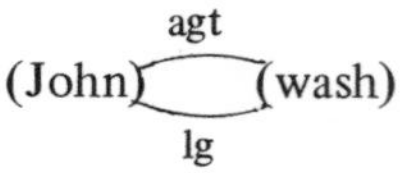

$$\text{(John)} \overset{\text{agt}}{\underset{\text{lg}}{\bigcirc}} \text{(wash)}$$

in which the 'agent' of '(wash)' has the same referent as the 'patient' of '(wash)', we want to derive the sentence *John washed himself.*

1. The reflexive pronoun *himself* refers anaphorically to *John*, so in the linearisation of fig. 39 we must have an anaphoric link. However, if we replaced the second occurrence of '(John)' by '(pro)' and made the normal 'ana' link to '(John)' then we could only derive the simple pronoun *him* with our present rules. Therefore, we introduce a new link, an 'anp' link. The linearisation of 39 is, thus:

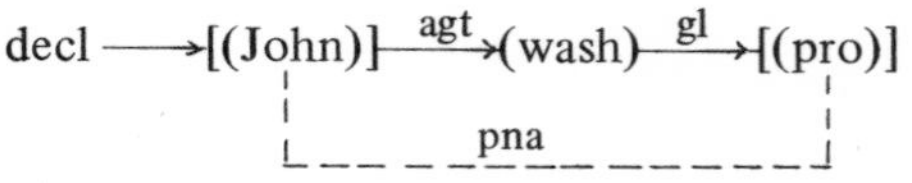

$$\text{decl} \longrightarrow [\text{(John)}] \overset{\text{agt}}{\longrightarrow} \text{(wash)} \overset{\text{gl}}{\longrightarrow} [\text{(pro)}]$$

with *pna* link connecting (John) and (pro).

Whereas 'ana' connects two SFs or two parts of a SF which could stand independently, 'anp' is found when a 'cyclic' SF is linearised: it connects elements separated in a linearisation but originating from the same node in a SF.

2. The semolexemic rule for the reflexives is

$$(45) \quad \text{anp} \quad : \quad N^0(\text{pro}) \rightarrow \text{Rfpron}$$

According to the 'gender' semon in the node to which it is attached, 'Rfpron(x)' is variously realised as *himself, herself, ourselves*, etc. Unlike 'ana', we can derive no definite article realisation through 'anp'.

3. The close relationship between the reflexive and the ergative or passive has been noted by many linguists and discussed at greatest length, perhaps, by Tesnière (1959: 272 ff.).
    The equivalent expression for the English ergative *The stone moves* is in French the reflexive *La pierre se meut*. German also has a reflexive in this

case: *Der Stein bewegt sich*. In general it seems that French (and Russian) tend to prefer the reflexive construction when English prefers an ergative or a passive construction and that German takes an intermediate position, sometimes using a reflexive and sometimes an ergative or a passive. Compare for example:

La porte s'ouvrit — Die Tür öffnete — The door opened/was opened

Le blé se sème en printemps — Korn wird in Frühling gesäet — Corn is sown in spring

Ce livre se vend facilement — Dieses Buch verkauft sich leicht — This book sells easily

For any given language it is probably incorrect to establish a relationship of 'sememic equivalence' between a SF such as 40 (i) realised as an ergative or passive and a SF such as 40 (ii) realised as a reflexive.

Fig. 40 (i) Fig. 40 (ii)

$$(a) \xrightarrow{\text{lg}} (b) \qquad (a) \overset{\text{agt}}{\underset{\text{lg}}{\rightleftharpoons}} (b)$$

However, in the process of translating from one language to another it seems clear that a conversion of 40 (i) into 40 (ii) or vice versa is often required. Equally clear is that the determining factor is the type of sememe found at node '(b)' because the transformation does not appear to be automatic (unconditional) in all circumstances.

D. Trivalent verbs

We turn now to the 'two-object' verbs, or, as Tesnière more felicitously calls them, the trivalent verbs — in contrast to the monovalent (= intransitive) and bivalent (= transitive) verbs. In sentences such as *John gives Mary a book* and *John gives a book to Mary* it is clear that the 'object' of the verb is *book* and can therefore be linked to '(give)' by a 'gl' link in the SF. On the other hand, *Mary* is the beneficiary of the action or, following traditional terminology, the indirect object or dative of *give*. We may represent this relationship by a 'dat' link, thus producing for the two sentences the following SF:

Fig. 41

$$(\text{John}) \xrightarrow{\text{agt}} (\text{give}) \overset{\text{gl} \diagup (\text{book})}{\diagdown_{\text{dat}} (\text{Mary})}$$

This may be linearised and realised in the following ways:

1.   decl $\longrightarrow$[(John)]$\xrightarrow{\text{agt}}$(give)$\xrightarrow{\text{gl}}$[(book)] b(give)$\xrightarrow{\text{dat}}$[(Mary)]

agt : $NP(...) \rightarrow NP(...) + V$

gl : $V(give) \rightarrow V(give) + NPt$

(70) dat : $V(\Delta) \rightarrow V(\Delta) + Pr(to) + NP[obl]$

John gives a book to Mary

decl $\longrightarrow$[(John)]$\xrightarrow{\text{agt}}$(give)$\xrightarrow{\text{dat}}$[(Mary)] b(give)$\xrightarrow{\text{gl}}$[(book)]

(69) dat : $V(give) \rightarrow V(give) + NP[obl]$

gl : $V(\Delta) \rightarrow V(\Delta) + NPt$

John gives Mary a book

2.   The significance of '[obl]' has been pointed out already (III.A.2 fn. 4). We are now in a position to describe the derivation of the 'oblique' pronouns more exactly. If the node '(Mary)' in fig. 41 is replaced by '(pro)$\xrightarrow{\text{ana}}$(Mary)' then the rule which follows either (69) or (70) must be:

(42) ana : $N[obl]^0(pro) \rightarrow Oblpron$

Since '(Mary)' contains the 'gender' semon '⟨fem⟩', the graphemic realisation of 'Oblpron(Mary)' will be *her*; hence: *John gives a book to her, John gives her a book.*

3.   decl $\longrightarrow$[(book)]$\xrightarrow{\text{lg}}$(give)$\xrightarrow{\text{tga}}$[(John)] b(give)$\xrightarrow{\text{dat}}$[(Mary)]

lg : $NP(...) \rightarrow NP(...) + V(be) + Vpp^0$

tga : $Vpp^0(give) \rightarrow Vpp^0(give) + Pr(by) + NP$

(77) dat : $Vpp^0(\Delta) \rightarrow Vpp^0(\Delta) + Pr(to) + NP[obl]$

A book is given by John to Mary

decl $\longrightarrow$[(book)]$\xrightarrow{\text{lg}}$(give)$\xrightarrow{\text{dat}}$[(Mary)] b(give)$\xrightarrow{\text{tga}}$[(John)]

(76) dat : $Vpp^0(give) \rightarrow Vpp^0(give) + Pr(to) + NP[obl]$

tga : $Vpp^0(\Delta) \rightarrow Vpp^0(\Delta) + Pr(by) + NP$

A book is given to Mary by John

4.   decl $\longrightarrow$[(Mary)]$\xrightarrow{\text{tad}}$(give)$\xrightarrow{\text{gl}}$[(book)] b (give)$\xrightarrow{\text{tga}}$[(John)]

     (350)   tad   : $NP(\ldots) \rightarrow NP(\ldots) + V(be) + Vpp^3$

     (213)   gl   : $Vpp^3(give) \rightarrow Vpp^0(give) + NPt$

              tga   : $Vpp^0(\Delta) \rightarrow Vpp^0(\Delta) + Pr(by) + NP$

                     Mary is given a book by John

decl $\longrightarrow$[(Mary)]$\xrightarrow{\text{tad}}$(give)$\xrightarrow{\text{tga}}$[(John)]b (give)$\xrightarrow{\text{gl}}$[(book)]

     (383)   tga   : $Vpp^3(give) \rightarrow Vpp^0(give) + Pr(by) + NP$

             gl   : $Vpp^0(\Delta) \rightarrow Vpp^0(\Delta) + NPt$

                     Mary is given by John a book

The last sentence is without doubt stylistically awkward as it stands, but if we append a relative clause it is more acceptable: *Mary is given by John a book which had once belonged to his grandfather.*

XIV. CAUSATIVE CONSTRUCTIONS

A. Relationships with other verbal constructions

1. Tesnière (1959) and Lyons (1968: 368) have shown that one-place constructions (monovalent) can be made two-place (bivalent), two-place constructions can be made three-place (trivalent) and three-place constructions can be made four-place (tetravalent) by an operation involving the notion of 'causativity'. The derivations are obtained either by using a verb such as *make* and *cause* (or *faire* in French) or by 'lexicalization'. For example

 (i) *The book falls*   → (a) *John makes the book fall* (b) *John drops the book*

 (ii) *The boy learns physics* → (a) *John makes the boy learn physics* (b) *John teaches the boy physics*

 (iii) *John gives Mary the book* → *Bill makes John give Mary the book*

In example (i) the monovalent construction is made bivalent in (a) by using *make* and in (b) by transforming *fall* into a causative *drop*, and by specifying the agent, *John*. In (ii) the bivalent construction is transformed into a trivalent construction in (a) by using *make* and in (b) by the 'lexicalization' of *make + learn* as *teach*. In (iii) only one kind of transformation is possible since English has no tetravalent verb forms.

2. It seems that there are many cases where a trivalent verb is the 'causative' form of a bivalent and a bivalent verb the 'causative' of a monovalent. We can represent the sememic origin of *make, cause*, etc. as the link '$\frac{\text{fe}}{}$(caus)$\frac{\text{ps}}{}$' e.g.

Fig. 42 (i)

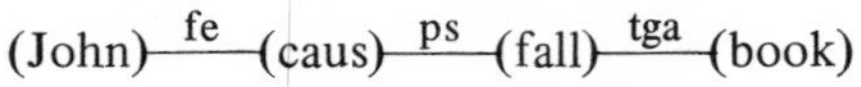

$$(\text{John}) \xrightarrow{\text{fe}} (\text{caus}) \xrightarrow{\text{ps}} (\text{fall}) \xrightarrow{\text{tga}} (\text{book})$$

John makes the book fall

Fig. 42 (ii)

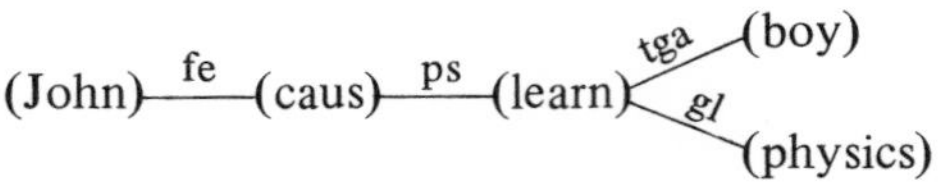

$$(\text{John}) \xrightarrow{\text{fe}} (\text{caus}) \xrightarrow{\text{ps}} (\text{learn}) \overset{\text{tga}}{\underset{\text{gl}}{<}} \begin{matrix} (\text{boy}) \\ (\text{physics}) \end{matrix}$$

John makes the boy learn physics

(The semolexemic rules for these realisations are given below.) As synonyms of 42 (i) and 42 (ii) we have the following SFs with bivalent and trivalent constructions respectively:

Fig. 43 (i)

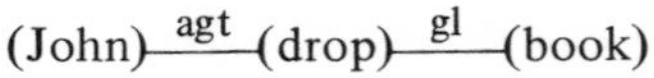

$$(\text{John}) \xrightarrow{\text{agt}} (\text{drop}) \xrightarrow{\text{gl}} (\text{book})$$

John drops the book

Fig. 43 (ii)

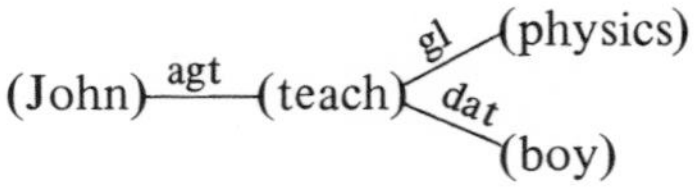

$$(\text{John}) \xrightarrow{\text{agt}} (\text{teach}) \overset{\text{gl}}{\underset{\text{dat}}{<}} \begin{matrix} (\text{physics}) \\ (\text{boy}) \end{matrix}$$

John teaches the boy physics

We can say, therefore, that SFs of the form in fig. 42 (i) are 'sememically equivalent' to those of the form in fig. 43 (i) if the verbal node in the latter (e.g. *drop*) is a 'causative' of the former (e.g. *fall*). Similarly there is a relationship of 'sememic equivalence' between figs. 42 (ii) and 43 (ii).

3. The relationship between the ergative *The stone moved* and the transitive *John moved the stone* was discussed above. Obviously the notion of 'causativity' operates here too and as a synonym for the transitive (bivalent) construction we have

Fig. 44

$$(\text{John}) \xrightarrow{\text{fe}} (\text{caus}) \xrightarrow{\text{ps}} (\text{move}) \xrightarrow{\text{gl}} (\text{stone})$$

John made the stone move

For both ergatives and intransitives, therefore, the transformation into bi-valent constructions is effected either by the addition of the 'causative' link (realised as *make* etc.) or by conversion into transitive forms, i.e. *fall → drop*, *move* (ergative) → *move* (transitive).

4. As Lyons has illustrated (1968: 359 ff.), we can extend the principle to the transformation of 'copula + adjective' constructions into bivalent constructions. For example, the SF:

Fig. 45 (i)

$$(\text{milk}) \xrightarrow{\text{sp}} (\text{mod}_2) \xrightarrow{\text{ef}} (\text{warm})$$

The milk is warm

may be transformed into:

Fig. 45 (ii)

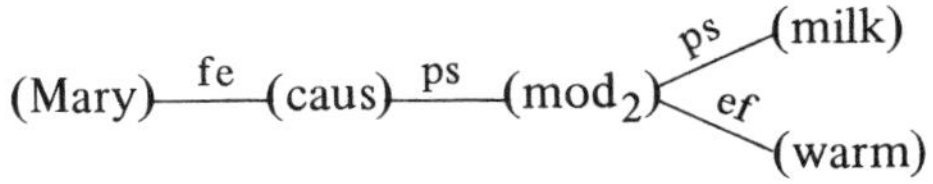

Mary makes the milk warm

or:

Fig. 45 (iii)

$$(\text{Mary}) \xrightarrow{\text{agt}} (\text{warm}) \xrightarrow{\text{gl}} (\text{milk})$$

Mary warms the milk

Once again, we find a relationship of 'sememic equivalence', between 45 (ii) and 45 (iii).

5. It would seem, therefore, that a very large number of trivalent verbs can be broken down into 'causative' constructions with bivalent verbs, e.g. the SF of fig. 43 (ii) can be analysed as the SF of fig. 42 (ii), and that very many bi-

valent verbs can be broken down into 'causative' constructions with monovalent verbs, e.g. the SF of fig. 43 (i) into the SF of fig. 42 (i). From this it
might be argued that there is no need to persist in proposing different kinds
of SF for datives, transitives, intransitives, ergatives, etc. Instead all SFs
would be made up of a central monovalent 'verbal' node to which a number
of 'causative' links are attached. Thus, the trivalent construction *Bill makes
John drop the book* would be derived from

Fig. 46 (i)

$$(\text{Bill}) \xrightarrow{\text{fe}} (\text{caus}) \underset{\text{fe}}{\overset{ps}{\diagdown}} (\text{caus}) \xrightarrow{ps} (\text{fall}) \xrightarrow{\text{tga}} (\text{book})$$
$$(\text{John})$$

and not from a SF in which the node '(drop)' occurred (as in fig. 43 (i)). The
implications of this procedure would be (a) that we would have no need for
the relationship of 'sememic equivalence' between SFs such as 42 (i) and
43 (i) since both the 'causative' construction and the bivalent construction
would have the same sememic origin, and (b) that we would no longer need
the 'gl' and 'dat' links, since they would be supplanted by the 'causative' link
' $\xrightarrow{\text{fe}} (\text{caus}) \xrightarrow{ps}$ '.

The proposal is undoubtedly very attractive but, in practice, it has proved
so far impossible to formulate semolexemic rules to deal with the complex
interlocking of 'causative' links which would arise. Consider for example, the
likely SF for the tetravalent construction *Bill made John teach the boy physics* (a sentence not uncommon by any means):

Fig. 46 (ii)

$$(\text{boy})$$
$$(\text{Bill}) \xrightarrow{\text{fe}} (\text{caus}) \underset{\text{fe}}{\overset{ps}{\diagdown}} (\text{caus}) \xrightarrow{ps} (\text{caus}) \xrightarrow{ps} (\text{x}) \xrightarrow{\text{tga}} (\text{physics})$$
$$(\text{John})$$

The node '(x)' represents a monovalent verb underlying the bivalent '(learn)',
cf. fig. 42 (ii).

In the realisation of such a SF there are not only numerous complex syntactic transformations but also the difficulties involved in 'lexicalizing' the
monovalent '(x)' into the trivalent '(teach)'.

For the present, therefore, it is argued that simpler semolexemic rules can
be formulated if we retain the different kinds of SF for monovalent, bivalent
and trivalent constructions. The consequence of this is that the relationship

of 'sememic equivalence' must be kept. In the approach adopted here, then, the SF of 46 (ii) is a more 'abstract' form of semantic graph and is a possible first approximation to the form of semon networks (see the next chapter).

B. *Have* and *make* in causative constructions

The various realisations of the 'causative' link will now be illustrated with the following SF

Fig. 47

$$(\text{Bill}) \xrightarrow{\text{fe}} (\text{caus}) \xrightarrow{\text{ps}} (\text{give}) \overset{\text{tga}}{\underset{\text{dat}}{\overset{\text{gl}}{<}}} \begin{matrix} (\text{John}) \\ (\text{book}) \\ (\text{Mary}) \end{matrix}$$

Firstly, there are the verbal realisations using *make* and *have*.

1. $\text{decl} \longrightarrow [(\text{Bill})] \xrightarrow{\text{fe}} (\text{caus}) \xrightarrow{\text{ps}} [(\text{give}) \xrightarrow{\text{tga}} [(\text{John})] \, b \, (\text{give}) \longrightarrow$

$\xrightarrow{\text{gl}} [(\text{book})] \, b \, (\text{give}) \xrightarrow{\text{dat}} [(\text{Mary})]\,]$

		fe	:	$NP(...) \rightarrow NP(...) + J$
1.1.	(272)	ps	:	$J(\text{caus}) \rightarrow V(\text{have}) + NPi$
	(26)	[	:	$NPi \rightarrow NP(Vnt^1)$
	(377)	tga	:	$Vnt^1(\text{give}) \rightarrow NP[\text{obl}] + Vnt^0(\text{give})$
	(206)	gl	:	$Vnt^0(\text{give}) \rightarrow Vnt^0(\text{give}) + NPt$
	(74)	dat	:	$Vnt^0(\Delta) \rightarrow Vnt^0(\Delta) + Pr(\text{to}) + NP[\text{obl}]$

Bill had John give a book to Mary

or, instead of rule (272) we may apply:

1.2.	(273)	ps	:	$J(\text{caus}) \rightarrow V(\text{make}) + NPj$
	(27)	[	:	$NPj \rightarrow NP(Vnt^2)$
	(378)	tga	:	$Vnt^2(\text{give}) \rightarrow NP[\text{obl}] + Vnt^0(\text{give})$

then by rules (206) and (74) to produce *Bill made John give a book to Mary*.

2. $\text{decl} \longrightarrow [(\text{Bill})] \xrightarrow{\text{fe}} (\text{caus}) \xrightarrow{\text{ps}} [(\text{give}) \xrightarrow{\text{tga}} [(\text{John})] \, b \, (\text{give})$ ——

     $\xrightarrow{\text{dat}} [(\text{Mary})] \, b \, (\text{give}) \xrightarrow{\text{gl}} [(\text{book})] \,]$

2.1. as in 1.1, i.e. by rules (272), (26) and (377) until:

> (73)   dat   : $\text{Vnt}^0(\text{give}) \rightarrow \text{Vnt}^0(\text{give}) + \text{NP[obl]}$
>
> (207)   gl   : $\text{Vnt}^0(\Delta) \rightarrow \text{Vnt}^0(\Delta) + \text{NPt}$
>
> *Bill had John give Mary a book*

2.2. or, as in 1.2 by rules (273), (27) and (378) and then by rules (73) and (207):

> *Bill made John give Mary a book*

3. $\text{decl} \longrightarrow [(\text{Bill})] \xrightarrow{\text{fe}} (\text{caus}) \xrightarrow{\text{ps}} [(\text{give}) \xrightarrow{\text{gl}} [(\text{book})] \, b \, (\text{give})$ ——

     $\xrightarrow{\text{tga}} [(\text{John})] \, b \, (\text{give}) \xrightarrow{\text{dat}} [(\text{Mary})] \,]$

3.1.   ps   : $\text{J}(\text{caus}) \rightarrow \text{V}(\text{have}) + \text{NPi}$

> (208)   gl   : $\text{Vnt}^1(\text{give}) \rightarrow \text{NP[obl]} + \text{Vpp}^0(\text{give})$

then, by (380) and (77), for *Bill had a book given by John to Mary*

3.2.   ps   : $\text{J}(\text{caus}) \rightarrow \text{V}(\text{make}) + \text{NPj}$

> (209)   gl   : $\text{Vnt}^2(\text{give}) \rightarrow \text{NP} + \text{Vergnt}(\text{give})$

No realisation is produced because (a) '(give)' has no ergative form and (b) 'tga' cannot operate on 'Verg' (by definition ergative forms have no agents).

4. $\text{decl} \longrightarrow [(\text{Bill})] \xrightarrow{\text{fe}} (\text{caus}) \xrightarrow{\text{ps}} [(\text{give}) \xrightarrow{\text{gl}} [(\text{book})] \, b \, (\text{give})$ ——

     $\xrightarrow{\text{dat}} [(\text{Mary})] \, b \, (\text{give}) \xrightarrow{\text{tga}} [(\text{John})] \,]$

as in 3.1, by rules (272) and (208), and then by (76) and (381) for:

> *Bill had a book given to Mary by John*

For the same reasons as in 3.2 there are no realisations with *make*: thus, * *Bill made a book given to Mary by John* (except, of course, in the 'non-causative' use of *make* when it is a synonym of *Bill made a book which was given by John to Mary*).

5.　　decl $\longrightarrow$ [(Bill)] $\xrightarrow{\text{fe}}$ (caus) $\xrightarrow{\text{ps}}$ [(give) $\xrightarrow{\text{dat}}$ [(Mary)] b (give) $\longrightarrow$:

$\xrightarrow{\text{gl}}$ [(book)] b (give) $\xrightarrow{\text{tga}}$ [(John)]]

5.1.　　　　　　ps　：　$J(\text{caus}) \to V(\text{have}) + NPi$

(75)　　dat　：　$Vnt^1(\text{give}) \to NP[\text{obl}] + Vpp^2(\text{give})$

(212)　　gl　：　$Vpp^2(\text{give}) \to Vpp^0(\text{give}) + NPt$

　　　　tga　：　$Vpp^0(\Delta) \to Vpp^0(\Delta) + Pr(\text{by}) + NP$

Bill had Mary given a book by John

5.2.　　　　　　ps　：　$J(\text{caus}) \to V(\text{make}) + NPj$

is unproductive because 'dat' cannot operate on '$Vnt^2(x)$'; thus, we do not have * *Bill made Mary given a book by John.*

6.　From the linearisation:

decl $\longrightarrow$ [(Bill)] $\xrightarrow{\text{fe}}$ (caus) $\xrightarrow{\text{ps}}$ [(give) $\xrightarrow{\text{dat}}$ [(Mary)] b (give) $\longrightarrow$

$\xrightarrow{\text{tga}}$ [(John)] b (give) $\xrightarrow{\text{gl}}$ [(book)]]

there are no realisations because (a) after the application of rules (272) and (75), 'tga' cannot operate on '$Vpp^2(x)$' and (b), as in 5.1, 'dat' cannot operate on '$Vnt^2(x)$': * *Bill had Mary given by John a book* and * *Bill made Mary given by John a book* are not acceptable.

7.　The new rules introduced enable constructions following *have* to be distinguished from those following *make*. This is done by having recourse again to the use of superscripts.

　　The reader will be able to confirm that with the rules illustrated above the folllowing realisations, among others, can be derived from the SFs in figs. 42 (i) and 42 (ii): *John made the book fall, John had the book fall, John made the boy learn physics, John had the boy learn physics, John had physics learnt by the boy,* etc.

8.　The SF of fig. 44 has one linearisation:

decl $\longrightarrow$ [(John)] $\xrightarrow{\text{fe}}$ (caus) $\xrightarrow{\text{ps}}$ [(move) $\xrightarrow{\text{gl}}$ [(stone)]]

8.1.   ps   :   J(caus) → V(have) + NPi

    (208)   gl   : Vnt^1(move) → NP[obl] + Vpp^0(move)

John had the stone moved

8.2.   ps   :   J(caus) → V(make) + NPj

    (209)   gl   : Vnt^2(move) → NP + Vergnt(move)

John made the stone move

Whereas in 3.2 above the application of rule (209) was unproductive because '(give)' has no ergative form, here it enables the realisation of the ergative *move* in 'causative' constructions.

9.   The realisation of the SF in fig. 45 (ii) and in other SFs with '(mod)' nodes requires additional rules

9.1.   decl $\longrightarrow$[(Mary)]$\xrightarrow{\text{fe}}$(caus)$\xrightarrow{\text{ps}}$[$(mod_2)$$\xrightarrow{\text{ps}}$(milk)

        b(mod_2) $\xrightarrow{\text{ef}}$(warm)]

          ps   :   J(caus) → V(make) + NPj

    (285)   ps   : $Vnt^2(mod_2)$ → $N[obl]^0$ + $Ynt(mod_2)$

    (166)   ef   : $Ynt(mod_2)$ → Adj_2

Mary made the milk warm

The presence of any form of the copula *be* is clearly unacceptable: * *Mary made the milk (to) be warm.*

9.2.   decl $\longrightarrow$[(Mary)]$\xrightarrow{\text{fe}}$(caus)$\xrightarrow{\text{ps}}$[$(mod_2)$$\xrightarrow{\text{ef}}$(warm)

        b$(mod_2)$$\xrightarrow{\text{ps}}$(milk)]

          ps   :   J(caus) → V(make) + NPj

    (101)   ef   : $Vnt^2(mod_2)$ → Adj_2 + $Jnt(mod_2)$

    (282)   ps   : $Jnt(mod_2)$ → N^0

Mary made warm the milk

The closeness of this realisation to *Mary warmed the milk*, in which the causative verb *warm* occurs, highlights the relationship of 'sememic equivalence' between the SF of fig. 45 (iii), from which the sentence is derived, and the SF of fig. 45 (ii).

9.3. For neither linearisation is the application of rule (272) productive since neither 'ps' nor 'ef' can operate on 'Vnt^1(x)': hence we do not find * *Mary had the milk warm* or * *Mary had warm the milk* (except, of course, in the 'non-causative' sense of *have*, e.g. as synonyms of *Mary drank the milk warm*).

C. Other causative realisations

The remaining realisations of the 'causative' link can be briefly described.

1. Firstly, there are those containing the transitive verb *cause*. In addition to rules (272) and (273) 'ps' may operate on 'J(caus)' as follows:

$$(271) \quad ps \quad : \quad J(caus) \rightarrow V(cause) + NPt$$

As normal, the application of '[' on 'NPt' produces, by rules (35–37), 'NP(N^0', 'NP(Vinf^0' and 'NPr(Conj(that) + Vrel'. The operations of 'tga', 'gl', 'ps' and 'ef' on these categories have already been amply illustrated. With the following additional rules for 'dat':

$$(65) \quad dat \quad : \quad Nv^0(x) \rightarrow Nv^3(x) + Pr(to) + NP[obl]$$

$$(66) \quad dat \quad : \quad Nv^1(x) \rightarrow Nv^3(x) + Pr(to) + NP[obl]$$

$$(67) \quad dat \quad : \quad Nv^2(\Delta) \rightarrow Nv^2(\Delta) + Pr(to) + NP[obl]$$

$$(68) \quad dat \quad : \quad Nv^3(\Delta) \rightarrow Nv^3(\Delta) + Pr(to) + NP[obl]$$

$$(71) \quad dat \quad : \quad Vinf^0(x) \rightarrow NP[obl] + Vinf(be) + Vpp^2(x)$$

$$(72) \quad dat \quad : \quad Vinf^0(\Delta) \rightarrow Vinf^0(\Delta) + Pr(to) + NP[obl]$$

$$(78) \quad dat \quad : \quad Vrel(x) \rightarrow NP + V(be) + Vpp^2(x)$$

it can be easily confirmed that from the SF of fig. 47 these realisations, among others, can be derived:

Bill caused John to give a book to Mary
Bill caused a book to be given to Mary by John
Bill caused Mary to be given a book by John
Bill caused that John gave a book to Mary
Bill caused that a book was given to Mary by John
Bill caused John's giving of a book to Mary
Bill caused the giving of a book by John to Mary
Bill caused the giving to Mary of a book by John

Many of these realisations are stylistically awkward, perhaps even for a large number of speakers quite unacceptable. This suggests that in English causative constructions *make* and *have* are preferred to *cause*.

2. Like many sememes occurring in 'sp–ef' links, '(caus)' has realisations as a preposition and as a subordinate conjunction.

2.1. An example of a prepositional realisation can be illustrated with the SF of fig. 47 linearised as follows:

$$\text{decl} \longrightarrow [(\text{John})] \xrightarrow{\text{agt}} (\text{give}) \xrightarrow{\text{gl}} [(\text{book})] \text{ b } (\text{give}) \xrightarrow{\text{dat}} [(\text{Mary})]$$

$$\text{b } (\text{give}) \xrightarrow{\text{sp}} (\text{caus}) \xrightarrow{\text{ef}} (\text{Bill})$$

(112)
sp	:	$V(\Delta) \rightarrow V(\Delta) + W_0$
ef	:	$W_0(\text{caus}) \rightarrow \text{Pr}(\text{because of}) + N^0$

John gave a book to Mary because of Bill

As we have described in chapters V and XI, a prepositional phrase may head a sentence by selecting '(caus)' as theme node and using the category 'NPk':
Because of Bill John gave a book to Mary.

2.2. A subordinate conjunction realisation can be illustrated with the following SF:

Fig. 48

The rules for the generation of subordinate clauses have been demonstrated in V.B. and VI.9. Employing the rule:

(111)   ef   : $W_0(\text{cause}) \rightarrow \text{Conj}(\text{because}) + \text{NPp}$

the reader can confirm that the following may be derived:

John rented a garage because he had bought a car and
Because he had bought a car John rented a garage

2.3. With the rules introduced above for verbal realisations of '(caus)', from the SF of fig. 48 may be derived also:

John's buying of a car made him rent a garage
John's buying of a car caused him to rent a garage
John's buying of a car caused his renting of a garage

Once again, the sentences with *cause* are stylistically awkward. Whatever the reason for this it may explain why the prepositional realisations in 2.1 are also in some way peculiar. Semantically and grammatically the realisations all seem to be quite acceptable, so their oddity must be attributed to a stylistic preference for other constructions; i.e. although the option is open to them, speakers and writers make other choices (see chapter II.B.2).

XV. SEMEMIC FORMULAE AND LOGICAL FORMULAE

On a number of occasions we have touched upon relationships between sememic formulae, i.e. in the notions of 'sememic equivalence', 'sememic implication' and 'inference', upon questions of sememic incompatibility and upon certain relationships between sememic formulae and logical formulae. All these aspects will be seen to be connected ultimately with interrelations between sememic formulae, semon networks and extralinguistic reference.

A. 'Sememic equivalence' and 'sememic implication'

1. Within the context of the general language model as outlined in chapter II, sememic formulae are but one stage in the processes of expression in language. It will be recalled from the outline that sememic formulae are derived from semon networks. For any given network of semons there are available to a speaker (writer) a number of different sememic formulae — just as for any given SF there are a number of different lexemic realisations — and since they are all derived from the same source all the SFs are synonymous, in the same way that all realisations of a single SF are synonymous. Which particular SF a speaker selects depends on factors such as his knowledge of the language (especially its semantic structure) and the social context and emotional state he finds himself in at the time.

2. If two SFs are synonymous it may be assumed that they must be derived from the same set of semons organised in a specific way as a semon network. One might say then that the SF underlying *John is a historian*, viz.

$$(\text{John})\underline{\quad\text{fe}\quad}(\text{cop, mem})\underline{\quad\text{ps}\quad}(\text{historian})$$

is synonymous with the SF underlying *John writes history*, viz.

$$(\text{John})\underline{\quad\text{agt}\quad}(\text{write})\underline{\quad\text{gl}\quad}(\text{history})$$

because the organisation of semons from which the sememe '(historian)' is derived is also the source for the sememic structure '(write)$\underline{\quad\text{gl}\quad}$(history)'. And so on for the other sememes in the two SFs.

3.   However, it is often possible to explain the synonymy of SFs at the sememic level. This was done in those cases where relationships of 'sememic equivalence' and 'sememic implication' were postulated. In chapter X, for example, we said that the SF in fig. 31 (i), namely:

$$(\text{John})\underline{\quad\text{agt}\quad}(\text{sell})\underline{\quad\text{gl}\quad}(\text{book, pl})$$
$$\underline{\quad\text{sp}\quad}(\text{quant})\underline{\quad\text{ef}\quad}(\text{non})$$

was synonymous with the SF in fig. 31 (iii):

$$(\text{John})\underline{\quad\text{agt}\quad}(\text{sell})\underline{\quad\text{gl}\quad}(\text{book, pl})$$
$$\{\varsigma(\text{non})\}\text{-----}^{\pi\quad\text{pt}}$$

If the three nodes '(John)', '(sell)' and '(book, pl)' were replaced by any other sememes the synonymy would still hold. Thus, we were able to make the generalisation that SFs of the following kinds

$$(\text{a})\underline{\quad\text{agt}\quad}(\text{b})\underline{\quad\text{gl}\quad}(\text{c})$$
$$\text{sp}$$
$$(\text{quant})$$
$$\text{ef}$$
$$(\text{non})$$

$$(\text{a})\underline{\quad\text{agt}\quad}(\text{b})\underline{\quad\text{gl}\quad}(\text{c})$$
$$\{\varsigma(\text{non})\}\text{-----}^{\pi\quad\text{pt}}$$

are always synonymous as long as the same sememes '(a)', '(b)' and '(c)' occur in both. In other words: from the semon network which is the source of any one of these SFs it is always possible to derive the other SF, i.e. the derivation of one necessarily implies the possibility of deriving the other — they are 'sememically equivalent'. Other examples of 'sememic equivalence' were found in IX.7 between SFs expressing modality, in XII.C.4 between SFs expressing a particular kind of 'similarity', and at greatest length in the chapter on causativity.

4.   In that chapter we were able to propose a form of SF which might approximate to a semon network. Fig. 46 (ii) is still a sememic formulae because all its nodes and links are sememes. However, it does illustrate how sememes might be broken down into their constituent semons: 'causative' verbs were divided into a sememe (or semon?) '(caus)' linked by 'ps' to 'noncausative' forms of the same verbs, and the links 'gl' and 'dat' were shown to be derived from 'agt', 'sp' and 'ef' in combination with the '(caus)' sememe. As a possible procedure for the discovery of semon networks, namely by the comparison of synonymous SFs, it is analogous to that adopted in the discovery of SFs themselves from synonymous lexemic strings. The procedure is, therefore, an extension of the process of componential and distributional analysis to syntagmatic relationships at the sememic level.

5.   The relationship of 'sememic implication' is a little more complex. Examples came from a number of sections, but perhaps the best were given in the chapter on co-ordination. Three basic kinds of SF were found for structures in which a verb has two 'subjects' co-ordinated in some way:

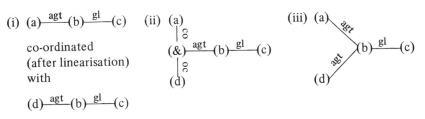

Whether all three can be derived from a given semon network depends on the kind of co-ordination being referred to. If it is 'comitative' then all three may be derived — however, only in (iii) is the nature of the co-ordination made explicit. If it is not 'comitative' but the events expressed are 'concurrent' then (i) and (ii) can be derived but not (iii) — only in (ii) is the concurrency made explicit. If neither 'comitation' nor 'concurrency' is present in the co-ordination then only (i) is possible. Finally, if the co-ordinated items are 'indivisible', e.g. *John and Bill are twins*, then only (ii) can be derived.

6. Clearly, the conditions surrounding the derivation of these SFs are complex and depend to a large extent on the sememes concerned. Ultimately, of

course, the conditions are determined by the presence or absence of certain
semons in the underlying semon network. In this respect the relationship of
'sememic implication' differs considerably from that of 'sememic equivalence'.
Whereas in the latter we are able to explain SF synonymy entirely in terms of
sememic structure, in the case of 'sememic implication' the final explanation
lies at a deeper level in the semon network. However, as a means of SF comparison for the discovery of semon networks, the relationship of 'sememic
implication' is no less important than that of 'sememic equivalence', although
naturally it must be used with rather greater caution.

B. 'Inference'

1. There is another relationship between SFs which can be explained largely
in terms of sememes with little or no recourse to underlying semons and that
is the 'inference' relationship. From a SF of the form:

$$(a) \xrightarrow{\text{agt}} (b) \xrightarrow{\text{gl}} (c)$$
$$\quad\quad\;\; \big\downarrow\!\!\xrightarrow{\text{sp}} (\text{on}) \xrightarrow{\text{ef}} (d)$$

we can 'infer' a SF of the form: $(c) \xrightarrow{\text{sp}} (\text{pos, on}) \xrightarrow{\text{ef}} (d)$. E.g. from *John put
a book on the table* can be 'inferred' *The book is on the table.*

The 'inference' is from a SF containing a dynamic sememe, '(on)', to a SF
containing a static sememe, '(pos, on)'. Similar inferential relationships probably exist between SFs with other spatial sememes, e.g. from one with '(in)'
to one with '(pos, in)', from '(pre)' to '(pos, pre)', from '(inter)' to '(pos,
inter)', etc. (cf. Quillian, 1966).

To describe these transformations at the sememic level we might propose
an 'inference' rule which would involve the elimination of the sememes '(a)'
and '(b)'.

2. Other 'inferences' involving the elimination of sememes can be illustrated.
2.1. Firstly, one in which a 'causative' link is removed. From a SF such as
that in fig. 42 (i):

$$(\text{John}) \xrightarrow{\text{fe}} (\text{caus}) \xrightarrow{\text{ps}} (\text{fall}) \xrightarrow{\text{tga}} (\text{book})$$

John made the book fall

we may infer:

$$(\text{book}) \underline{\quad \text{agt} \quad} (\text{fall})$$

The book fell

The 'inference' is from a SF in which the 'cause' of a process is specified to one in which it is not. The 'inference' rule would eliminate '$\underline{\quad \text{fe} \quad}$(cause)$\underline{\text{ps}}$' and the sememe attached to 'ef' in the source SF to produce the 'inferred' SF. The same rule could be applied to other SFs with 'causative' links, e.g. from fig. 42 (ii) to infer the SF: (boy)$\underline{\quad \text{agt} \quad}$(learn)$\underline{\quad \text{gl} \quad}$(physics); from fig. 45 (ii) (*Mary makes the milk warm*) to fig. 45 (i) (*The milk is warm*), from fig. 47 to fig. 41, etc.

2.2. Secondly, a case in which an 'instrumental' link is eliminated. From a SF such as fig. 16:

$$(\text{John}) \underline{\quad \text{agt} \quad} (\text{break}) \underline{\quad \text{gl} \quad} (\text{window})$$
$$\underline{\quad \text{sp} \quad} (\text{instr}) \underline{\quad \text{ef} \quad} (\text{hammer})$$

  (i) *John broke the window with a hammer*   or
  (ii) *The window was broken by John with a hammer*

we may infer the SF:

$$(\text{hammer}) \underline{\quad \text{agt} \quad} (\text{break}) \underline{\quad \text{gl} \quad} (\text{window})$$

  (iii) *A hammer broke the window*
  (iv) *The window was broken by a hammer* [14]

The 'inference' is from a SF in which the 'agent' is specified to one in which it is not. The 'inference' rule would eliminate '$\underline{\quad \text{sp} \quad}$(instr)$\underline{\quad \text{ef} \quad}$' and replace the sememe at the end of 'tga' by the sememe at the end of 'ef'.

3.   However, in earlier sections, we found an example of an 'inference' relationship which can only be explained in terms of semons. In XIII.A.4 we inferred from the SF:

---

[14] It may be argued, with some justification (Fillmore, 1968), that since *hammer* is 'non-agentive' the construction is ergative. However, if this view were taken semo-lexemic rules would have to be devised in order to deal with what is apparently the 'object' of an ergative verb (*window* in (iii)). Furthermore, the derivation from a transitive construction accounts more easily for the preposition *by* followed by an 'instrument' (in (iv)) which may occur instead of the usual *with* (as in (ii)).

$$(\text{John}) \xrightarrow{\text{sp}} (\text{become}) \xrightarrow{\text{ef}} (\text{rich})$$

the SF: $(\text{John}) \xrightarrow{\text{sp}} (\text{mod}_2) \xrightarrow{\text{ef}} (\text{rich})$

by postulating the elimination of a semon '⟨inceptive⟩' from the sememe '(become)'.

4.   Ultimately, of course, any 'inference' explicable in terms of sememes can always be explained in terms of semons — just as 'sememic equivalence' can be explained by either sememes or semons. Therefore, the operation of any 'inference' rule through the elimination of sememes from a SF can be equally well described as an operation eliminating semons from a network.

Strictly speaking the 'inference' relationship is not between SFs or even semon networks but between the events to which they refer. This is evident from the temporal element present in the relationship: the reference of an 'inferred' SF succeeds in time the reference of its source SF. [15] Thus, *The book is on the table* is an event coming after *John puts the book on the table*. Similarly: after *John dropped the book, The book fell*; and: after *John became rich, John was rich*. Although the temporal element is perhaps rather weak — it seems to be quite absent in *John broke the window with a hammer* and *A hammer broke the window* — it is sufficient reason for not regarding the 'inference' relationship as non-temporal and for avoiding analogies with logical operations of 'inference' or 'deduction' (since logic is by convention (and definition?) non-temporal).

C. Semantic anomaly and logic

On the other hand we have found that there are analogies which can be made between some sememic structures and certain formulae of logic.

1.   The copula-construction showed a clear parallel: the threefold distinction made by logicians between equivalence, class-membership and class-inclusion was also found in the SFs underlying copula sentences (chapter XII). Similarly, in chapter VII.A.4 we found that the logical distinction between

---

[15] Because of this the relationship might in many cases be more aptly called 'expectancy' or 'presupposition' (Lyons, 1968: 469).

'A & (B v C)' and '(A & B) v C' is present also in the SFs underlying sentences containing two co-ordinators *and* and *or*.

As a further example, the different treatment of SF-negation and sememe-negation has parallels in logic. In a proposition '$(x)(Fx)$' either the whole may be negated '$\sim(x)(Fx)$' or only one element '$(x)(\sim Fx)$'. In a SF '(a)———^{agt}(b)———^{gl}(c)' either the whole may be negated:

$$(a) \xrightarrow{\text{agt}} (b) \xrightarrow{\text{gl}} (c)$$
$$\vdots \pi$$
$$\{\varsigma(\text{non})\}$$

or only one element (a)———^{agt}(b)———^{gl}(c)———^{sp}(quant)———^{ef}(non).

2. It should not be surprising that such parallelisms can be found. The formulae of logic are used to clarify the processes of valid argument and deductive thinking. In so far as part of natural language is used in argumentation and deduction it follows that much of the work in logical analysis has been concerned with the analysis of some aspects of the semantics of sentences. The analogies with sememic formulae which we have encountered have been in the areas of negation, co-ordination, class-membership, class-inclusion and equivalence — all areas in which logicians have been long active and where their formulations are solidly based. It is probable that further parallelisms between sememic formulae and logical propositions will be found in other areas in which logicians have been very active such as quantification and modality.

3. At a rather more abstract level, a further parallel between SFs and logical formulae can be demonstrated by considering the status of sentences which are grammatically correct (well-formed) but semantically anomalous.

Some well-known examples, first introduced into the literature of linguistics by Chomsky (1957), are:

(i) *Sincerity admires John*
(ii) *John frightens sincerity*
(iii) *Colourless green ideas sleep furiously*

The grammaticality of these sentences was shown by Chomsky within the framework of transformational grammar. In my model, their grammaticality can be demonstrated by the fact that there are semolexemic rules available for their generation from the SFs:

Fig. 49 (i) $(\text{sincerity}) \xrightarrow{\text{agt}} (\text{admire}) \xrightarrow{\text{gl}} (\text{John})$

(ii) $(\text{John}) \xrightarrow{\text{agt}} (\text{frighten}) \xrightarrow{\text{gl}} (\text{sincerity})$

(iii) $(\text{ideas}) \xrightarrow{\text{agt}} (\text{sleep}) \xrightarrow{\text{sp}} (\text{mod}_4) \xrightarrow{\text{ef}} (\text{fury})$

$\Big|_{\text{sp}} \xrightarrow{\text{sp}} (\text{mod}_1) \xrightarrow{\text{ef}} (\text{green})$

(poss)

$\Big|_{\text{ef}}$

$(\text{colour}) \xrightarrow{\text{sp}} (\text{quant}) \xrightarrow{\text{ef}} (\text{non})$

3.1. There are two possible explanations for the semantic anomaly of these SFs and their realisations: 'sememic incompatibility' and 'referential implausibility' (see XI.E.1). According to the first, the sememe '(admire)' in 49 (i) is incompatible with '(sincerity)' because '(admire)' may be linked by 'tga' only to sememes containing the semon '⟨animate⟩', and '(sincerity)' does not contain this semon. Similarly, in 49 (ii) '(frighten)' is incompatible with '(sincerity)' because the sememe linked to it by 'gl' must contain the semon '⟨animate⟩'. (Compare the acceptability of *John admires sincerity* and *Sincerity frightens John*). In the case of 49 (iii), the SF underlying *Colourless green ideas sleep furiously*, the sememe '(green)' is incompatible with the sememic structure '(colour) $\xrightarrow{\text{sp}}$ (quant) $\xrightarrow{\text{ef}}$ (non)' since they both modify the same node, '(ideas)'. Also, '(fury)' is incompatible '(sleep)' when it is linked to it by 'sp–ef'.

3.2. In the explanation by 'referential implausibility', the semantic anomalies of our examples are attributed simply to the unlikelihood, even impossibility, that in the 'real world' (as perceived and conceived by members of the language community) such referents can be found. Thus, it is difficult to conceive of any referent about which it can be said to be both *colourless* and *green*. Similarly it is difficult to believe that *ideas* can be *green* and *sleep furious* or that *sincerity* is capable of admiration or of being frightened.

3.3. The 'referential implausibility' explanation, though vague, is more flexible than that of 'sememic incompatibility'. Although it is difficult to attach any meaning (reference) to them, it is undoubtedly true that anomalous sentences can in fact be expressed. Furthermore, it is possible to express contradictions *Some bachelors are married, Her green dress is red*, etc. From this we must conclude that the language model must permit the formulation of the SFs underlying such sentences. It should not forbid their formation by any kind of 'incompatibility rule'. [16] In this way, the model does not exclude any metaphor or poetic image on the grounds that by a 'cognitive' reading some of its elements may appear to be incompatible.

The concept of 'sememic incompatibility' has its place in a semantic theory, as Katz (1966) and others have shown, to explain why and how sentences are tautologous, analytic, synthetic, anomalous, etc. In these 'logical' or 'cognitive' analyses sememic compatibility and incompatibility must play an important role. But, although the semantic anomaly of a SF can be largely explained at the sememic level in terms of 'sememic incompatibility' the final arbiter must be its 'referential implausibility' and this rests ultimately on the social and cultural condition of the language community. [17]

4. We turn now to logical propositions. An argument can be well-formed (syntactically correct) but nonsensical. For example, the syllogism:

> Napoleon was a German
>
> All Germans are short and dark-haired
>
> Therefore, Napoleon was short and dark-haired

derives a true conclusion from false premises using the formula: $Fa, (x)(Fx \rightarrow Gx) \vdash Ga$. The validity of the formula does not depend on the truth of the propositions *Napoleon was a German* or *All Germans are short and dark-haired* but only on its logical well-formedness.

If we assert that *Some bachelors are married* is contradictory (i.e. false) we imply that *bachelors* are by definition *unmarried*. From the proposition '$(x)(Bx \rightarrow \sim Mx)$' (*All bachelors are unmarried*) we cannot derive by any valid logical argument '$(\exists x)(Bx \& Mx)$' (*Some bachelors are married*). Similarly, in an explanation by 'sememic incompatibility': if the sememe '(bachelor)' contains all the semons present in the sememic structure for *unmarried* then a sentence such as *Some bachelors are married* is anomalous.

Both demonstrations of the contradiction in the sentence depend on the definition of *bachelor*. If the definition is accepted by the language commu-

---

[16] Allowing the co-occurrence of incompatible sememes in SFs does not necessarily imply that they are realisable. The realisation of any SF depends in the last resort on the existence of a graphic form for a given lexeme plus category group − numerous examples have illustrated this point, e.g. in III.C.8 we found that 'Adv(computer)' has no graphemic realisation. On the other hand, English is remarkably flexible in this respect − recall Shakespeare's "But me no buts".

[17] 'Referential implausibility' thus explains why phrases once considered anomalous and without reference are now quite acceptable, e.g. as a result of cultural or technological change: would not an eighteenth century speaker have considered the elements in *nuclear energy* and *atomic bomb* as incompatible?

nity as 'referentially' true then the semantic anomaly of *Some bachelors are* *married* is also universally accepted. However, if the definition does not stand up to comparison with 'reality' then the sentence is no longer contradictory. Similarly with a proposition such as *Napoleon was a German:* only an examination of the facts can show that the proposition is false.

5.   Neither logical propositions nor sememic formulae are inherently true or false; they are merely vehicles for the expression (in the case of logic, in abstract terms) of external events, percepts and concepts as these are seen by speakers or observers. Relationships between sememic formulae, such as 'sememic equivalence', 'sememic implication' and 'inference', and examination of SFs for 'sememic incompatibility' are based upon definitions (analysed into semons) of vocabulary which are accepted by the community at large (chapter II). The characteristics attributed to referents and incorporated into the definitions of the sememes which express them are by no means necessarily 'real' or 'true' [18] — all that matters is that the community accepts them for the purposes of communication (or rather, to be precise, for the purposes of communicating 'cognitive experiences'). In the case of logic, definitions of terms are accepted for the purposes of argument and for no other motive. Therefore, a logical proposition is not necessarily 'referentially' true. Of course, logicians usually select definitions which are acceptable in the context in which they are working. When dealing with mathematics, they choose definitions acceptable to mathematicians. When dealing with natural language they try to find definitions acceptable to the majority of the users of the language. However, because of the imprecision and doubtfulness of many semantic analyses logicians have been forced to conduct their own analyses of language in those areas where they have most interest. In doing this they have made valuable contributions to the semantics of natural language (cf. section 2 above).

   In brief, a well-formed logical formula or a well-formed sememic formula (e.g. one without incompatible sememes) is not necessarily true and an ill-formed logical formula or an ill-formed sememic formula is not necessarily false. In logic, as in linguistics, the distinction between 'sense' and 'reference' must be kept constantly in mind.

---

[18] What a language community considers 'true' at one time it may later consider 'false'. Thus, whereas once *Whales are fish* would have been universally accepted as a true statement this is now no longer so.

XVI. CONCLUSION

The basic aim of this monograph has been to present the capacity of the model to deal with a wide variety of linguistic structures. Although it is hoped that the analyses of English represent a reasonable consensus in most cases I make no claim to their accuracy in all instances. Indeed I am well aware that the analyses I have provided are frequently inadequate. Furthermore I do not claim to have covered more than a small part of the various forms of English structures. In the first place the presentation has been limited to declarative forms: interrogatives and imperatives have been ignored. Nothing has been said about 'sequence of tenses'. Chapter IX dealt with the modification of verbs in the 'pivotal' position but not with verb modification in subordinate clauses. The problems of modals and comparative constructions have been skirted. The generic *the* needs more extensive treatment and no account has been made of the deictic *the* or indeed of deixis in general. Verb forms such as *it rains* and *it snows*, called by Tesnière 'avalent', have not been treated: it is fairly obvious that they must be derived from a SF with no 'agt' or 'gl' links from the sememes '(rain)' and '(snow)' although the exact formulation of the semolexemic rules might cause difficulties.

Despite these omissions and many others which will occur to any reader it is believed that the flexibility of the model has been demonstrated and that it is capable of coping with most other structures. Naturally, in many cases additions and alterations will have to be introduced to deal with the more complex ones, and some of these alterations may be far-reaching in their consequences.

This monograph will have achieved its purpose if it stimulates further investigation into the semantic properties of syntactic structures. Hopefully, it has shown how these properties can be represented and has provided a basis for the analysis of deeper semantic problems — problems which are of concern not only to linguists but also to logicians and workers in other fields dealing with problems of communication and the transfer of information by language.

XVII. REFERENCES

Abraham, S. and F.Kiefer (1966) *A theory of structural semantics.* (Janua Linguarum, Series Minor, 49.) The Hague, Mouton.

Anderson, J. (1969) 'Adjectives, datives and ergativisation'. *Foundations of Language* 5, 301–323.

Antal, L. (1963) *Questions of meaning.* (Janua Linguarum, Series Minor, 27.) The Hague, Mouton.

Baldinger, K. (1966) 'Sémantique et structure conceptuelle'. *Cahiers de Lexicologie* 8, 3–46.

Bar-Hillel, Y. (1964) *Language and information.* Reading, Mass., Addison-Wesley.

Bickerton, D. (1969) 'The linguistic validity of verb-nominalising transformations'. *Lingua* 22, 47–62.

Boyd, J. and J.P.Thorne (1969) 'The semantics of modal verbs'. *J. of Linguistics* 5, 57–74.

Chomsky, N. (1957) *Syntactic structures.* (Janua Linguarum, Series Minor, 4.) The Hague, Mouton.

Chomsky, N. (1965) *Aspects of the theory of syntax.* Cambridge, Mass., M.I.T. Press.

Cros, R.C., J.C.Gardin and F.Levy (1964) *L'automatisation des recherches documentaires: un modèle général 《Le Syntol》.* Paris, Gauthiers-Villars.

Daneš, F. (1968) 'Some thoughts on the semantic structure of the sentence'. *Lingua* 21, 55–69.

Dik, S.C. (1968a) *Co-ordination: its implications for the theory of general linguistics.* Amsterdam, North-Holland.

Dik, S.C. (1968b) 'Referential identity'. *Lingua* 21, 70–97.

Fillmore, C.J. (1966) 'A proposal concerning English prepositions'. *Proceedings of the 17th Annual Round Table Meeting on Linguistics and Language Studies, Georgetown Univ.,* 19–33.

Fillmore, C.J. (1968) 'The case for case' In: Bach, E. and R.T.Harms (eds.), *Universals in linguistic theory,* 1–88. New York, Holt, Rinehart and Winston.

Gleason, H.A. (1964) 'The organization of language: a stratificational view'. *Report of the 15th Annual (1st International) Round Table Meeting on Linguistics and Language Studies, Georgetown Univ.,* 75–95.

Greenberg, J.H. (1966) 'Language universals'. In: Sebeok, T.A. (ed.), *Current trends in linguistics 3: theoretical foundations,* 61–112, The Hague, Mouton.

Halliday, M.A.K. (1967–68) 'Notes on transitivity and theme in English'. *J. of Linguistics* 3, 37–81, 199–244; 4, 179–216.

Hill, A.A. (1966) 'A re-examination of the English articles'. *Proceedings of the 17th Annual Round Table Meeting on Linguistics and Language Studies, Georgetown Univ.,* 217–31.

Hjelmslev, L. (1961) *Prolegomena to a theory of language.* Transl. by F.J.Whitfield. Rev. ed. Madison, Univ. of Wisconsin Press.

Hockett, C.F. (1967) *Language, mathematics, and linguistics.* (Janua Linguarum, Series Minor, 60.) The Hague, Mouton.

Ikegami, Y. (1967) 'Structural semantics: a survey and problems'. *Linguistics* 33, 49–67.

Jackendoff, R.S. (1968) 'Quantifiers in English'. *Foundations of Language* 4, 422–42.

Jackendoff, R.S. (1969) 'An interpretive theory of negation'. *Foundations of Language* 5, 218–241.

Katz, J.J. (1966) *Philosophy of language.* New York, Harper and Row.

Katz, J.J. and J.A.Fodor (1963) 'The structure of a semantic theory'. *Language* 39, 170–210.

Katz, J.J. and P.M.Postal (1964) *An integrated theory of linguistic descriptions.* Cambridge, Mass., M.I.T. Press.

Klima, E.S. (1964) 'Negation in English'. In: Fodor, J.A. and J.J.Katz (eds.), *The structure of language: readings in the philosophy of language,* 246–323. Englewood Cliffs, N.Y., Prentice-Hall.

Lamb, S.M. (1964) 'The sememic approach to structural semantics'. *American Anthropologist* 66, No. 3, Pt. 2, 57–78.

Lamb, S.M. (1966) *Outline of stratificational grammar.* Washington, Georgetown Univ. Press.

Leech, G.N. (1969) *Towards a semantic description of English.* London, Longmans.

Lees, R.B. (1960) 'The grammar of English nominalizations'. *International Journal of American Linguistics* 26, No. 3, Pt. 2.

Lyons, J. (1963) *Structural semantics.* (Publications of the Philological Society, 20.) Oxford, Blackwell.

Lyons, J. (1968) *Introduction to theoretical linguistics,* Cambridge, Univ. Press.

Minsky, M. (1968) ed: *Semantic information processing.* Cambridge, Mass., M.I.T. Press.

Morris, C.W. (1938) 'Foundations of the theory of signs'. *International Encyclopedia of Unified Science,* Vol. 1, No. 2. Chicago, Univ. of Chicago Press.

Quillian, M.R. (1966) *Semantic memory.* (Air Force Cambridge Research Laboratories, AFCRL-66-189) Cambridge, Mass., Bolt, Beranek and Newman. (Also, a shortened version in Minsky, 1968.)

Quine, W.V. (1960) *Word and object,* Cambridge, Mass., M.I.T. Press.

Robbins, B.L. (1968) *The definite article in English transformations.* (Papers on Formal Linguistics, 4.) The Hague, Mouton.

Russell, B.A.W. (1940) *An inquiry into meaning and truth.* London, Allen and Unwin.

Salton, G. (1968) *Automatic information organization and retrieval.* New York, McGraw-Hill.

Šaumjan, S.K. (1965) 'Outline of the applicational generative model for the description of language'. *Foundations of Language* 1, 189–222.

Schwartz, A. (1968) 'Derivative functions in syntax'. *Language* 44, 747–783.

Sgall, P. (1966) 'Zur Frage der Ebenen im Sprachsystem'. *Travaux Linguistiques de Prague* 1, 94–106.

Simmons, R.F. (1965) 'Answering English questions by computer: a survey'. *Communications of the Association for Computing Machinery* 8, 53–70.

Sparck-Jones, K. (1965) 'Experiments in semantic classification'. *Mechanical Translation* 8, 97–112.

Tesnière, L. (1959) *Eléments de syntaxe structurale*. Paris, Klincksieck.

Vater, H. (1963) *Das System der Artikelformen im gegenwärtigen Deutsch*. Tübingen, Niemeyer.

Vendler, Z. (1968) *Adjectives and nominalizations*. (Papers on Formal Linguistics, 5.) The Hague, Mouton.

Weinreich, U. (1966) 'Explorations in semantic theory'. In: Sebeok, T.A. (ed.) *Current trends in linguistics 3: theoretical foundations*, 395–477. The Hague, Mouton.

White, J.H. (1964) 'The methodology of sememic analysis with special application to the English preposition'. *Mechanical Translation* 8, 15–31.

Yngve, V.H. (1960) 'A model and a hypothesis for language structure'. *Proceedings of the American Philosophical Society* 104, 444–67.

APPENDIX A: LEXICAL CATEGORIES

(a) Terminal categories:

Adj $\overline{\text{Adj}}$ Adv Conj N $\overline{\text{N}}$ Nab Nag Ngen Nv Oblpron
Pr Pron Prov Rfpron V Verg Vergnt Vger Vinf Vnt
Vprp Vpp Wh ʃ

(b) Non-terminal categories:

A Ap B G J Jnt K L Vfor Vof Vrel W_n X X_n
Y Y_n Yger Ynt Z_n

APPENDIX B: SEMOLEXEMIC RULES

Note: C   = any 'lexical' category, i.e. any included in appendix A,
       K   = any 'non-lexical' category,
      (x) = any sememe,
      (...) = any lexemic string enclosed in brackets.

(1) (x) : $C \rightarrow C(x)$

(2) $]$: $K(... \rightarrow K(...)$

(3) $b(x)$: $C(x) \rightarrow C(x)$

(4) $b(x)$: $C(y) \rightarrow C(y) + C_x(\Delta)$

(5) (mod_n): $C_n \rightarrow C_n(mod_n)$

(6)   decl : $S \rightarrow NPk$

(7)   decl : $S \rightarrow NPs$

(8)   decl : $S \rightarrow Pron(it) + V(be) + AJ$

(10) $[$: $Adj_n \rightarrow AJ(Adj_n$

(11) $[$: $Adv \rightarrow ADV(Adv$

(12) $[$: $AJ \rightarrow AJ(Adj$

(13) $[$: $ADV \rightarrow ADV(Adv$

(14) $[$: $N^0 \rightarrow NPw(N^0$

(15) $[$: $N^1 \rightarrow NPw(N^1$

(16) $[$: $N^2 \rightarrow NPw(N^2$

(17)	[	:	$Ngen \rightarrow NPgen(Ngen$
(18)	[	:	$NP \rightarrow NP(N^0$
(19)	[	:	$NPgen \rightarrow NPgen(Ngen$
(20)	[	:	$NP[gen] \rightarrow NP[gen](N[gen]^0$
(21)	[	:	$NP[obl] \rightarrow NP[obl](N[obl]^0$
(22)	[	:	$NPc \rightarrow NPc(Vger$
(23)	[	:	$NPe \rightarrow NPe(Vfor$
(24)	[	:	$NPf \rightarrow NPf(Vinf^1$
(25)	[	:	$NPh \rightarrow NPh(Vof$
(26)	[	:	$NPi \rightarrow NP(Vnt^1$
(27)	[	:	$NPj \rightarrow NP(Vnt^2$
(28)	[	:	$NPk \rightarrow NPk(W_0$
(29)	[	:	$NPp \rightarrow NPp(Vrel$
(30)	[	:	$NPs \rightarrow NP(N^0$
(31)	[	:	$NPs \rightarrow NPc(Vger$
(32)	[	:	$NPs \rightarrow NPe(Vfor$
(33)	[	:	$NPs \rightarrow NPf(Vinf^1$
(34)	[	:	$NPs \rightarrow NPr(Conj(that) + Vrel$
(35)	[	:	$NPt \rightarrow NP(N^0$
(36)	[	:	$NPt \rightarrow NPq(Vinf^0$
(37)	[	:	$NPt \rightarrow NPr(Conj(that) + Vrel$
(40)	ana	:	$N^0(pro) \rightarrow Pron$
(41)	ana	:	$N^0(pro) \rightarrow D(the) + N^0$
(42)	ana	:	$N[obl]^0(pro) \rightarrow Oblpron$
(43)	ana	:	$V(pro) \rightarrow Prov$
(45)	anp	:	$N^0(pro) \rightarrow Rfpron$
(50)	agt	:	$NP(...) \rightarrow NP(...) + V$
(51)	agt	:	$NP(...) \rightarrow NP(...) + V(be) + Nag$
(52)	agt	:	$NP(...) \rightarrow NP(...) + P + Pr(at) + Vger$
(53)	agt	:	$NPw(...) \rightarrow NP(...) + Wh(s) + V$

(54) agt : $NPw(...) \rightarrow NP(...) + Pr(by) + Wh(s) + Vrel$

(55) agt : $NPw(...) \rightarrow Vprp^1 + NP(...)$

(60) co : $N^0(x) \rightarrow N^0(x) + L$

(61) co : $NP(...) \rightarrow NP(...) + L$

(62) co : $V(x) \rightarrow V(x) + L$

(65) dat : $Nv^0(x) \rightarrow Nv^3(x) + Pr(to) + NP[obl]$

(66) dat : $Nv^1(x) \rightarrow Nv^3(x) + Pr(to) + NP[obl]$

(67) dat : $Nv^2(\Delta) \rightarrow Nv^2(\Delta) + Pr(to) + NP[obl]$

(68) dat : $Nv^3(\Delta) \rightarrow Nv^3(\Delta) + Pr(to) + NP[obl]$

(69) dat : $V(x) \rightarrow V(x) + NP[obl]$

(70) dat : $V(\Delta) \rightarrow V(\Delta) + Pr(to) + NP[obl]$

(71) dat : $Vinf^0(x) \rightarrow NP[obl] + Vinf(be) + Vpp^2(x)$

(72) dat : $Vinf^0(\Delta) \rightarrow Vinf^0(\Delta) + Pr(to) + NP[obl]$

(73) dat : $Vnt^0(x) \rightarrow Vnt^0(x) + NP[obl]$

(74) dat : $Vnt^0(\Delta) \rightarrow Vnt^0(\Delta) + Pr(to) + NP[obl]$

(75) dat : $Vnt^1(x) \rightarrow NP[obl] + Vpp^2(x)$

(76) dat : $Vpp^0(x) \rightarrow Vpp^0(x) + Pr(to) + NP[obl]$

(77) dat : $Vpp^0(\Delta) \rightarrow Vpp^0(\Delta) + Pr(to) + NP[obl]$

(78) dat : $Vrel(x) \rightarrow NP + V(be) + Vpp^2(x)$

(80) ef : $Ap(cop) \rightarrow N^0$

(81) ef : $Ap(mod_n) \rightarrow Comma + Adj_n + Comma$

(82) ef : $J(cop, diff, sb) \rightarrow V(be) + Adj(different) + Pr(from) + N^0$

(83) ef : $J(cop, sim, sb) \rightarrow V(be) + Pr(like) + N^0$

(84) ef : $K(about) \rightarrow Pr(about) + N^0$

(85) ef : $K(about) \rightarrow Pr(on) + N^0$

(86) ef : $K(diff) \rightarrow Adj(different) + Pr(from) + Pron(that) + Pr(of) + N^0$

(87) ef : $K(diff, sb) \rightarrow Adj(different) + Pr(from) + N^0$

(88) ef : $K(orig) \rightarrow Pr(of) + N^0$

(89)   ef   : $K(\text{orig}) \rightarrow Vpp(\text{make}) + Pr(\text{of}) + N^0$

(90)   ef   : $K(\text{pos, in}) \rightarrow Pr(\text{in}) + N^0$

(91)   ef   : $K(\text{pos, on}) \rightarrow Pr(\text{on}) + N^0$

(92)   ef   : $K(\text{pos, pre}) \rightarrow Pr(\text{in front of}) + N^0$

(93)   ef   : $K(\text{pos, sub}) \rightarrow Pr(\text{under}) + N^0$

(94)   ef   : $K(\text{posh}) \rightarrow Pr(\text{with}) + N(\text{shape}) + Pr(\text{of}) + N^0$

(95)   ef   : $K(\text{posq}) \rightarrow Pr(\text{with}) + Adj(\text{much}) + N^0$

(96)   ef   : $K(\text{poss}) \rightarrow Pr(\text{with}) + N^0$

(97)   ef   : $K(\text{sim}) \rightarrow Pr(\text{like}) + Ngen$

(98)   ef   : $K(\text{sim}) \rightarrow Pr(\text{like}) + Pron(\text{that}) + Pr(\text{of}) + N^0$

(99)   ef   : $K(\text{sim, sb}) \rightarrow Pr(\text{like}) + N^0$

(100) ef   : $NPk(\ldots) \rightarrow NP(\ldots) + NPp$

(101) ef   : $Vnt^2(\text{mod}_n) \rightarrow Adj_n + Jnt(\text{mod}_n)$

(102) ef   : $W_n(\text{mod}_n) \rightarrow Pr(\text{with}) + N^0$

(103) ef   : $W_0(\text{ab}) \rightarrow Pr(\text{from}) + N^0$

(104) ef   : $W_0(\text{ad}) \rightarrow Pr(\text{to}) + N^0$

(105) ef   : $W_0(\text{ad}) \rightarrow Pr(\text{until}) + N^0$

(106) ef   : $W_0(\text{although}) \rightarrow Conj(\text{although}) + NPp$

(107) ef   : $W_0(\text{although}) \rightarrow Pr(\text{in spite of}) + NPc$

(108) ef   : $W_0(\text{ante}) \rightarrow Conj(\text{before}) + NPp$

(109) ef   : $W_0(\text{ante}) \rightarrow Pr(\text{before}) + N^0$

(110) ef   : $W_0(\text{bene}) \rightarrow Pr(\text{for}) + N^0$

(111) ef   : $W_0(\text{caus}) \rightarrow Conj(\text{because}) + NPp$

(112) ef   : $W_0(\text{caus}) \rightarrow Pr(\text{because of}) + N^0$

(113) ef   : $W_0(\text{diff}) \rightarrow Adv(\text{different}) + Pr(\text{from}) + N^0$

(114) ef   : $W_0(\text{from}) \rightarrow Pr(\text{out of}) + N^0$

(115) ef   : $W_0(\text{instr}) \rightarrow Pr(\text{with}) + N^0$

(116) ef   : $W_0(\text{inter}) \rightarrow Pr(\text{between}) + N^0$

(117) ef   : $W_0(\text{on}) \rightarrow Pr(\text{onto}) + N^0$

(118) ef   : $W_0(\text{pos, on}) \rightarrow Pr(\text{on}) + N^0$

(119) ef : $W_0(\text{pre}) \rightarrow \text{Pr(in front of)} + N^0$

(120) ef : $W_0(\text{sim}) \rightarrow \text{Pr(like)} + N^0$

(121) ef : $W_0(\text{sub}) \rightarrow \text{Pr(under)} + N^0$

(122) ef : $W_0(\text{temp}) \rightarrow \text{Conj(while)} + \text{NPp}$

(123) ef : $W_0(\text{temp}) \rightarrow \text{Pr(on)} + N_\theta^0$

(124) ef : $X(\text{mod}_n) \rightarrow \text{Adj}_n$

(125) ef : $X_n(\text{mod}_n) \rightarrow \text{Adj}_n$

(126) ef : $X(\text{about}) \rightarrow N^1$

(127) ef : $X(\text{num}) \rightarrow \text{Adj}$

(128) ef : $X(\text{orig}) \rightarrow \text{Adj}$

(129) ef : $X(\text{pos, from}) \rightarrow \text{Adj}$

(130) ef : $X(\text{pos, in}) \rightarrow \text{Adj}$

(131) ef : $X(\text{posh}) \rightarrow \text{Adj}$

(132) ef : $X(\text{posq}) \rightarrow \text{Adj}$

(133) ef : $X(\text{poss}) \rightarrow \text{Adj}$

(134) ef : $X(\text{quant}) \rightarrow \text{Adj}$

(135) ef : $X(\text{sim}) \rightarrow \text{Adj}$

(136) ef : $X(\text{sim, sb}) \rightarrow \text{Adj}$

(138) ef : $Y(\text{mod}_n) \rightarrow V(\text{be}) + \text{Adj}_n$

(139) ef : $Y_n(\text{mod}_n) \rightarrow V(\text{be}) + \text{Adj}_n$

(140) ef : $Y(\text{about}) \rightarrow V(\text{be}) + \text{Pr(about)} + N^0$

(141) ef : $Y(\text{ante}) \rightarrow V(\text{be}) + \text{Vpp(follow)} + \text{Pr(by)} + N^0$

(142) ef : $Y(\text{ante}) \rightarrow V(\text{precede}) + N^0$

(143) ef : $Y(\text{caus}) \rightarrow V(\text{be}) + \text{Vpp(cause)} + \text{Pr(by)} + N^0$

(144) ef : $Y(\text{cop}) \rightarrow V(\text{be}) + N^0$

(145) ef : $Y(\text{diff}) \rightarrow V(\text{be}) + \text{Adj(different)} + \text{Pr(from)}$
$+ \text{Pron(that)} + \text{Pr(of)} + N^0$

(146) ef : $Y(\text{diff, sb}) \rightarrow V(\text{be}) + \text{Adj(different)}$
$+ \text{Pr(from)} + N^0$

(147) ef : $Y(\text{num}) \rightarrow V(\text{be}) + \text{Adj} + \text{Pr(in)} + N(\text{number})$

(148)	ef	:	$Y(\text{orig}) \rightarrow V(\text{be}) + \text{Adj}$
(149)	ef	:	$Y(\text{orig}) \rightarrow V(\text{be}) + V\text{pp}(\text{make}) + Pr(\text{of}) + N^0$
(150)	ef	:	$Y(\text{pos, in}) \rightarrow V(\text{be}) + Pr(\text{in}) + N^0$
(151)	ef	:	$Y(\text{pos, on}) \rightarrow V(\text{be}) + Pr(\text{on}) + N^0$
(152)	ef	:	$Y(\text{pos, pre}) \rightarrow V(\text{be}) + Pr(\text{in front of}) + N^0$
(153)	ef	:	$Y(\text{pos, sub}) \rightarrow V(\text{be}) + Pr(\text{under}) + N^0$
(154)	ef	:	$Y(\text{posh}) \rightarrow V(\text{be}) + \text{Adj}$
(155)	ef	:	$Y(\text{posh}) \rightarrow V(\text{have}) + N(\text{shape}) + Pr(\text{of}) + N^0$
(156)	ef	:	$Y(\text{posq}) \rightarrow V(\text{be}) + \text{Adj}$
(157)	ef	:	$Y(\text{posq}) \rightarrow V(\text{have}) + \text{Adj}(\text{much}) + N^0$
(158)	ef	:	$Y(\text{poss}) \rightarrow V(\text{be}) + \text{Adj}$
(159)	ef	:	$Y(\text{poss}) \rightarrow V(\text{have}) + N^0$
(160)	ef	:	$Y(\text{sim}) \rightarrow V(\text{be}) + \text{Adj}$
(161)	ef	:	$Y(\text{sim}) \rightarrow V(\text{be}) + Pr(\text{like}) + N\text{gen}$
(162)	ef	:	$Y(\text{sim}) \rightarrow V(\text{be}) + Pr(\text{like}) + \text{Pron}(\text{that})$ $+ Pr(\text{of}) + N^0$
(163)	ef	:	$Y(\text{sim, sb}) \rightarrow V(\text{be}) + \text{Adj}$
(164)	ef	:	$Y(\text{sim, sb}) \rightarrow V(\text{be}) + Pr(\text{like}) + N^0$
(165)	ef	:	$Y\text{ger}(\text{mod}_n) \rightarrow V\text{ger}(\text{be}) + \text{Adj}_n$
(166)	ef	:	$Y\text{nt}(\text{mod}_n) \rightarrow \text{Adj}_n$
(167)	ef	:	$Z_n(\text{mod}_n) \rightarrow \text{Adv}_n$
(168)	ef	:	$Z_0(\text{quant}) \rightarrow \text{Adv}$
(169)	ef	:	$Z_8(\text{quant}) \rightarrow \zeta$
(170)	ef	:	$Z_0(\text{sim}) \rightarrow \text{Adv}$
(180)	fe	:	$\text{AJ}(...) \rightarrow \text{AJ}(...) + G$
(181)	fe	:	$N^0(x) \rightarrow A + N^0(x)$
(182)	fe	:	$N^0(x) \rightarrow N^0(x) + B$
(183)	fe	:	$N^0(x) \rightarrow N^0(x) + Wh(s) + J$
(184)	fe	:	$N^0(x) \rightarrow N^0(x) + \text{Comma} + \text{Ap} + \text{Comma}$
(185)	fe	:	$\text{Nab}^0(x) \rightarrow A + \text{Nab}^0(x)$

$$(186) \quad \text{fe} \quad : \quad \text{Nab}^0(x) \to \text{Nab}^0(x) + \text{B}$$

$$(187) \quad \text{fe} \quad : \quad \text{NP}(...) \to \text{NP}(...) + \text{J}$$

$$(188) \quad \text{fe} \quad : \quad \text{NP}_w(...) \to \text{NP}_w(...) + \text{B}$$

$$(189) \quad \text{fe} \quad : \quad \text{V}(\Delta) \to \text{V}(\Delta) + \text{W}_0$$

$$(190) \quad \text{gl} \quad : \quad \text{Nag}(x) \to \text{Nag}(x) + \text{Pr}(\text{of}) + \text{NP}$$

$$(191) \quad \text{gl} \quad : \quad \text{Nag}(x) \to \text{NP}[\text{gen}] + \text{Nag}(x)$$

$$(192) \quad \text{gl} \quad : \quad \text{Nv}^0(x) \to \text{Nv}^2(x) + \text{Pr}(\text{of}) + \text{NP}$$

$$(193) \quad \text{gl} \quad : \quad \text{Nv}^0(x) \to \text{NP}[\text{gen}] + \text{Nv}^2(x)$$

$$(194) \quad \text{gl} \quad : \quad \text{Nv}^1(x) \to \text{Nv}^2(x) + \text{Pr}(\text{of}) + \text{NP}$$

$$(195) \quad \text{gl} \quad : \quad \text{Nv}^1(x) \to \text{NP}[\text{gen}] + \text{Nv}^2(x)$$

$$(196) \quad \text{gl} \quad : \quad \text{Nv}^2(x) \to \text{Nv}^2(x) + \text{Pr}(\text{of}) + \text{NP}$$

$$(197) \quad \text{gl} \quad : \quad \text{Nv}^2(x) \to \text{NP}[\text{gen}] + \text{Nv}^2(x)$$

$$(198) \quad \text{gl} \quad : \quad \text{Nv}^3(\Delta) \to \text{Nv}^2(\Delta) + \text{Pr}(\text{of}) + \text{NP}$$

$$(199) \quad \text{gl} \quad : \quad \text{V}(x) \to \text{V}(x) + \text{NPt}$$

$$(200) \quad \text{gl} \quad : \quad \text{V}(\Delta) \to \text{V}(\Delta) + \text{NPt}$$

$$(201) \quad \text{gl} \quad : \quad \text{Vfor}(x) \to \text{Pr}(\text{for}) + \text{NP}[\text{obl}] + \text{Vinf}(\text{be}) + \text{Vpp}^0(x)$$

$$(202) \quad \text{gl} \quad : \quad \text{Vger}(x) \to \text{Vger}(x) + \text{NPt}$$

$$(203) \quad \text{gl} \quad : \quad \text{Vinf}^0(x) \to \text{Vinf}^0(x) + \text{NPt}$$

$$(204) \quad \text{gl} \quad : \quad \text{Vinf}^1(x) \to \text{Vinf}^0(x) + \text{NPt}$$

$$(205) \quad \text{gl} \quad : \quad \text{Vinf}^2(\Delta) \to \text{Vinf}^0(\Delta) + \text{NPt}$$

$$(206) \quad \text{gl} \quad : \quad \text{Vnt}^0(x) \to \text{Vnt}^0(x) + \text{NPt}$$

$$(207) \quad \text{gl} \quad : \quad \text{Vnt}^0(\Delta) \to \text{Vnt}^0(\Delta) + \text{NPt}$$

$$(208) \quad \text{gl} \quad : \quad \text{Vnt}^1(x) \to \text{NP}[\text{obl}] + \text{Vpp}^0(x)$$

$$(209) \quad \text{gl} \quad : \quad \text{Vnt}^2(x) \to \text{NP} + \text{Vergnt}(x)$$

$$(210) \quad \text{gl} \quad : \quad \text{Vpp}^0(x) \to \text{Vpp}^0(x) + \text{Pr}(\text{with}) + \text{NP}$$

$$(211) \quad \text{gl} \quad : \quad \text{Vpp}^0(\Delta) \to \text{Vpp}^0(\Delta) + \text{Pr}(\text{with}) + \text{NP}$$

$$(212) \quad \text{gl} \quad : \quad \text{Vpp}^2(x) \to \text{Vpp}^0(x) + \text{NPt}$$

$$(213) \quad \text{gl} \quad : \quad \text{Vpp}^3(x) \to \text{Vpp}^0(x) + \text{NPt}$$

$$(214) \quad \text{gl} \quad : \quad \text{Vprp}^1(x) \to \text{NP} + \text{Vprp}^1(x)$$

$$(215) \quad \text{gl} \quad : \quad \text{Vrel}(x) \to \text{NP} + \text{V}(\text{be}) + \text{Vpp}^0(x)$$

(216)	lg	:	$NP(...) \rightarrow NP(...) + V(be) + Vpp^0$
(217)	lg	:	$NP(...) \rightarrow NP(...) + Verg$
(218)	lg	:	$NPw(...) \rightarrow NP(...) + Wh(s) + V(be) + Vpp^0$
(219)	lg	:	$NPw(...) \rightarrow NP(...) + Wh(s) + Vrel$
(220)	lg	:	$NPw(...) \rightarrow NP(...) + Vrel$
(221)	lg	:	$NPw(...) \rightarrow NP(...) + Vpp^0$
(222)	lg	:	$NPw(...) \rightarrow Vpp^1 + NP(...)$
(225)	oc	:	$C^0(\&) \rightarrow C^0 + C^1(\&)$
(226)	oc	:	$C^1(\&) \rightarrow Comma + C^0 + C^1(\&)$
(227)	oc	:	$C^1(\&) \rightarrow Conj(and) + C^0$
(228)	oc	:	$C^1(\&) \rightarrow Conj(and) + C^0 + C^1(\&)$
(229)	oc	:	$C^0(vel) \rightarrow C^0 + C^1(vel)$
(230)	oc	:	$C^0(vel) \rightarrow Conj(either) + C^0 + C^1(vel)$
(231)	oc	:	$C^1(vel) \rightarrow Comma + C^0 + C^1(vel)$
(232)	oc	:	$C^1(vel) \rightarrow Conj(or) + C^0$
(233)	oc	:	$C^1(vel) \rightarrow Conj(or) + C^0 + C^1(vel)$
(234)	oc	:	$L(\&) \rightarrow Conj(and) + NPs$
(235)	oc	:	$L(\&) \rightarrow Conj(and) + V$
(238)	ps	:	$A(cop, mem) \rightarrow N^1$
(239)	ps	:	$A(mod_n) \rightarrow Ngen$
(240)	ps	:	$A(orig) \rightarrow Ngen$
(241)	ps	:	$A(posh) \rightarrow Ngen$
(242)	ps	:	$A(posq) \rightarrow Ngen$
(243)	ps	:	$A(poss) \rightarrow Ngen$
(244)	ps	:	$Ap(cop) \rightarrow N^0$
(245)	ps	:	$Ap(cop, mem) \rightarrow N^0$
(246)	ps	:	$Ap(cop, sb) \rightarrow N^0$
(247)	ps	:	$B(mod_n) \rightarrow Pr(of) + N^0$
(248)	ps	:	$B(mod_3) \rightarrow Pr(with) + Wh(s) + NPp$
(249)	ps	:	$B(mod_4) \rightarrow Pr(with) + Wh(s) + NPp$

(250)　ps　:　$B(\text{mod}_7) \rightarrow Pr(\text{of}) + NPc$

(251)　ps　:　$B(\text{mod}_8) \rightarrow Pr(\text{of}) + NPc$

(252)　ps　:　$B(\text{mod}_9) \rightarrow Pr(\text{of}) + NPc$

(253)　ps　:　$B(\text{num}) \rightarrow Pr(\text{of}) + N^0$

(254)　ps　:　$B(\text{orig}) \rightarrow Pr(\text{of}) + N^0$

(255)　ps　:　$B(\text{pos, pre}) \rightarrow Pr(\text{behind}) + N^0$

(256)　ps　:　$B(\text{pos, sub}) \rightarrow Pr(\text{over}) + N^0$

(257)　ps　:　$B(\text{posh}) \rightarrow Pr(\text{of}) + N^0$

(258)　ps　:　$B(\text{posq}) \rightarrow Pr(\text{of}) + N^0$

(259)　ps　:　$B(\text{poss}) \rightarrow Pr(\text{of}) + N^0$

(260)　ps　:　$B(\text{quant}) \rightarrow Pr(\text{of}) + N^0$

(261)　ps　:　$G(\text{mod}_4) \rightarrow NPe$

(262)　ps　:　$G(\text{mod}_4) \rightarrow NPf$

(263)　ps　:　$G(\text{mod}_6) \rightarrow NPh$

(264)　ps　:　$G(\text{mod}_7) \rightarrow NPe$

(265)　ps　:　$G(\text{mod}_7) \rightarrow NPf$

(266)　ps　:　$G(\text{mod}_8) \rightarrow NPe$

(267)　ps　:　$G(\text{mod}_8) \rightarrow NPf$

(268)　ps　:　$G(\text{mod}_9) \rightarrow NPh$

(269)　ps　:　$J(\text{ante}) \rightarrow V(\text{be}) + Vpp(\text{precede}) + Pr(\text{by}) + N^0$

(270)　ps　:　$J(\text{ante}) \rightarrow V(\text{follow}) + N^0$

(271)　ps　:　$J(\text{caus}) \rightarrow V(\text{cause}) + NPt$

(272)　ps　:　$J(\text{caus}) \rightarrow V(\text{have}) + NPi$

(273)　ps　:　$J(\text{caus}) \rightarrow V(\text{make}) + NPj$

(274)　ps　:　$J(\text{cop}) \rightarrow V(\text{be}) + N^0$

(275)　ps　:　$J(\text{cop, mem}) \rightarrow V(\text{be}) + N^0$

(276)　ps　:　$J(\text{cop, mem}) \rightarrow V(\text{be}) + N^2$

(277)　ps　:　$J(\text{cop, sb}) \rightarrow V(\text{be}) + N^0$

(278)　ps　:　$J(\text{pos, in}) \rightarrow V(\text{contain}) + N^0$

(279)　ps　:　$J(\text{pos, pre}) \rightarrow V(\text{be}) + Pr(\text{behind}) + N^0$

(280)   ps   : $J(pos, sub) \rightarrow V(be) + Pr(over) + N^0$

(281)   ps   : $J(poss) \rightarrow V(be) + Ngen$

(282)   ps   : $Jnt(mod_n) \rightarrow N^0$

(283)   ps   : $NPk(...) \rightarrow NP(...) + NPp$

(284)   ps   : $Vger(mod_n) \rightarrow Ngen + Yger(mod_n)$

(285)   ps   : $Vnt^2(mod_n) \rightarrow N[obl]^0 + Ynt(mod_n)$

(286)   ps   : $Vrel(mod_n) \rightarrow N^0 + Y(mod_n)$

(287)   ps   : $W_0(ante) \rightarrow Conj(after) + NPp$

(288)   ps   : $W_0(ante) \rightarrow Pr(after) + N^0$

(289)   ps   : $W_0(pre) \rightarrow Pr(behind) + N^0$

(290)   ps   : $W_0(sub) \rightarrow Pr(over) + N^0$

(295)   sp   : $Adj_n(x) \rightarrow Z_0 + Adj_n(x)$

(296)   sp   : $Adj_n(x) \rightarrow Adj_n(x, Z_8)$

(297)   sp   : $Adv_n(x) \rightarrow Z_0 + Adv_n(x)$

(298)   sp   : $Adv_n(x) \rightarrow Adv_n(x, Z_8)$

(299)   sp   : $N^0(x) \rightarrow N^0(x) + K$

(300)   sp   : $N^0(x) \rightarrow N^0(x) + Wh(s) + Y$

(301)   sp   : $N^0(x) \rightarrow X + N^0(x)$

(302)   sp   : $N^0(x) \rightarrow N^0(x) + Comma + Ap + Comma$

(303)   sp   : $N^1(x) \rightarrow X + N^1(x)$

(304)   sp   : $N^2(x) \rightarrow X_2 + Pr(for) + N^0$

(305)   sp   : $N^2(x) \rightarrow X_3 + Pr(as) + N^0$

(306)   sp   : $Nag(x) \rightarrow Nag(x) + Wh(s) + Y$

(307)   sp   : $Nag(x) \rightarrow X_3 + Nag(x)$

(308)   sp   : $Ngen(x) \rightarrow X + Ngen(x)$

(309)   sp   : $Nv^0(x) \rightarrow Nv^4(x) + Wh(s) + Y$

(310)   sp   : $Nv^0(x) \rightarrow X + Nv^2(x)$

(311)   sp   : $Nv^1(x) \rightarrow Nv^4(x) + Wh(s) + Y$

(312)   sp   : $Nv^1(x) \rightarrow X + Nv^2(x)$

(313)   sp   : $Nv^2(x) \rightarrow Nv^4(x) + Wh(s) + Y$

(314) sp : $Nv^2(\Delta) \to Nv^4(\Delta) + Wh(s) + Y$

(315) sp : $Nv^3(\Delta) \to Nv^4(\Delta) + Wh(s) + Y$

(316) sp : $NP(...) \to NP(...) + Y$

(317) sp : $\dot{N}Pc(...) \to NPc(...) + Y_{46789}$

(318) sp : $NPe(...) \to NPe(...) + Y_{46789}$

(319) sp : $Npf(...) \to NPf(...) + Y_{478}$

(320) sp : $NPr(...) \to NPr(...) + Y_{69}$

(321) sp : $P \to Y_3$

(322) sp : $R \to Y_6$

(323) sp : $T \to Y_{4789}$

(324) sp : $V(x) \to V(x) + W_{034}$

(325) sp : $V(x) \to V(x) + Z_{034}$

(326) sp : $V(x) \to Z_{469} + V(x)$

(327) sp : $V(x) \to V(be) + X_{69} + Vinf^0(x)$

(328) sp : $V(\Delta) \to V(\Delta) + W_{034}$

(329) sp : $V(\Delta) \to V(\Delta) + Z_{034}$

(330) sp : $Verg(x) \to Verg(x) + W_{034}$

(331) sp : $Verg(x) \to Verg(x) + Z_{034}$

(332) sp : $Verg(x) \to Z_{469} + Verg(x)$

(333) sp : $Vinf^0(x) \to Vinf^0(x) + W_{034}$

(334) sp : $Vinf^0(x) \to Vinf^0(x) + Z_{034}$

(335) sp : $Vinf^0(\Delta) \to Vinf^0(\Delta) + W_{034}$

(336) sp : $Vinf^0(\Delta) \to Vinf^0(\Delta) + Z_{034}$

(337) sp : $Vinf^1(x) \to Vinf^2(x) + Z_{034}$

(338) sp : $Vnt^0(x) \to Vnt^0(x) + W_{034}$

(339) sp : $Vnt^0(x) \to Vnt^0(x) + Z_{034}$

(340) sp : $Vnt^0(\Delta) \to Vnt^0(\Delta) + W_{034}$

(341) sp : $Vnt^0(\Delta) \to Vnt^0(\Delta) + Z_{034}$

(342) sp : $Vpp^0(x) \to Vpp^0(x) + W_{034}$

(343) sp : $Vpp^0(x) \to Vpp^0(x) + Z_{034}$

$$(344) \quad \text{sp} \quad : \quad V_{pp}^0(x) \to V_{pp}^0(x, X_7)$$

$$(345) \quad \text{sp} \quad : \quad V_{pp}^0(x) \to X_{478} + V_{inf}^1(x)$$

$$(346) \quad \text{sp} \quad : \quad V_{pp}^0(x) \to Z_{3469} + V_{pp}^0(x)$$

$$(347) \quad \text{sp} \quad : \quad V_{pp}^0(\Delta) \to V_{pp}^0(\Delta) + W_{034}$$

$$(348) \quad \text{sp} \quad : \quad V_{pp}^0(\Delta) \to V_{pp}^0(\Delta) + Z_{034}$$

$$(349) \quad \text{sp} \quad : \quad V_{pp}^2(x) \to Z_{3469} + V_{pp}^0(x)$$

$$(350) \quad \text{tad} \quad : \quad NP(...) \to NP(...) + V(be) + V_{pp}^3$$

$$(355) \quad \text{tga} \quad : \quad N_v^0(x) \to AJ + N_v^1(x)$$

$$(356) \quad \text{tga} \quad : \quad N_v^0(x) \to N_v^3(x) + Pr(by) + NP$$

$$(357) \quad \text{tga} \quad : \quad N_v^0(x) \to NPgen + N_v^1(x)$$

$$(358) \quad \text{tga} \quad : \quad N_v^2(x) \to N_v^3(x) + Pr(by) + NP$$

$$(359) \quad \text{tga} \quad : \quad N_v^2(x) \to N_v^2(x)) + R + PRP(Pr(of) + NP$$

$$(360) \quad \text{tga} \quad : \quad N_v^2(x) \to N_v^2(x)) + T + PRP(Pr(for) + NP$$

$$(361) \quad \text{tga} \quad : \quad N_v^2(\Delta) \to N_v^3(\Delta) + Pr(by) + NP$$

$$(362) \quad \text{tga} \quad : \quad N_v^2(\Delta) \to N_v^2(\Delta)) + R + PRP(Pr(of) + NP$$

$$(363) \quad \text{tga} \quad : \quad N_v^2(\Delta) \to N_v^2(\Delta)) + T + PRP(Pr(for) + NP$$

$$(364) \quad \text{tga} \quad : \quad N_v^3(\Delta) \to N_v^3(\Delta) + Pr(by) + NP$$

$$(365) \quad \text{tga} \quad : \quad V(x) \to V(x) + Pr(with) + NP$$

$$(366) \quad \text{tga} \quad : \quad V(\Delta) \to V(\Delta) + Pr(with) + NP$$

$$(367) \quad \text{tga} \quad : \quad V_{for}(x) \to Pr(for) + NP[obl] + V_{inf}^1(x)$$

$$(368) \quad \text{tga} \quad : \quad V_{ger}(x) \to NPgen + V_{ger}(x)$$

$$(369) \quad \text{tga} \quad : \quad V_{ger}(x) \to V_{ger}(x) + Pr(by) + NP$$

$$(370) \quad \text{tga} \quad : \quad V_{ger}(\Delta) \to V_{ger}(\Delta) + Pr(by) + NP$$

$$(371) \quad \text{tga} \quad : \quad V_{inf}^0(x) \to NP[obl] + V_{inf}^1(x)$$

$$(372) \quad \text{tga} \quad : \quad V_{inf}^0(\Delta) \to V_{inf}^0(\Delta) + Pr(by) + NP$$

$$(373) \quad \text{tga} \quad : \quad V_{inf}^0(\Delta) \to V_{inf}^0(\Delta)) + R + PRP(Pr(of) + NP$$

$$(374) \quad \text{tga} \quad : \quad V_{inf}^0(\Delta) \to V_{inf}^0(\Delta)) + T + PRP(Pr(for) + NP$$

$$(375) \quad \text{tga} \quad : \quad V_{inf}^1(x) \to Pr(for) + NP[obl] + V_{inf}^1(x)$$

$$(376) \quad \text{tga} \quad : \quad V_{inf}^1(x) \to V_{inf}^0(x) + Pr(by) + NP$$

$$(377) \quad \text{tga} \quad : \quad V_{nt}^1(x) \to NP[obl] + V_{nt}^0(x)$$

(378)	tga	:	$Vnt^2(x) \rightarrow NP[obl] + Vnt^0(x)$.
(379)	tga	:	$Vof(x) \rightarrow Pr(of) + NP[obl] + Vinf^1(x)$
(380)	tga	:	$Vpp^0(x) \rightarrow Vpp^0(x) + Pr(by) + NP$
(381)	tga	:	$Vpp^0(\Delta) \rightarrow Vpp^0(\Delta) + Pr(by) + NP$
(382)	tga	:	$Vpp^1(x) \rightarrow ADV + Vpp^1(x)$
(383)	tga	:	$Vpp^3(x) \rightarrow Vpp^0(x) + Pr(by) + NP$
(384)	tga	:	$Vrel(x) \rightarrow NP + V(\dot{x})$
(390)	tp	:	$N^0(x) \rightarrow \overline{Adj} + N^0(x)$
(391)	tp	:	$N^0(pro) \rightarrow \overline{N} + Pr(of) + N^0(pro)$

APPENDIX C: VERB MODIFICATION RULES

(400) π : $V(x) \rightarrow V^1(x)$

(401) $\alpha(\text{pot})$: $V^1(x) \rightarrow V^2(\text{pot}) + Vnt^0(x)$

(402) $\beta(\text{cont})$: $V^1(x) \rightarrow V^2(\text{be}) + Vger(x)$

(403) $\beta(\text{cont})$: $V^2(x) \rightarrow V^2(\text{be}) + Vger(x)$

(404) $\gamma(\text{perf})$: $V^1(x) \rightarrow V^2(\text{have}) + Vpp^2(x)$

(405) $\gamma(\text{perf})$: $V^2(x) \rightarrow V^2(\text{have}) + Vpp^2(x)$

(406) $\delta(\text{fut})$: $V^1(x) \rightarrow V^2(\text{will}) + Vnt^0(x)$

(407) $\delta(\text{fut})$: $V^2(x) \rightarrow V^2(\text{will}) + Vnt^0(x)$

(408) $\delta(\text{pot})$: $V^1(x) \rightarrow V^2(\text{pot}) + Vnt^0(x)$

(409) $\delta(\text{pot})$: $V^2(x) \rightarrow V^2(\text{pot}) + Vnt^0(x)$

(410) $\epsilon(\text{past})$: $V^1(x) \rightarrow V^1(\text{past}, x)$

(411) $\epsilon(\text{past})$: $V^2(x) \rightarrow V^2(\text{past}, x)$

(412) $\zeta(\text{non})$: $V^1(x) \rightarrow V^1(\text{do}) + Adv(\text{non}) + Vnt^0(x)$

(413) $\zeta(\text{non})$: $V^1(\text{past}, x) \rightarrow V^1(\text{past}, \text{do}) + Adv(\text{non})$
                                               $+ Vnt^0(x)$

(414) $\zeta(\text{non})$: $V^2(x) \rightarrow V^2(x) + Adv(\text{non})$

(415) $\zeta(\text{non})$: $V^2(\text{past}, x) \rightarrow V^2(\text{past}, x) + Adv(\text{non})$

(416) $\eta(y)$: $V^1(x) \rightarrow V^1(y, x)$

(417) $\eta(y)$: $V^2(x) \rightarrow V^2(y, x)$